Data Analysis
with Spreadsheets

David A. Patterson

University of Tennessee

Randall E. Basham

University of Texas–Arlington

PEARSON

Boston ■ New York ■ San Francisco

Mexico City ■ Montreal ■ Toronto ■ London ■ Madrid ■ Munich ■ Paris

Hong Kong ■ Singapore ■ Tokyo ■ Cape Town ■ Sydney

Series Editor: *Patricia Quinlin*
Series Editorial Assistant: *Sara Holliday*
Marketing Manager: *Kris Ellis-Levy*
Production Administrator: *Anna Socrates*
Editorial-Production Service: *Omegatype Typography, Inc.*
Composition Buyer: *Linda Cox*
Manufacturing Buyer: *JoAnne Sweeney*
Cover Administrator: *Joel Gendron*
Electronic Composition: *Omegatype Typography, Inc.*

For related titles and support materials, visit our online catalog at www.ablongman.com.

Between the time Website information is gathered and then published, it is not unusual for some sites to have closed. Also, the transcription of URLs can result in unintended typographical errors. The publisher would appreciate notification where these errors occur so that they may be corrected in subsequent editions.

Many of the designations used by manufacturers and sellers to distinguish their products are claimed as trademarks. Where those designations appear in this book, and Allyn and Bacon was aware of a trademark claim, the designations have been printed in initial or all caps.

Library of Congress Cataloging-in-Publication Data

Patterson, David A.
    Data analysis with spreadsheets / David A. Patterson, Randall E. Basham.
      p. cm.
    Includes bibliographical references.
    ISBN 0-205-40751-X
    1. Social service—Data processing.   2. Human services—Data processing.   3. Electronic spreadsheets.   I. Basham, Randall E.   II. Title.
    HV29.2.P368 2006
    005.54—dc22

                                            2004065070

Printed in the United States of America

10 9 8 7 6 5 4 3 2 1   10 09 08 07 06 05

To Eunice Fisher Patterson, who after
nearly ninety-nine trips around the sun and a life of service to others,
slipped the bonds of the physical world in May of 2004.
—D. A. P.

To my wife, Sharon, and to my writing companion, Wylie.
—R. E. B.

CONTENTS

PREFACE

Social workers and human services professionals are increasingly called on to evaluate the outcomes of their practice, to measure changes in their clients over time, to determine if one type of approach to services delivery in an agency is better than another, and to respond to requests for evaluative data from managed care companies and other funding sources. Unfortunately, one of the great deficits in the educational preparation of students in social work and the human services is that they are commonly taught limited data analysis skills using conventional statistical analysis software such as SPSS. The problem with this approach is that social service and health care agencies seldom have expensive statistical software such as SPSS available for agency research projects and program evaluation. Conversely, most personal computers have installed spreadsheet software.

While the utility of spreadsheet software in budgetary procedures is commonly recognized, the social work and human services professions have been slow to recognize the efficacy of spreadsheets in data analysis. There exist a number of textbooks in business and science that describe the use of spreadsheets in data analysis for business and scientific applications. We wrote *Data Analysis with Spreadsheets* and created the accompanying CD-ROM as a comprehensive guide to the application of spreadsheets to commonly encountered data analysis problems in practice evaluation, statistical analysis, and program evaluation. In this text and on the CD-ROM, we demonstrate the use of spreadsheets in the full-spectrum of data analysis skills requisite for the evaluation of practice, agency-based research, and program evaluation.

Microsoft Excel

As is described in Chapter 1, there are both commercial and noncommercial publishers of spreadsheets. Most of them are roughly equivalent in appearance and functionality. The most widely used spreadsheet around the globe is Microsoft Excel. This market dominance means that social work and human services professionals are far more likely to have Microsoft Excel on their home and office computers than any other spreadsheet. For that reason, we have limited our description of spreadsheet data analysis procedures to how to perform these procedures in Microsoft Excel. Many of the procedures we describe here can be readily adapted for other types of spreadsheets, depending on the feature richness of the particular spreadsheet.

Microsoft Excel for Windows was originally released in 1987. Since that time there have been at least eight subsequent versions of this spreadsheet software. The challenge in writing any book about information technology is that it is a bit like trying to comprehend and describe a river by examining the contents of a cup recently dipped into the river. One can carefully observe the temperature, clarity, purity, acidity, salinity, and taste of the water in the cup. However, by the time one has come to know and write about the qualities of the river in the cup, the river at one's feet is no longer the same water. In *Data Analysis with Spreadsheets* we have consciously chosen to not link our description of data analysis procedures with Excel to a particular version of this software. While successive versions of Excel have added features, enhanced the functionality, and improved its appearance, the operation of the data analysis tools of Excel, listed in Chapter 1, has remained relatively consistent in the last three or four iterations of this software. We believe that almost all of the data analysis procedures described in the text and demonstrated on the accompanying CD-ROM can be accomplished with very little adaptation on versions of Excel released in this millennium.

Data Analysis with Spreadsheets: Multimedia Modules CD-ROM

The *Data Analysis with Spreadsheets: Multimedia Modules* CD-ROM that comes with this book contains videos demonstrating the spreadsheet data analysis procedures described in the 12 chapters. The CD-ROM has a "Read me first" file that should be read before using the CD-ROM for the first time. It will acquaint you with the procedures for viewing the videos and spreadsheets found under Bonus Materials on the CD-ROM.

The web browsers Microsoft Internet Explore or Netscape Navigator will open the file on the CD-ROM entitled *Data Analysis with Spreadsheets,* from which you can start your exploration of the content of the CD-ROM. All of the videos on the CD-ROM are recorded in the QuickTime format. If your computer does not have QuickTime player installed, you can download a free copy from www.apple.com/quicktime/download/standalone. Quick-Time players are available for Windows and Apple Macintosh operating systems. The QuickTime videos of this CD-ROM will play within the Microsoft Internet Explore or Netscape Navigator browser windows. Be sure to turn up the sound on your computer. Listening with headphones may be particularly helpful. The videos are 800×600 pixels in size, so expand your web browser window to its largest size in order to fully see the videos.

The Application of Spreadsheets to Practice-Related Data Analysis

The utility spreadsheets in data analysis extend beyond research applications into the everyday challenges of information management for social work and human service practitioners. A quick reference of the linkage between the chapters of this book and the practice-related issues addressed within them follows:

Chapter 1
- The role of data collection, analysis, and information dissemination in practice
- Uses of spreadsheets in practice settings as tools of practice
- Evaluation of practice
- Spreadsheets as a practice alternative to statistical software

Chapter 2
- The use of spreadsheets for information/data collection in practice settings
- Levels of measurement common to practice settings
- Sources of practice information/data

Chapter 3
- Selecting samples in social services agency data

Chapter 4
- Data cleaning challenges of information from practice settings

Chapter 5
- Graphically representing frequency distributions such as observations or behaviors
- Evaluating educational efforts that may be applied to service settings that provide education

Chapter 6
- Describing caseloads, performance, and productivity using descriptive statistics
- Measures of central tendency and variation in evaluating interventions

Chapter 7
- Evaluating practice interventions
- Spreadsheets as a tool for developing evidence-based practice
- Practice-level research sample selection and evaluating distributions

Chapter 8
- Comparing sample means to population means in practice
- Comparing observed versus expected frequencies across group services

Chapter 9
- Using pivot tables for social service data summary and exploration

Chapter 10
- Single system designs for practice evaluation
- Advantages of spreadsheets in single system design practice evaluation
- Single system design data collection with spreadsheets
- Single system design charting with spreadsheets
- Evaluating change in practice outcomes with single system design spreadsheets
- Spreadsheets for evaluating groups using single system designs

Chapter 11
- Determining change through evaluating associations between variables in interventions
- Using spreadsheet graphing tools to evaluate distributions and trends
- Evaluating and predicting change using regression analysis capabilities within spreadsheets

Chapter 12
- Spreadsheet production of practice graphics
- Applications of graphics in social service practice
- Spreadsheet-produced ecomaps
- Spreadsheet-produced genograms

Acknowledgments

This book is the result of the efforts, input, feedback, and support of many people without whom this book and CD-ROM would not have been possible. We offer our heartfelt thanks to John Orme, Jim Post, Mary Ellen Cox, and Vaughn DeCoster. Thanks as well to our most excellent editor Patricia Quinlin and our equally excellent editorial assistant, Annemarie Kennedy. Your patience and support were greatly appreciated. Now see if you can get us a spot on Oprah. We would also like to thank the reviewers of this book: Margaret E. Ademek, Indiana University; John Goad, Arizona State University; Stephen Marson, University of North Carolina, Pembroke; and Bibhuti K. Sar, Kent School of Social Work. As professors we are indebted as well to our students who have taught us how to teach the material presented here.

We greatly appreciate the profound love, support, and nurturance of our families. We offer our countless thanks to Melanie McGhee, Kaitlyn Sage Patterson, Hannah McGhee Patterson, and Sharon Basham, without whom this project may never have begun and certainly would not have been finished.

1

An Introduction
to Spreadsheets

Spreadsheets—First Facts

An inescapable task of the early 21st century in social service practice is the management of information. Most social workers, counselors, and human service workers likely enter their respective professional roles with the desire to provide necessary services to a particular client population, having neither the intention nor the wish to devote their time and energy to the collection, analysis, and dissemination of information. The emerging practice reality is that data have to be collected that document to whom what specific services are delivered, for what duration, in what quantity, and resulting in what outcomes. Governmental agencies, public and private insurers, managed care companies, as well as agency administrators and program evaluators, require the capture, analysis, and reporting of social services delivery information. Further, budgetary analysis and financial reporting requirements of social service agencies require skills in the evaluation of possible budget scenarios, the preparation of viable budget reports, and the monitoring of resources and expenditures over the life of the budget. Computers and the spectrum of information technology software and hardware now available are the essential tools for each of these information management tasks. Consequently, the ability to use information technology in the gathering, examination, and presentation of information regarding the provision of social services is now a requisite skill set for social service professionals.

Spreadsheet applications, or simply "spreadsheets," are computer programs that display a matrix of rows and columns of cells into which information, in the form of numbers, text, or formulas, is entered and displayed. The size of this rows and columns matrix is generally only limited by the available memory of the computer in which the spreadsheet software resides. As a result of the ever-growing power of personal computers, manifest in processing speed, storage capacity, and memory (RAM), spreadsheets are now capable of holding and manipulating vast amounts of information. Beyond the simple storage of information, the usefulness of spreadsheets stems from the ease with which they allow users to interact with data. For instance, spreadsheets can be used in social services practice settings to (a) record and graph the changes clients make over the course of service delivery, (b) collect and analyze data on how groups and individuals within the groups change over time, (c) record and analyze agency income and expenses, and (d) generate graphs and tables reporting agency service delivery and financial status to private and governmental funding sources, oversight boards, and constituents.

Spreadsheets are a rather neglected tool for the evaluation of social service practice and practice-based research. Social service practice settings have seen a growing movement toward greater accountability over the last generation. Accountability standards have been recommended for the purposes of determining intervention effectiveness, reducing risk of harm to clients, providing cost-effectiveness information on services provided, and for tracking overall program progress at various levels in social service agencies. Spreadsheets, which are commonly found on almost all modern-day computers, are a ready instrument for accomplishing each of these data analysis tasks. The inattention in social service practice to the utility and versatility of spreadsheets is explored below.

The Brief History of Spreadsheets

The history of spreadsheets is paradoxically both long and short. Over the course of civilization dating back to the Babylonian Empire (4,500 B.C), the recording of information in ledgers or registers has been a means to account for financial transactions, inventory objects, assess taxes, and list the births, actions, and deaths of individuals. Such ledgers were pragmatic tools for recording and tracking information, both fiscal and demographic, as well as means to preserve and convey the actions and transactions of individuals, families, communities, businesses, and nations. More recently, though prior to the advent of electronic computers, accountants and others have used worksheets composed of matrices of columns and rows to record credits and debts, to note financial transactions, and to track the fiscal well-being of individuals, enterprises, and institutions.

The trouble with paper-based ledgers or spreadsheets is that they are static. A change of a number in a column or the removal or addition of information located in a row requires the recalculation of the bottom line, the manual re-entry of new figures. It is hardly surprising that prior to the introduction of the electronic spreadsheet, two of the essential tools of any accountant were an eraser and a sharp pencil, requisite instruments of the impermanent tasks of preliminary calculations. Further, it is of little wonder that with the advent of computers, researchers and academics turned their attention to how the tasks of accounting and inventory control might be automated and made more flexible.

It is generally recognized that one of the pioneers in the development of computer-based spreadsheets was Richard Mattessich. Mattessich's groundbreaking work appeared first in a paper (Mattessich, 1961) and later in two books (Mattessich, 1964a; Mattessich, 1964b). In these publications he laid out the basic elements of computerized financial spreadsheets, including the use of matrices, formulas calculating cell values, and simulations of "what if" scenarios (Gaffikin, 1996; Legg, 1988; Murphy, 1997). The fundamental limitation of Mattessich's early work was not conceptual but instead pragmatic. His methods required mainframe computers (the only type available at the time) and complex programming, both of which had significant associated costs.

The birth of modern, personal computer-based spreadsheets occurred in 1978 when a Harvard Business School student, Dan Bricklin, balked at the complexity involved in doing a "case study" project either by hand or on a mainframe computer (Power, 2000). As an alternative he envisioned an interactive electronic spreadsheet. He initially created a "working prototype" composed of 20 rows and 5 columns in which a user could input numbers and produce calculations. He then joined with Bob Frankston, whom he knew from MIT, to improve the functioning of the original prototype by adding the ability to scroll, increase the speed of calculations, enhance the arithmetic, and optimize the program code so it would run on an affordable personal computer, one of the first Apple Computer machines. The resulting program was called VisiCalc, which was short for "visible calculator."

Bricklin (2003) points out that prior to the development of VisiCalc, there existed other row and column tabulation programs. VisiCalc, however, was unique as the first "electronic spreadsheet" having interactive features including scrolling, automatic recalculation of values in cells based on stored formulas, and ease of data input, formatting, and output. The introduction of VisiCalc had a catalytic sales effect on the blossoming personal computer industry, as it was a software product with real utility for organizations in the business and finance sectors of the economy. Further, the VisiCalc user interface became the prototype for all spreadsheet programs subsequently developed. Bricklin and Frankston formed Software Arts in January, 1979 and eventually sold over 500,000 copies of this first "electronic spreadsheet." Readers interested in seeing screenshots of the original VisiCalc program should visit Bricklin's website, www.bricklin.com/firstspreadsheetquestion.htm. A copy of the original VisiCalc is available for downloading at www.bricklin.com/history/vcexecutable.htm.

The VisiCalc dominance of the spreadsheet market was eclipsed in the early 1980s by a new product, Lotus 1-2-3, which offered an easier to use interface, the ability to create charts, and database functions. Lotus 1-2-3 soon became a best-selling software application and the de facto standard for spreadsheets during that time period (Power, 2000). In the mid-1980s Microsoft introduced Excel, which was developed for an early version of the Apple Macintosh. At that time, the Apple Macintosh was the only personal computer with a graphical user interface and a pointing device, the now ubiquitous mouse. The software programmers of Excel took advantage of these features unique to the Macintosh by incorporating into Excel design elements such as pulldown menus and point-and-click data entry. Microsoft released its first version of Windows in 1987 along with an early version of Excel for Windows. In 1989, Version 3.0 of Windows was released along with a much-improved version of Excel, which was the only Windows spreadsheet until 1992. Lotus 1-2-3 and other spreadsheet applications ran on the MS-DOS operating system.

Over the course of the mid- to late-1990s, there were three major spreadsheets available for the Windows operating system: Microsoft Excel, Lotus 1-2-3, and Quattro Pro. Each of these spreadsheets was incorporated into an office suite of software by its respective publisher. Software office suites usually contain a word processor, spreadsheet, presentation software, and sometimes a database. Lotus 1-2-3 was purchased in 1995 (Power, 2000) by IBM and included in its Lotus SmartSuite software package. Quattro Pro became part of Corel's WordPerfect Office suite. Excel, which has long been a part of the Microsoft Office suite, became the dominant spreadsheet on the market, accounting for about 90 percent of all spreadsheet sales (Krazit, 2002; Walkenbach, 2003).

More recently, low-cost and open source office suites have become available over the web that include spreadsheets. Open source software is developed collectively by volunteers in the worldwide programming community and made freely available to the public. Sun Microsystems' StarOffice 7.0 is available at no cost to academic and research institutions and is very competitively priced for businesses (www.sun.com/software/star/staroffice/index.xml). OpenOffice is an open source, feature-rich office suite that contains Calc, a fully functional spreadsheet. It is available at www.openoffice.org/product. The spreadsheets in these two office suites contain the full array of common spreadsheet tools; can read, write, and export Microsoft Excel files; and represent viable alternatives for individuals and agencies seeking lower-cost options in spreadsheet software.

The brief history of personal computer spreadsheets evidences three noteworthy trends. First, since the development of VisiCalc, spreadsheets have continued to expand the array of tools and features available to users. Spreadsheet users are no longer limited to simply calculating formulas for columns and rows of numbers. They can import data from multiple sources including databases and other types of spreadsheets. They can analyze complex data sets with descriptive and inferential statistics and then graphically represent the results with the charting tools of spreadsheets. Moreover, the tables, charts, and diagrams that users can now create with modern-day spreadsheets can be readily exported to other tools of electronic communication, including word processing, presentation, and web-authoring software (Patterson, 2000).

This integration of spreadsheets with other types of software is the second noteworthy trend in the history of spreadsheets. Early spreadsheets could generally produce printed output, but had no capacity to interact with other forms of software in sharing information. This electronic isolation was partially a function of the limitations of the MS-DOS and early Windows operating systems. The barrier between word processing and spreadsheets was broken by the release of Microsoft Word and Excel for the Apple Macintosh, which allowed for the cutting and pasting of charts and tables from Excel to Word. Since then, spreadsheet publishers have continued to expand the range of data and graphics exchange capabilities of their respective products. Most spreadsheets can now import data in a wide range of spreadsheet, database, and text file formats and export or share data, summary tables, charts, and graphics to word processors, databases, and web pages, and many other applications. These capabilities are described in greater depth in subsequent chapters.

The third trend evident over the history of spreadsheets is their increasingly widespread utilization. Though it is difficult to measure directly the change over time in the use of spreadsheets by either professionals or in the general population, several facts are suggestive of their increased utilization. A search of www.amazon.com database using "spreadsheet" as the search term found listings for 3,058 available books. An identical search of www.barnesandnoble.com resulted in a list of 3,373 books related to spreadsheets. A search of Business Source Premier, an electronic database of business publications, found 4,253 articles that included the terms "spreadsheet" or "spreadsheets." A search of PsychInfo, an electronic database of journal articles, dissertations, and books related to psychology, found 177 listings of sources using the terms "spreadsheet" or "spreadsheets." An identical search of Social Sciences Abstracts, a multidisciplinary index of journals in the social sciences, found 64 articles. Rather remarkably, a search of Social Work Abstracts found only four articles using either of the two search terms. A search of www.google.com using the term "spreadsheet" found 1,970,000 web pages in which the word appeared. When "social work" was added to the Google "spreadsheet" search, 8,600 web pages were found. A mere 0.004 percent of all references to spreadsheets on the World Wide Web also include content somehow related to social work. In contrast, if the term "psychology" is added to "spreadsheet" on a Google search, 47,000 web pages are located. A search of World Wide Web Resources for Social Workers (www.nyu.edu/socialwork/wwwrsw) found only three articles using the search term "spreadsheet," none of which was directly related to social work.

It seems safe to conclude this brief history of spreadsheets with two observations. First, the sheer volume of spreadsheet-related publications, whether electronic or hard copy, is indicative of the widespread interest in their use and applicability to a broad spectrum of data analysis and information dissemination tasks. Second, if the dearth of academic literature and low volume of web pages are valid indicators, then it appears that social workers have yet to fully appreciate the utility of spreadsheets and take them up as tools of social work practice. It is this unfortunate neglect of a highly versatile tool that we seek to redress with this text.

Why Use Spreadsheets for Data Analysis in the Social Services?

In order to address the robust potential of spreadsheets as data analysis tools in the social services, it is perhaps necessary to first address the question of why social service professionals should concern themselves with "data analysis" in the first place. In the opening paragraph of this chapter we describe how information management, manifest in the collection, analysis, and subsequent communication of findings or information, is becoming a required skill set for social service professionals.

The necessity of social service information management skills is driven by three key factors: professional and fiscal accountability, ethics, and decision making (Montcalm & Royse, 2002). Social service agencies and professionals are increasingly being called on by funding sources, whether local, state, federal, or private insurers, to demonstrate both the actual delivery of services and efficacy of the services provided. In other words, it has become increasingly important to measure the outcomes of services provided. The accountability expectations of funding sources necessitates the collection of service delivery information, its subsequent analysis and evaluation, and the lucid communication of results.

For social workers, the confluence of ethics and social services information management skills arises from their Code of Ethics. The 1999 revision of the National Association of Social Workers (NASW) Code of Ethics states in section 5.02, Evaluation and Research (2003):

(a) Social workers should monitor and evaluate policies, the implementation of programs, and practice interventions.

(b) Social workers should promote and facilitate evaluation and research to contribute to the development of knowledge.

The ethical imperative conveyed in this section of the Code of Ethics is unequivocal. Social workers are expected to "monitor and evaluate" and "promote and facilitate evaluation and research." The intersection of this ethical obligation and information management is borne of pragmatism. The most efficient way to monitor and evaluate practice and facilitate research is with the employment of information technology.

The third factor driving the need for information management skills in the social services is the ever-present need to make decisions (Montcalm & Royse, 2002). Social workers and social services professionals are called on daily to make critical decisions on matters including child protection, staff allocation for service delivery, agency fiscal resources utilization, and governmental policy recommendations, just to name a few. There are of course many ways to make a decision. Caprice, gut hunches, and intuition are means to arrive at a decision, albeit perhaps an ill-informed and intellectually unsupportable one. Proctor (2002) states, "Decision making in social work is high-stakes work" (p. 3). She asserts as well that decision quality can be impaired by the lack of information, as well as other factors. All too often, social service agencies have a wealth of information that is collected and stored on paper, an unfortunate decision that amplifies the complexity of information retrieval and synthesis. The point here is that decision making in the social services can and should be improved by information management skills that include electronic data collection, analysis/synthesis, and reporting. As we will see, social service practitioners can employ spreadsheets in each of these three domains of information management.

One of the great advantages offered to social service practitioners by spreadsheets is that they are commonly available on most personal computers. Today they are almost always part of an office suite of software applications. Sometimes the office suite is included on the computer as part of the original software and in other instances the office suite is purchased separately and loaded onto the computer. As described previously, there are now low-cost and open source office suites that are downloadable from the World Wide Web. It is now increasingly difficult to find a personal computer without some form of spreadsheet software on it. Consequently, social service practitioners and agencies have the readily available potential to employ spreadsheets for a spectrum of information management tasks.

Spreadsheet Basics

The overarching purpose of this book is the demonstration of spreadsheets' flexibility and data analytic power as tools of practice. In preparation to do that, it may be helpful to review the basic elements of spreadsheets. A spreadsheet is essentially a table composed of rows, columns, and cells. A column is a vertical line of boxes with a letter identifying each column (maranGraphics, 1996). A row is a horizontal line of boxes with a number identifying each row. A cell is a single box in the spreadsheet, which is the intersection of a row and a column. The cell reference is the address of the cell, which is composed of the column letter and the row number. For instance, cell B4 is located in column B on row 4. Figure 1.1 shows a spreadsheet in which cell B4 is highlighted (see the accompanying CD-ROM video animation: "Spreadsheet Tour").

Three types of information may be entered into a cell: labels, values, and formulas. Labels are explanatory text such as the name of a variable that appears at the top of a column and identifies the information contained in the column. Values are the data, both numerical and text, that are collected in the spreadsheet. Formulas perform calculations,

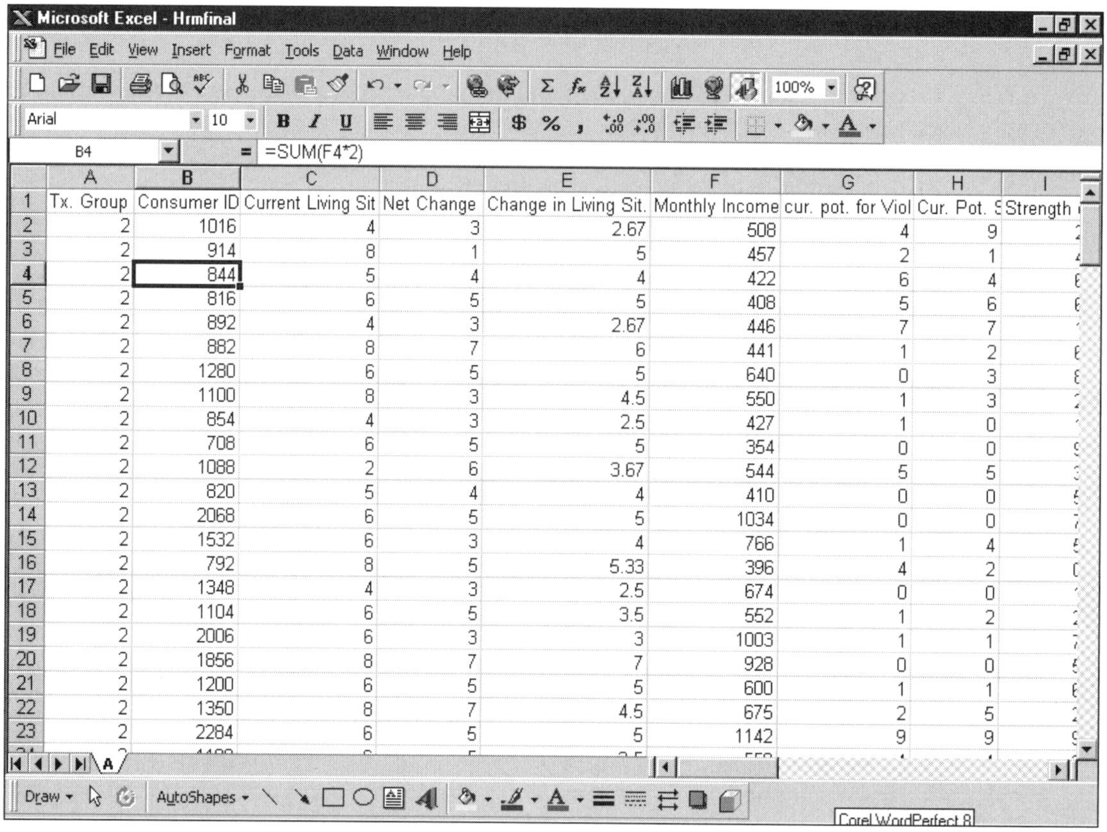

	Tx. Group	Consumer ID	Current Living Sit	Net Change	Change in Living Sit.	Monthly Income	cur. pot. for Viol	Cur. Pot. S
2	2	1016	4	3	2.67	508	4	9
3	2	914	8	1	5	457	2	1
4	2	844	5	4	4	422	6	4
5	2	816	6	5	5	408	5	6
6	2	892	4	3	2.67	446	7	7
7	2	882	8	7	6	441	1	2
8	2	1280	6	5	5	640	0	3
9	2	1100	8	3	4.5	550	1	3
10	2	854	4	3	2.5	427	1	0
11	2	708	6	5	5	354	0	0
12	2	1088	2	6	3.67	544	5	5
13	2	820	5	4	4	410	0	0
14	2	2068	6	5	5	1034	0	0
15	2	1532	6	3	4	766	1	4
16	2	792	8	5	5.33	396	4	2
17	2	1348	4	3	2.5	674	0	0
18	2	1104	6	5	3.5	552	1	2
19	2	2006	6	3	3	1003	1	1
20	2	1856	8	7	7	928	0	0
21	2	1200	6	5	5	600	1	1
22	2	1350	8	7	4.5	675	2	5
23	2	2284	6	5	5	1142	9	9

FIGURE 1.1 Spreadsheet of Client Data

such as the average or sum of a column or row of values. Formulas are one of the means through which data in a spreadsheet is analyzed. Formulas make it possible to test a range of "what if" scenarios. For instance, in planning a budget, a manager might examine the impact of a 2 percent, 4 percent, or 5 percent salary increase for staff from her available annual resources. The formula would automatically recalculate her personnel budget as she multiplied current salary cost by the possible 2 percent, 4 percent, or 5 percent salary increase. See Table 1.1 for an example. A caseworker also might help a client plan a household budget through exploring a range of "what if" scenarios around spending for the month. This capacity to test scenarios makes the spreadsheet a valuable tool in testing financial options in both administration and clinical practice settings.

TABLE 1.1 Spreadsheet for Salary Increases

Employee	Present Salary	2% Increase	4% Increase	5% Increase
J. P. Dole	32,000	32,640	33,280	33,600
Q. A. Smith	23,500	23,970	24,440	24,675
U. R. Wright	19,800	20,196	20,592	20,790
D. A. Day	18,000	18,360	18,720	18,900
Total	93,300	95,166	97,032	97,965
Net Increase in Personnel Cost		1,866	3,732	4,665

The following features are commonly found in spreadsheets.

1. Data Import/Export—The importation/exportation of data to and from a variety of sources, including database tables.
2. Functions—Built-in, predefined formulas for deriving specific mathematical, logical, informational, or statistical results.
3. Graphing—Data in the spreadsheet visually represented in a range of graph and chart formats, such as bar charts and area graphs.
4. Formatting—Options in formatting of cell contents including bold, italics, underline, justification (right, left, center), number representation (percentage, scientific, decimal places, etc.), row and column height and width, and specification of cell border styles.
5. Data Management—Information in spreadsheets sorted in a variety of ways, analyzed and summarized in pivot (cross-tabulation) tables, selected based on specified filters (e.g., all men over 50), and grouped in a variety of ways.
6. Statistical Analysis Tools—A collection of statistical procedures ranging from simple descriptive statistics, frequency counts, and histograms to inferential statistics.
7. Drawing Tools—A range of graphics tools available to enhance visually spreadsheet documents including lines, arrows, shapes, colors, and graphically augmented text tools, which add shape, color, and dimension to text.
8. Multidimensionality—Most spreadsheet programs create workbooks of spreadsheets (a.k.a. worksheets) that allow the linkage of a series of spreadsheets by formulas. The result is that a change in one spreadsheet will affect all the other spreadsheets to which it is connected by a formula. For instance, an administrator could create a spreadsheet with the agency's budget on it. This spreadsheet would be linked to three other spreadsheets in the same workbook, each spreadsheet representing a department's budget. The four spreadsheets might be linked by a formula that allocates a percentage of the agency's personnel budget to each of the three departments. Any change in the spreadsheet cell that contains the agency's budget would alter, in turn, the budget allocation for each department.

Data In

The aggregation of data into a spreadsheet can occur through many routes. Data may be directly input by typing it into the cells of the sheet. Many spreadsheets have the option of creating a data entry form, making it possible to enter data in much the same manner as one would enter data into a database.

Most spreadsheets allow for the importing of data files from databases. This feature makes it possible to pull data drawn from a database into a spreadsheet in order to analyze and summarize it in ways that are not possible with most databases. This data importation from databases to spreadsheets is an extremely useful option. Many progressive or better-funded social service agencies now have databases to track client demographics, services delivered, and services outcomes data. These databases can be queried for information of interest. A query is the extraction of data from database tables based on specifically defined criteria. For instance, if one wished to understand what services are delivered to a subset of the population served by an agency (e.g., all clients living in a particular geographic region), then one might request from the agency's database administrator a file containing a list of all clients from that geographic region along with demographic information and a listing of the services they received. Once the database query is run, the resulting file, often called a "flat file," could be imported into a spreadsheet for an analysis of services delivered by a demographic group. The specific steps of such an analysis are presented in Chapter 9.

Using Formulas and Functions

Regardless of the means by which data arrives in a spreadsheet, whether by direct data entry, a data entry form, or importation from a database, formulas and functions are commonly the

TABLE 1.2 Simple Formula Example

	A	B	C
1		45	53
2		56	76
3		75	15
	Sum	176	=sum(C1:C3)

first tools used to understand the data. Formulas and functions enable spreadsheet users to conduct data analysis procedures ranging from the simple to the dreadfully complex. For now, we will limit our introduction of formulas and functions to the simple end of the continuum.

Simple Formulas. Formulas define the calculations the spreadsheet is to perform (Parsons, Oja, & Auer, 1995). A formula is initiated by clicking on the cell in which the results of the calculation is to appear. Every formula has an operation symbol indicating to the spreadsheet the presence of a formula. In Microsoft Excel, the operation symbol that appears at the beginning of any formula is the equal sign (=), whereas Lotus 1-2-3 and Corel Quattro Pro use the "at" symbol (@). For instance, this formula in an Excel spreadsheet tells the application to add the numbers contained in the formula =45+56+75. In Lotus 1-2-3 and Quattro Pro the formula would be @(45+56+75). Once the values are entered into the formula, pressing the Enter key returns the numerical result of the formula's calculations. Likewise, formulas can use values in other cells by entering their cell references into the formula. For example, in Table 1.2 the formula summing the three numbers could be expressed as =(B1+B2+B3) or as =(B1:B3). Column C contains a set of values that will be added with the formula in cell C4. See the accompanying CD-ROM video animation: *Formulas and Functions.*

Operators in Formulas. The formulas in the preceding paragraph contain several symbols, including =, +, (, and). These symbols are referred to as operators. Operators are used in formulas for arithmetic calculations, to reference cells, to link portions of equations, and to segment portions of equations. Table 1.3 contains a list of commonly used operators. Technically speaking, parentheses are not operators but instead indicate in the formula the order of operation. When calculating a formula, the spreadsheet will first calculate the portion of the formula contained within parentheses and then use the results to calculate the remainder of the formula. For instance, in the equation =(5+7+9*2), the formula adds 5+7 and then adds 18, the results of 9*2, to produce a product of 30. Whereas, if the equation is written as =(5+7+9)*2, the sum of the numbers within the parentheses is 21, which is then multiplied by 2 for a product of 42 (Dretzke & Heilman, 1998). Basic algebraic order of operations procedures are applied in spreadsheet formulas. This means that operations in

TABLE 1.3 Operators for Formulas

Symbol	Meaning	Formula Example
=	Equal—Used at the start of every equation	=(53+76+15)
+	Plus sign—Used for addition	=(C1+C2+C3)
–	Subtraction or a negative number	=(76–15)
*	Asterisk—Used for multiplication	=(C1*C2) or =(53*76)
/	Forward slash—Used for division	=(76/15) or =(C2/C3)
%	Percent	=(76*10%)
^	Caret—Used for exponentiation, e.g., to square or cube a number	=(76^2) or =(76*76) =(76^3) or =(76*76*76)
:	Colon—Used to indicate a range of cells	=sum(C1:C3)
,	Comma—Used to combine two or more references	=sum(B1:B3,C1:C3)
( )	Parentheses—Used to segment portions of an equation and to specify the order of operation	=sum(B1:B3)*(C1^2)

parentheses are calculated first, then exponential expressions (10^2), next division and multiplication operations, and finally addition and subtraction.

Functions. Some spreadsheet calculations are most readily accomplished with functions, instead of writing a formula or equation. "A 'function' is a special prewritten formula that provides a shortcut for commonly used calculations" (Parsons, Oja, & Auer, 1995, p. 32). Essentially, functions are mathematical or logical procedures that are inserted in one or more cells and perform a calculation or logical operation. Examples of functions include statistical functions such as average, standard deviation, random, median, and logical functions such as "if," "and," and "true." In Excel, functions are found in the menu bar under Insert, Function. When Function is selected from the menu bar, a pop-up window appears with categories of functions listed on the left and function names listed on the right. Categories of functions include Math & Trig, Logical, Financial, and Statistical. For our purposes, Statistical is the category of function we will most commonly employ. It offers a wide range of statistical formulas from which we will use a limited number. The great utility of functions is that they allow one to quickly and accurately perform simple to complex calculations and analyses on data. Functions also reduce formula typing errors. Further, each function provides step-by-step information and instructions necessary to employ the selected function for its intended purpose (Black, 1999). We will use functions for a number of data analysis purposes in this book.

Advanced Tools for Understanding Data

In addition to formulas and functions, spreadsheets offer a number of other data analysis tools. Each of these data analysis tools is demonstrated in subsequent chapters, but in the service of this overview of the versatility of spreadsheets, some of them are described in Table 1.4. Taken together, this collection of data analysis tools makes it possible to conduct a spectrum of data analysis tasks ranging from simple data sorting to complex inferential statistical analysis.

One of the tools in Table 1.4 is both (for our purposes) unfortunately named and particularly important to understanding the power and versatility of spreadsheets as tools of social service practice, particularly in data analysis. This collection of statistical procedures is rather indistinctly named Data Analysis Tools in Excel. Microsoft's use of this poorly differentiating label for Excel's statistical tools obscures both the data analytic power of the other tools listed in Table 1.4 and the statistical utility of the collection of procedures found in the Data Analysis Tools.

TABLE 1.4   Data Analysis Tools of MS Excel

Chart Wizard	A step-by-step guide for the creation of charts. Enables the graphical representation and exploration of data.
Data Analysis Tools	A collection of tools for the organization, statistical analysis, and interpretation of numeric data.
AutoFilter	A tool for filtering data sets for subsets of data based on selected criteria from the data set.
Functions	A predefined formula to perform a calculation on a specified range of values.
Pivot Table	A tool to collapse and summarize data in order to understand the relationships between variables. The means to create cross-tabulation tables.
Sort	A tool for sorting data sets or subsets of data in specified order (ascending or descending).

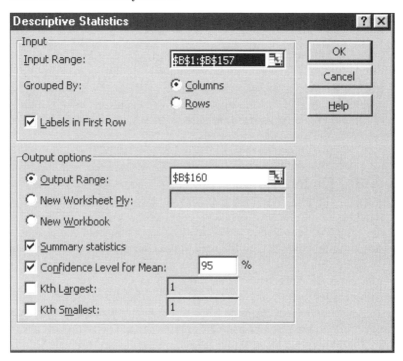

FIGURE 1.2   Data Analysis Tools

FIGURE 1.3   Data Analysis Tools—Descriptive Statistics

TABLE 1.5   Data Analysis Tools—Descriptive Statistics Output

AGE	
Mean	62.99
Standard Error	0.75
Median	64.00
Mode	70.00
Standard Deviation	9.40
Sample Variance	88.37
Kurtosis	1.68
Skewness	−0.44
Range	64.00
Minimum	23.00
Maximum	87.00
Sum	9827.00
Count	156.00
Confidence Level (95.0%)	1.49

The Data Analysis Tools are found in Excel's menu bar Tools, Data Analysis. If Data Analysis does not appear under the Tools menu, then select Add-Ins. The Add-Ins window will appear; in that window, select Analysis ToolPak, then click OK. This will add the Data Analysis Tools to the Tools menu. Figures 1.2 and 1.3 display the Data Analysis Tools window and the Descriptive Statistics dialog box. Table 1.5 contains the statistical results produced by the Descriptive Statistics tool.

Though Figure 1.2 does not show the entire selection of statistical procedures available in Data Analysis Tools, it in fact contains a robust collection of statistical procedures. These statistical procedures are widely used in business, scientific, research, and financial settings. As will be demonstrated in subsequent chapters, they are more than sufficient to address the data analytic requirements of most social service professionals and agencies.

A Comparison of Spreadsheets
to Statistical Analysis Software

The alternative data analysis tool to the spreadsheet is statistical analysis software. There are many brands of statistical analysis software, including SPSS, STATISTICA, SYSTAT, all of which are commercially available products. There are also a number of statistical software packages available in the public domain at no or low cost. See http://members.aol.com/johnp71/javasta2.html#General for a list of no- or low-cost packages. There is, of course, a great deal of variability in the appearance of, functionality of, and statistical producers included in statistical software applications. Some of the commonalities among most statistical software packages include a graphical user interface, ability to create and edit data files, import/export data tools, charting tools, pivot tables (cross-tabulation), and a range of statistical procedures and tests.

There are many commonalities and some differences between spreadsheets and statistical analysis software. Spreadsheets and statistical analysis software are compared in Table 1.6.

TABLE 1.6 Spreadsheets Compared to Statistical Software

Assessment Category	Spreadsheets	Statistical Software
Ease of use	Ranges from easy to challenging depending on the task	Ranges from easy to challenging depending on the task
Graphical user interface	Yes	Yes for most packages
Versatility	Capable of multiple tasks	Statistical analysis/graphing
Direct data entry	Yes	Yes
Data entry form tool	Yes	May require add-on tool
Mathematical/statistical functions	Preformatted equations available for rapid calculations/data analysis tools	Simple to sophisticated set of statistical procedures selected from pulldown menus
Charting and graphing	Flexible graphing tools with easy customization	Graphing tools selected from pulldown menu. Formatting and customization more challenging
Data sorting/filtering	Yes	Yes
Pivot tables (cross-tabulations)	Yes	Yes
Diagramming and drawing tools	Yes	No
Importation of data from database	Yes	Yes
Web output (html file format)	Yes	Yes
Budget analysis	Yes	No
What-if scenarios[1]	Yes	No

[1]A data analysis procedure to test different outcomes based upon a range of input options. For instance, one might test how an agency's total budget would be impacted by 2%, 4%, 6%, or 8% raises for all employees. As each of the raise percentages are input into the spreadsheet, formulas recalculate the total budget.

Sources: Johnson, 2001; Nash & Quon, 1996.

The Paradox of Spreadsheets and
Statistical Software in Social Service Practice

It is quite common in social work and other human and social services professional education programs for students to be taught to use statistical software such as SPSS. SPSS is a powerful statistical software package that is widely used in undergraduate and graduate education. Faculty members, especially those who teach research and statistical classes, often have some level of proficiency with SPSS because they likely had to use it in the data analysis required for their doctoral research. The cycle of learning pattern is that faculty learn SPSS or some other statistical software package in their doctoral education and then they teach the use of the same software in their undergraduate and graduate classes. The question then arises, Why should social workers and other social service professionals learn spreadsheets for data analysis when SPSS works so well and so many professors teach its use? This question is perhaps best answered by a simple bit of research. If you work in a social service agency or if you are a student doing a field placement or internship in a social service agency, examine the available programs on any computer to which you have approved access. See if you can find a spreadsheet or a statistical software package on the machines available to you. If the machines you are examining have the Windows operating system, then under the Start, select Programs. If you are using an Apple Macintosh, then click on the hard drive and look in the Applications folder. You may also want to ask a supervisor or information technology (IT) person in the agency whether computers in the agency have available spreadsheets or statistical software packages. Some supervisors may be better prepared or more technologically proficient and able to answer this question. Most agency IT staff should be able to offer a reasonably accurate answer.

The point of this small research project is that it is much more likely that you will find a spreadsheet on the social service agency computers you examine than a statistical software package. There are a number of good reasons for this likely fact. First, as described previously, spreadsheets are commonly installed on personal computers either by the vendor, the agency, or the personal owner, usually as part of an office suite. Second, the intended function of statistical software packages is too specific for them to be broadly installed on personal computers. The third factor is that widely taught statistical software packages such as SPSS are relatively expensive. There are less expensive, but perhaps less robust and powerful, statistical software packages available. However, a careful examination of social work research texts we conducted indicates that SPSS is the most commonly referenced statistical package (Patterson, Basham, & DeCoster, in preparation). It is our hypothesis that within social work, the use of statistical packages such as SPSS for data analysis is widely taught in undergraduate and graduate programs; paradoxically, students and professionals are far more likely to have access in social service practice settings to spreadsheets for data analysis than statistical packages. The unfortunate likely consequence of this mismatch between education and practice is that professionals are less likely to engage in practice and program evaluation and research. We believe practice and program evaluation are critical to the vitality of the profession. The purpose of this book is to prepare students and professionals to conduct the data analysis necessary to produce high-quality practice and program evaluation with the tools most readily available to them: spreadsheets.

Summary

This chapter provides an introduction to spreadsheets and their potential as a tool of practice in the social services. The chapter describes the history of the development of spreadsheets in their pre-electronic and electronic forms. Three trends in the development of spreadsheets are noted: the expansion of tools and features, improving ability to import and export information in multiple forms and formats, and increasingly widespread utilization. This chapter presents a rationale for the greater adoption of spreadsheets in social service practice. An overview of the basic features, functions, and data analysis tools of spreadsheets is presented. Finally, this chapter provides a comparison between spreadsheets with statistical software followed by an examination of spreadsheets' paradoxical underutilization in the social services despite their widespread availability.

REVIEW QUESTIONS

1. Who created the first personal computer-based spreadsheet for what purpose, and what was it called?

2. What are the three noteworthy trends in the history of personal computer spreadsheets?

3. How can the ethical imperatives to "monitor and evaluate" and "promote and facilitate evaluation and research" be accomplished with spreadsheets?

4. What types of information can be entered into spreadsheet cells?

5. What does the term "multidimensionality" mean in reference to spreadsheets?

6. What do formulas and functions do in spreadsheets?

7. How are the Data Analysis Tools activated in Excel and, once activated, where are they found in the menu bar?

8. What has been the historical paradox of spreadsheets in social service education and practice?

2 Data Collection Ways and Means

The Many Paths of Data Acquisition

The requisite precursor of data analysis is data acquisition. Social service professionals collect data in a wide variety of settings and for a broad array of purposes. Sadly and too frequently, the data they collect are not in a form amenable to ready data analysis, as it is often recorded on paper, a commonly available information medium (witness this book in your hands) that is distinctly lacking in information fluidity. Information fluidity refers to the fact that information in the form of electronic bits processed by computers can be readily moved between computer software applications or around the globe to other computers (Patterson, 2000; Negroponte, 1995). A bit is the presence or absence of an electronic pulse, a magnetized spot on a disk or hard drive, or a microscopic pit on the plastic-coated aluminum disk of a CD-ROM.

The collection of information in electronic form, as bits, maximizes its fluidity. Alternatively, the collection of information, especially large amounts of numerical information on atoms in the form of paper, impairs or inhibits one's capacity to summarize, statistically analyze, or in most other ways quickly make sense of the information. It commonly becomes necessary to transfer paper-based data to a computer, to translate it from atoms to bits, to accomplish meaningful data analysis. The point here is that if the eventual goal is extraction of information and meaning from data, it is far more efficient to begin with collecting the information as bits, not atoms, in spreadsheets, not on paper.

This chapter describes multiple ways to use spreadsheets for collection of data relevant to social service practice. Before we proceed, it might be helpful to consider the many paths of data acquisition. The fact is that data of interest and importance to social work practitioners and agencies comes from many sources. We collect information during home visits with clients and their families. We record the important facts of client visits to clinics and agencies. We document services delivered in hospitals, school, jails, prisons, and offices. We are called on to summarize information from agency databases, financial records, and surveys of customer satisfaction. Data from each of these sources may be either recorded directly in a spreadsheet or imported into a spreadsheet for summarization. Increasing availability and declining cost of laptops and PDAs (personal digital assistants) with spreadsheet software makes the collection of data from home visits and out of office work ever more feasible. Data collected from the laptops and PDAs of multiple workers can be pooled into a single spreadsheet for summarization and report generation. Data drawn from agency databases can be imported into spreadsheets for analysis and graphical representation. This chapter provides the basic spreadsheet procedures for this spectrum of data acquisition tasks, which are applicable to the collection of data from multiple sources and social service practice settings.

Levels of Measurement

Variables and Attributes

Before describing how to collect data in spreadsheets it is necessary to provide a much more specific definition of *data*. For our purposes we will define data as "factual information encoded into a form allowing for transmission and processing" (Patterson, 2000, p. 322). This "factual information" is commonly organized into variables. A variable is something that can change or varies. Examples include age, weight, level of depression, and so on. A variable is composed of two or more attributes. An attribute is a quality, property, or characteristic of something or somebody. Note that as stated above, a variable is composed of two or more attributes. A variable with a single attribute does not vary and is therefore not a variable. The two fundamental characteristics of a variable are that its attributes are exhaustive and that the attributes in the variable are mutually exclusive. The attributes of a variable are said to be exhaustive if it includes all the possible responses, conditions, or categories. For instance, the U.S. Census Bureau (2003) defines the variable "marital status" as including the attributes never married, married, divorced, and widowed. Recognizing that the attribute "married" also may have variation, they define it as a secondary variable with the attributes "married, spouse present," "separated," and "other married, spouse absent." The exhaustive range of attributes for some variables are at times numerous but infrequent. Race is an example of a variable with a large number of possible attributes that in many settings will have low frequency counts. For such variables, it is often preferable to use the attribute "other" for attributes that infrequently occur.

The second requirement of attributes, "mutually exclusive," means that a respondent or client should not have or qualify for two or more attributes in a variable at the same time. For example, the attributes of "marital status" are mutually exclusive if considered from the perspective of one's status at the point of time when the question is asked. Alternatively, one might be "widowed" from a previous marriage and "married" at present. The mutual exclusivity of the attributes of the variable then becomes dependent on how the question is asked. The important point here is that when defining the attributes of a variable, it is critical to consider both their definitional independence and the manner in which the question eliciting information for the variable is structured or stated.

Variables have four possible levels of measurement: nominal, ordinal, interval, and ratio. The level of measure of a variable is an important factor to consider in both data collection and subsequently in data analysis. Level of measurement affects the type of statistics one can use in analysis of the data, the precision with which the variable is measured, and the manner in which the data may be transformed in subsequent analyses. Definitions of the four levels of data analysis follow, and constraints of level of measurement in all data analysis are described.

Nominal Data

Nominal data typically indicates differences in kind or type. It is sometimes referred to as qualitative or categorical data in that it specifies the differences in the attributes of the variable that are not quantifiable, but qualitative. Nominal-level variables are frequently used as sociodemographic descriptors. Examples of nominal measures include ethnicity, gender, occupation, political party, and city of birth.

It is common practice to assign a numerical value to the attributes of nominal level variables such as marital status, for instance, 1 = never married, 2 = married, 3 = divorced, and 4 = widowed. The numerical values assigned to the categories within this variable of marital status are merely a means of coding the data and have no quantitative meaning. In nominal level variables, numerical values are used only to indicate qualitative differences. One cannot calculate the mean, standard deviation, or median of a nominal level variable. One can, however, compute the frequency of each attribute in the variable. So, for instance, in a sample of 100 individuals, 33 may report never being married, 40 might be married, 20 are divorced, and 7 are widowed. In this case we know the relative frequency of marital status in the sample; however, it would be mathematically inappropriate to report the mean marital status. Reporting the standard deviation of marital status would make no sense either. Nonetheless, measuring the relative frequency of the attributes in a variable measured at the nominal level allows one to report the occurrence of each attribute in the sample being measured.

Ordinal Data

Ordinal data expresses information about the rank of the categories contained within the range of measurement in the variable. Unlike nominal data in which there is no ordering of the attributes of the variable, ordinal data expresses a rank ordering, providing information on the relative position of each attribute in relationship to the others, but not conveying information on the relative distance between the attributes. For example, clients might be asked to rank their level of marital satisfaction on a scale of 1 to 5 with 1 = highly dissatisfied, 2 = moderately dissatisfied, 3 = neutral, 4 = moderately satisfied, and 5 = highly satisfied, as in Figure 2.1. Each point in this 5-point scale represents a relative ranking of satisfaction with marriage. As such, clients rating their marital satisfaction at level 2 would be said to be less satisfied than clients rating their marital satisfaction at a level 4. However, because the relative distance between the points on an ordinal scale are not known one could not assume that the clients rating their group experience as a 4 are twice as satisfied as clients rating their marital satisfaction as a 2. In this example, the relative position of the respective ratings are known; however, the magnitude of difference remains unknown.

Ordinal level scales are commonly used in social service practice to measure variables of interest, especially when attempting to rate or evaluate variation based on judgment of either the client or that of a social service professional. One form of ordinal scale is the Likert scale. Likert scales are used to measure respondents' level of agreement with a specific statement. For instance, clients at a mental health clinic might receive a consumer satisfaction survey in which they are asked to respond to the statement, "I believe I am receiving the services I need from this clinic" with a Likert scale containing the following response categories (attributes): 1 = strongly disagree, 2 = disagree, 3 = undecided, 4 = agree, 5 = strongly agree.

Other examples of ordinal variables include quality of housing arrangement, symptom severity, current risk of rehospitalization, level of educational attainment, socioeconomic group, and medication compliance. Two of these variables, level of educational attainment and socioeconomic group, alternatively might be measured as either ordinal level variables or at the interval/ratio level.

Nominal Variable	Marital Status									
Attribute	Never Married	Married		Divorced		Widowed				
Value	1	2		3		4				

Ordinal Variable	Marital Satisfaction									
Attribute	Highly Dissatisfied	Moderately Dissatisfied			Neutral	Moderately Satisfied			Highly Satisfied	
Value	1	2			3	4			5	

Interval Variable	Marital Emotional Intelligence									
Attribute	0	5	10	15	20	25	30	35	40	

Ratio Variable	Years of Marriage									
Attribute	0	1	2	3	4	5	6	7	8	9	10

FIGURE 2.1   Levels of Measurement

For the time being, let us consider how educational attainment and socioeconomic status might be measured as ordinal variables and the intrinsic limitations of doing so. Educational attainment can be quantified by a ranking of 1 = less than high school completion, 2 = high school completion, 3 = some college, 4 = college completion, 5 = some graduate education, and 6 = graduate degree. Quantified in this way, the ordinal variable of educational attainment allows for the rating of an individual's level of educational attainment and the comparison of one or more individuals in terms of educational attainment. The limitation here in using an ordinal ranking is that there is a lack of precision. One semester of college represents a significantly lower level of educational attainment than three and one half years of college, yet individuals with these two very different levels of education would be lumped together with this ordinal scale. The more precise measurement of educational attainment would be to use a higher level of measurement ratio, in which the years of education are specified.

Likewise, one approach to measuring socioeconomic status is to rank individuals along a continuum ranging from poor to wealthy with additionally specified increments such as near poor, lower middle class, middle class, and upper middle class. Alternatively, an ordinal scale ranking socioeconomic status could be developed using annual household income increments of $10,000. The scale would allow for ranking individuals along their income level and comparing individuals or groups of individuals on income level. This type of ordinal ranking of income is commonly seen in social service settings where clients are asked at the time of intake to indicate their annual income on an ordinal scale with broad increments. As with educational attainment, this is a means to collect important data in a straightforward and easy manner. The problem again is a lack of precision. In attempting to analyze annual income, one may report the relative frequency of clients in each increment of income and the most commonly occurring level of income (mode). Unfortunately, income measured with this type of ordinal scale does not lend itself to commonly used and more precise statistics such as mean (average) and standard deviation. These descriptive statistics will be described in subsequent chapters. The important point here is that while it may occasionally be necessary or expedient to measure variables such as educational attainment and socioeconomic status with ordinal scales, from the point of view of data analysis it is preferable to use more precise interval or ratio level measures. It is to these levels of measurement that we will now turn our attention.

Interval Data

Interval level variables have characteristics and utility beyond variables measured at the ordinal level. Like ordinal level variables, the attributes of interval level variables are ordered by rank. An attribute with the corresponding value of 10 is greater than an attribute on the same scale with a corresponding value of 5. However, unlike ordinal variables, the distance between attributes of interval variables are equally spaced and constant. There is a known distance between attributes. Therefore, if one were to measure Marital Emotional Intelligence (presuming it actually exists) with the interval scale displayed in Figure 2.1, a wife receiving a score of 30 would be said to score 15 points higher on this marital emotional intelligence scale than a husband receiving a score of 15. Of course, this is a purely hypothetical example! However, for reasons related to the arbitrariness of the zero on interval level measures, the wife could not be said to have twice the marital emotional intelligence of her husband. Following is a discussion of this issue of the arbitrary zero.

Data derived from interval level measurement of variables allows for the use of more sophisticated statistics than are appropriate to use with nominal and ordinal variables. One can calculate the mean (average) and the standard deviation (a statistic indicating the dispersion of scores from the mean) for interval level variables. Interval level variables are commonly necessary for bivariate and multivariate statistical procedures, which we describe in subsequent chapters.

Examples of interval level variables include standardized intelligence tests, marital emotional intelligence, and temperature measured on Fahrenheit scale. What is common for each of these three measures and the feature that differentiates interval level measures from ratio level measures, discussed in the next section, is the absence of a true zero. The zero on any interval level measure is arbitrary. A zero on an intelligence test does not mean the subject is devoid of any form of intelligence; it only means that the subject answered each question on the test incorrectly. A temperature of zero on the Fahrenheit scale does not indicate the total absence of heat. As for the marital emotional intelligence scale, one would presume that as an interval level scale, a score of zero would not necessarily indicate a person totally devoid of any "marital emotional intelligence." Should future development and testing of such a scale find individuals totally devoid of "marital emotional intelligence," the scale would need to be reclassified as a ratio level measure. It is to the ratio level of measurement that we now turn our attention.

Ratio Data

Ratio level measures have all the attributes of interval level measures along with the presence of a true or absolute zero. Ratio level measures do not have negative values. Examples of ratio data include years of marriage, number of children, age, length of time in a residence, and number of therapy sessions. For each of these ratio level variables it is not possible to have a negative value. The zero is an absolute point.

Because a ratio level variable has a true zero, we are able to specify the magnitude of difference between values (attributes) in the variable. For instance, a fifty-year-old individual is twice the age of a twenty-five-year-old or a person who has lived in his or her apartment for three years has only a third of the length of residency of a person who has lived in his or her apartment for nine years. This capacity to measure magnitude of difference is distinct from interval level variables. Recall in the previous example of marital emotional intelligence, one could say that the wife scored 15 points higher than her husband on the scale, but that due to arbitrary zero of the scale, her score of 30 could not be said to be twice his score of 15. The distinction between interval and ratio level variables regarding the matter of an arbitrary versus absolute zero is a rather nuanced argument that is of consequence perhaps only to mathematicians and statisticians. For our data analytic and statistical purposes, we will typically treat interval and ratio level variables in the same manner.

A common mistake that novice researchers and data analysts make is treating a variable that could be either interval or ratio as an ordinal level variable. For example, as described previously, educational attainment can be quantified by a ranking of 1 = less than high school completion, 2 = high school completion, 3 = some college, 4 = college completion, 5 = some graduate education, and 6 = graduate degree. Alternatively, asking a respondents how many years of education they received allows the variable to be treated as ratio level data, which opens the possibility of conducting higher-level statistical analysis on the resulting data. It could be argued that a researcher may want to ask the question both ways, as many college students spend more than four years in college but do not move on to graduate education. Therefore, posing two questions, one with an ordinal attribute and the other with a ratio level answer, would yield more information for the researcher. It is extremely important to think through how questions are posed and, when possible, to use the highest level of measure appropriate for answers.

Data Coding

Data in social service practice and research are collected from numerous sources including electronic client records, surveys, direct observations, and chart reviews. Prior to initiating the collection of any form of data, an extremely important consideration is how the data will be coded to enable its subsequent analysis with a spreadsheet. Data coding is the process of organizing data through the creation and assignment of numerical values for nominal data and ordinal data. In the case of nominal data, numerical values are assigned to each attribute in the variable. For example, in Figure 2.1 the four categories of marital status are coded with numerical values. Ordinal data, especially from Likert scales on survey instruments, may take the form of standardized text categories such as Strongly Disagree, Disagree, Undecided, Agree, and Strongly Agree. As with nominal data, each category on this Likert scale would be assigned a numerical value.

Traditionally, researchers and data analysts have used codebooks to document information about a data set. Codebooks have typically been a document of one or more pages containing information about each variable, including a short form of each variable's name, a longer, more descriptive variable name, each question or instrument item, and each category or label in the variable with its respective numerical value. Spreadsheets offer several highly flexible alternatives to a traditional codebook, including comment windows, text boxes, and codebook sheets.

Comment Windows

Comment windows are containers into which information pertaining to a cell in a spreadsheet is entered. For data collection purposes, comment windows can be created containing all the codebook information germane to each variable. Typically the names of variables are entered in the first row of the spreadsheet (see Figure 2.2). A pop-up comment window is a useful tool by which to remember data codes when a questionnaire does not already have values assigned to each attribute of the variable. Comment windows are inserted by clicking "Insert" in the Menu bar and then clicking "Comment." Once the comment window appears, simply click in the window to enter the variable's attributes and assigned values. In some situations, such as in the case of a survey, it may be helpful to enter the question for each variable into the comment window as well as the attributes and assigned values. The variable "Marital Satisfactions" in Figure 2.2 is an example of including the question in the comment window. Comment windows may either be set to be visible all the time or to pop up when the cursor is moved over the top of a cell containing a comment window. A small triangle in the upper left corner of a cell indicates the presence of a hidden comment window. To see all the comment windows in a spreadsheet, select View, Comments from the menu bar. Repeating this command sequence hides all the comment windows in the spreadsheet. See the accompanying CD-ROM video animation: *Comment Windows.*

Text Boxes

A second alternative to a codebook is the use of text boxes in either the first or second row of a spreadsheet to hold the requisite codebook information for each variable. As its name implies, a text box is simply "a rectangular space in an application into which text may be

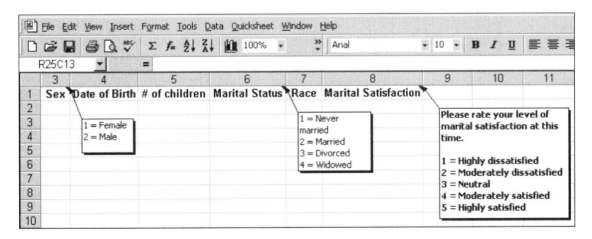

FIGURE 2.2   Pop-up Comment Windows for Data Coding

inserted or typed" (Patterson, 2000, p. 326). Configuring a spreadsheet with text boxes to receive data from a survey instrument or questionnaire requires the following steps:

1. Decide whether to place variable names in either the first or second row of the spreadsheet. Placement of text boxes for codebook information in the first row and variable names in the second row facilitates subsequent data analysis as this increases the ease of copying the variable names and data into another worksheet for data analysis.

2. Enlarge the height of the first row by moving the pointer of the line between rows 1 and 2 on the far left side of the spreadsheet, then clicking and dragging the line down until the row reaches the desired height. The actual height and width of the cell will depend on the length of the question the cell will contain. The width of each column can be expanded by moving the pointer to the line between the column identification numbers, then clicking and dragging the column to the desired width.

3. Insert a text box into each of the cells of the first row for each of the items in the survey. Text boxes are available in the spreadsheet's Drawing Tools toolbar. If the Drawing Tools toolbar is not present in the spreadsheet, from the menu bar select View, Toolbars, then Drawing. Simply typing or pasting a question into the cell inserts the text as a single line, which necessitates creating very wide cells in order to see the entire question. A text box wraps the text to fit the size of the box.

4. In the order they appear on the survey, type or paste each question from its word processing file into the text boxes created in the first row.

5. In the second row, type the variables names.

6. Locate the split box at the top of the vertical scroll bar. The split box is a small, rectangular box. When the pointer is placed over the top of the split box, the cursor changes it to a bi-directional, up and down arrow. After clicking on the box, drag it to above the third row. This will keep the first two rows visible as data are entered into succeeding rows.

7. See Figure 2.3 for an example of a spreadsheet configured with text boxes. Also see the accompanying CD-ROM video animation: "Text Boxes."

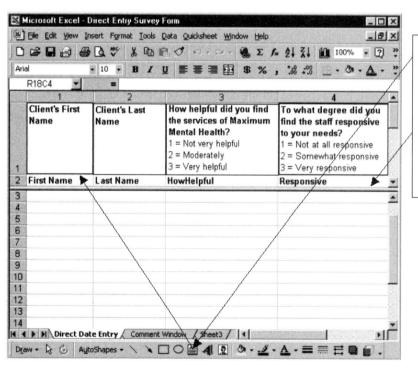

FIGURE 2.3   Text Boxes for Data Coding

Codebook Sheets

The third way to incorporate codebook information for a data set in a spreadsheet is to enter the information on the variables in a second worksheet in the spreadsheet. Spreadsheets typically allow for the creation of multiple worksheets within a single spreadsheet document. For instance, in Figure 2.4, there are four tabs labeling the four worksheets in that particular spreadsheet. The "Codebook" worksheet documents the column location of each variable, the variable name, the variable description or question, and the attributes and values of each variable. Figure 2.5 displays this codebook worksheet. The advantage of creating a separate worksheet for the codebook is that because of the virtually unlimited space of a worksheet, it allows for the inclusion of much more detailed information on each variable than is practical using either text boxes or comment windows. The disadvantage of a codebook worksheet is that if data are being entered directly into a spreadsheet, the values for the attributes are not displayed on the data worksheet, which could result in data entry errors, a topic covered in Chapter 3. Alternatively, one could configure the data worksheet with either text boxes or comment windows and create a codebook worksheet in which detailed information about each variable of the data set is documented.

Basic Data Entry

There are many ways to get data into a spreadsheet. In the following sections we will describe a number of ways to import or pull data into a spreadsheet for subsequent analysis. But first let us address perhaps the most simple and straightforward means of spreadsheet data entry: typing data into the cells of a spreadsheet formatted for data entry.

There are two spreadsheet formatting conventions that will facilitate the ease with which data analysis can proceed and enable the transfer of data from a spreadsheet into databases or statistical software. Additionally, most of the data analysis procedures described in subsequent chapters are predicated on the assumption that the spreadsheet is formatted in accordance with these conventions. First, the names of the variables in the data set are always entered into the first row of the spreadsheet. The second convention of data entry is that the case identifier should appear in the first column on the far left-hand side of the spreadsheet (Column A). In some instances, the case identifier will be the subject or client's first or last name. In other instances, the case identifier will be some numerical or alphanumeric code. Because one usually starts or searches the data with the case name or identifier, placing the primary case identifier in the first column facilitates both the ease of data entry as well as subsequent data retrieval.

Commonly, data sets or case records contain more records than there are rows on the spreadsheet as it initially appears on screen. If there are more records than the number of rows appearing on the screen, use the split screen tool as shown in Figure 2.3. Splitting the screen beneath the first or second row allows the variable names to remain visible as data are entered into rows that are not initially visible on the screen. This feature holds the first and second rows in place and visible while rows beneath them can be scrolled downward as data are entered.

An alternative to splitting the spreadsheet screen is to freeze a portion of the screen so it does not scroll. This is accomplished in Excel by selecting the row beneath the row where

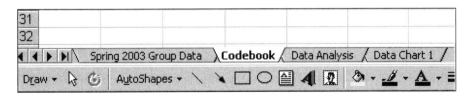

FIGURE 2.4 Worksheet Tabs

File   Edit   View   Insert   Format   Tools   Data   Quicksheet   Window   Help

Arial   ▼ 10 ▼   **B** *I* <u>U</u>   ≡ ≡ ≡ 国   **$** % ,   ⁺.₀ .₀₀   ⧗ ⧘   ▦ ▾ ◊ ▾ **A** ▾

R31C12   ▼   =

	1	2	3	4	5	6
1	**Column**	**Variable Name**	**Variable Description/Question**	**Attributes and Values**		
2		1 Session	Semester and Year of the Group	Fall or Spring/Year		
3						
4		2 Leader	Group Leader	1 = DP		
5				2 = MM		
6				3 = LD		
7						
8		3 InstruVer	Instrument Version	1 = Before Fall 2000		
9				2 = After Fall 2000		
10						
11		4 Subgroup#	Class Subgroup	1 = Odd		
12				2 = Even		
13		5 ID#	Group member unique identifier	Last four digits of SS#		
14						
15		6 Date	Date of the group session	month/day/year		
16						
17		7 Time	I feel _____ with the	1 = Very dissatisfied		
18			amount of time I had to talk in	2 = Moderately dissatisfied		
19			group today.	3 = Mildly dissatisfied		
20				4 = No feeling one way or the other		
21				5 = Mildly satisfied		
22				6 = Moderately satisfied		
23				7 = Very satisfied		
24						
25		8 Honesty	I feel _____ with the	1 = Very dissatisfied		
26			amount of group honesty today.	2 = Moderately dissatisfied		
27				3 = Mildly dissatisfied		
28				4 = No feeling one way or the other		
29				5 = Mildly satisfied		
30				6 = Moderately satisfied		
31				7 = Very satisfied		

FIGURE 2.5   Codebook Worksheet

the split is to appear. An entire row is selected by clicking on the row number in the far left-hand column. Once the row is selected, from the menu bar select Window, Freeze Pane. After these steps are complete, the frozen rows will remain visible, while the remainder can be scrolled through for data entry. One could freeze the top two rows so that text boxes containing data codes remain visible as data are entered in the rows below them.

Creating Data Entry Forms

An alternative procedure for entering data into a spreadsheet is to create a data entry form. A data entry form uses the variables' names from the first row in a spreadsheet to create a form to simplify data entry (Rutledge, 1997). Figure 2.6 specifies the steps of this process in Microsoft Excel. Also see the accompanying CD-ROM video animation: "Data Entry Forms."

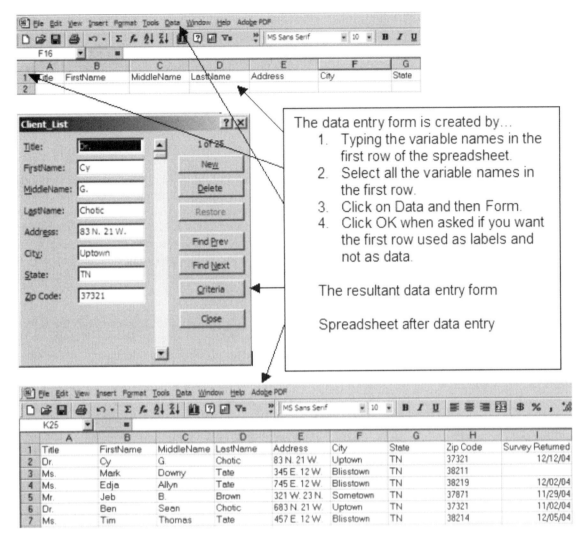

FIGURE 2.6   Data Entry Form Creation

Creating and using a data entry form to input data may increase the speed with which one can enter data. Additionally, using a data entry form instead of typing data directly into a spreadsheet may decrease data entry errors as one sees only the cells (fields) into which data are entered, thereby improving one's visual focus on the information entered and making it easier to detect errant data. The Tab key moves the cursor or data insertion point between cells. To enter a new case or record, click New and then type the data for each variable displayed in the form into the cell adjacent to the variable name. When the form is complete, press Enter on the keyboard. The data for that case is entered into the spreadsheet and the data entry form is cleared of the prior data, making the data entry form available for the next case.

One drawback of the data entry form in Excel is that the actual form is limited to 32 columns (variables). If there are more than 32 variables in the data set, one can either enter data directly into the spreadsheet as described previously or use one of the alternative procedures that follow.

Downloading Data

The collection of data for analysis does not always involve entering data into a spreadsheet in a case-by-case, row-by-row manner. Sometimes in social service practice, data acquisition necessitates the retrieval of information from an existing data source such as an agency database or web-based data source. *Downloading* is the term given to the process of copying data to a personal computer from a network filer server or from a computer on the Web (a web server). Most readers will certainly be familiar with the concept, if not the practice, of downloading music files from the Web. Both music files and data files are fundamentally a collection of 1s and 0s. Data files that can be read by spreadsheets simply have a different format and structure than music files such as MP3 files.

Format

One of the key factors in successfully downloading data files is knowing the format of the file and whether that file format can be read by the spreadsheet program one is using. Most spreadsheets are capable of reading a broad range of file formats including standard spreadsheet file formats (Excel–.xls, Lotus–.123), web pages (.html), text files (.txt), data interchange files (.dif), rich text files (.rtf), and MS Access database files (.mdb), to name a few. Spreadsheet file formats, text files, and some web pages can be opened directly into an Excel spreadsheet, while database files are downloaded into spreadsheets through a set of procedures for getting external data.

Sometimes Excel will not recognize the structure of the data and the Text Import Wizard will be activated. When this happens a Text Import Wizard window appears that directs the user through a step-by-step process of specifying the structure of the data so that it can be read into appropriate rows and columns. In regard to spreadsheets, the phrase "structure of the data" generally refers to the organization of the data within the file. Typically, the characters in a data file will either be "delimited" by commas or tabs that separate each field or the data file will have a "fixed width" where characters are aligned in columns with between fields. Delimited (also known as Tab-delimited) files and Fixed width (also known as Fixed ASCII) files can be recognized by their .dat file extension. The Text Import Wizard uses the information it obtains from the user in the three steps of the importation process to produce a spreadsheet with the imported data in the proper rows and columns.

If one encounters difficulty opening a data file from another software package, it is often possible to save such data files in an alternate format that can be opened by the spreadsheet. For instance, SPSS files can be saved as Excel, Tab-delimited, and Fixed ACSII files, all of which can be opened by most spreadsheets. If you are working in an agency that maintains client or fiscal information in one or more databases, it is possible to request that the database administrator query the appropriate database for the information from specific variables in the database germane to the analysis you wish to conduct. It is then important to request saving an electronic transmission of the resultant data file in a format that can be opened by your spreadsheet software. Most commercial database software can readily create and save this type of "flat file" in a format useable by spreadsheets.

Web-Based Data Retrieval

Publication of information in spreadsheets residing on either the Internet or on agency intranets has become an increasingly common practice for the dissemination of data to both limited and broad audiences. An intranet is a network internal to an organization or company that uses Internet software to share information on internal web servers (Patterson, 2000). Excel spreadsheets placed on Internet or intranet servers can accessed by standard web browsers such as Microsoft Internet Explorer or Netscape by simply typing the URL (universal resource locator—the address of a file on the Internet or on an intranet) into the address box of the web browser. The most recent versions of both Internet Explorer and Netscape will open spreadsheets directly into Microsoft Excel, as long as Excel is installed on that personal computer. Once the file is opened, it can be saved to the computer, thereby making it ready for data analysis. The U.S. government posts multiple spreadsheets with budgetary information at http://w3.access.gpo.gov/usbudget/fy2003/spreadsheets.html. Readers may wish to visit this site and experiment with opening and saving one or more of the available spreadsheets. This capacity to retrieve spreadsheet data from Internet public domain sources such as government websites enables social service providers to access and utilize data to support justifications of funding requests, provide information for client education initiatives, and compare local data to state, regional, and national data.

Excel Web Query

There are many data sources on the Web that do not use the Excel.xls file format. Instead these data sources format data in standard HTML (**h**ypertext **m**arkup **l**anguage—used for authoring web documents) formatting to present information in a table format. One option to retrieve data in HTML tables is to use the MS Excel's Web Query tool. The Web Query tool extracts data from a specified web page and imports it into an Excel spreadsheet. Before using this tool for the first time, select Tools in the Excel menu bar, and then select Add-Ins. A pop-up window titled Add-Ins appears. Click the check box beside MS Query Add-In. While this window is open, click the check box beside Analysis ToolPak. The Analysis ToolPak will be used in data analysis tasks in subsequent chapters, so go ahead and activate it now while the Add-Ins window is open. After the check boxes beside these two tools are selected, click OK and the Add-Ins window disappears. The process of doing a Web Query is illustrated in Figure 2.7. Also see the accompanying CD-ROM video animation: "Web Data Query."

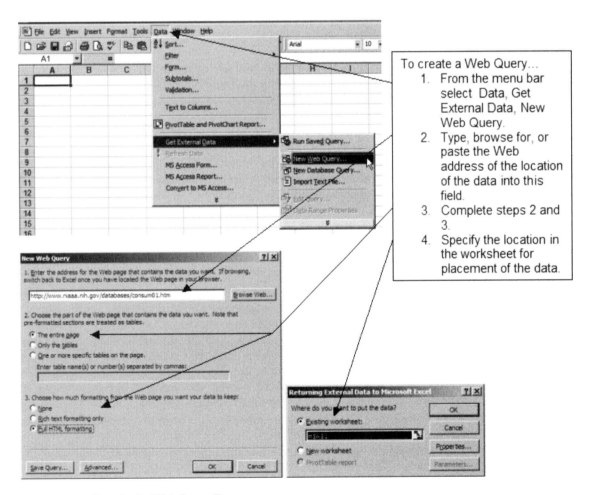

FIGURE 2.7   Steps in the Web Query Process

A number of useable tables can be found at www.niaaa.nih.gov/databases/qf.htm. Users may wish to experiment with the Web Query procedure using some of the data tables found at this site.

Relating to Database Software

One method of acquiring data for analysis in a spreadsheet is extracting the data from a database. Database software can manage large quantities of information. Databases are used in a wide range of areas related to social service practice, including mailing lists, client records, referral resources, financial transactions, and donor contributions. Databases are a means to store information, like an electronic filing system (Margolis, 1996). Beyond information storage, most databases provide options for summarizing data in reports, basic data analysis, sorting data on specified parameters, and finding specific information. Data queries search for information meeting designated criteria, such as every case in a certain Zip code area between 18 and 50 years old. Other examples are that a financial donor database could be queried to retrieve and calculate the total pledges of each donor in order to select those donors who have contributed more than a specified amount, or the financial donor database might be queried to sum the total amounts received from each donor or to provide the average amount pledged.

Databases store information in one or more tables. Each table is composed of fields and records. A field is a single type of information such as last name or city. In data analysis terms, fields are variables. Fields, like columns in spreadsheets, arrange information vertically in the table. A record is all the information about a single object or individual in the table.

There are two general types of databases: desktop databases and server databases. Generally speaking, desktop databases are used by a single user and are located on that user's personal computer (Chapple, 2003). It is possible to share access to a desktop database with other users on a network, though this functionality is not always employed. Desktop databases include Microsoft Access and FileMaker Pro. Server databases reside on a server on a network across which multiple users access the contents of the database. Examples of server databases include Oracle, MySQL, Microsoft Visual FoxPro, and FileMaker Server.

Although databases are excellent tools for the collection, storage, and retrieval of simple and complex datasets, spreadsheets are a much more robust and flexible tool for data analysis. Consequently, it is important to know how to move data from databases to spreadsheets for subsequent data analysis. It is beyond the scope of this discussion to review in detail how to extract and transfer data from each of the database applications named above into a spreadsheet. In most social service agencies utilizing server databases, the database administrator typically can query databases on specific search parameters and provide users with the query results in a spreadsheet format. For instance, an administrator of an outpatient intensive substance abuse treatment program conducting a year-end review of services delivered might request a query of the agency's database for a file listing every client served in the previous year, their diagnoses, admit dates, discharge dates, number of services delivered in each service category, admit severity ratings, discharge severity ratings, and follow-up outcome indicators. The database administrator would query the agency database for these specified fields (variables) and delimit the search for clients served in the previous year. This query could then be saved in a spreadsheet format and sent electronically to the program administrator for data analysis.

In an alternative scenario, the data for the query described above might reside in a desktop database shared by members of an outpatient intensive substance abuse treatment team. Extraction of the requisite data requires querying the database. In Microsoft Access, the Queries tool is used to select the data tables from which to pull data, specify the fields (variables) in which to search, and choose the parameters (e.g., after this date but before this date) with which to delimit the query. In Access, once the query is run, the resulting data can be sent to an Excel spreadsheet by selecting from the menu bar, Tools, Office Links, Analyze It with MS Excel. This simple procedure copies the queried data into an Excel spreadsheet for data analysis. For more information on querying MS Access databases, see Patterson (2000) and Fuller and Pagan (1997). Also see the accompanying CD-ROM video animation: "Database Query."

Saving What You Have and Using What You Need

Thus far we have described the many paths of data acquisition with spreadsheets. The collection of data, especially data collected from paper-based records or in field settings, can be a time- and labor-intensive process. Once data is in a spreadsheet, through any of the means described previously, it is critical to preserve the data before, during, and after the process of data analysis. The fundamental principle is to save a copy of the acquired data that will not be altered by any step of the data analysis. Preservation of a copy of the original data set ensures that effort expended toward its collection is not wasted should any calamity befall the data or the computer on which it resides.

There are a number of ways to retain a copy of a dataset before beginning data analysis. The easiest is to simply save a copy of the data using a slightly different name, indicating its status. For instance, a spreadsheet data file titled CaseMgn.xls might be preserved as CaseMgn-Original.xls. One would then conduct all data analysis on the CaseMgn.xls file, reserving CaseMgn-Orignal.xls for use if there was some unexpected corruption or loss of the CaseMgn.xls file or a catastrophic hardware failure. In the case of a catastrophic hardware failure, such as the malfunction of a hard drive, recovery of the original data file is contingent on saving it to a backup medium other than a single hard drive. The important point is to create backup copies of all critical data files on data storage media such as CD-ROMs, Zip disks, external hard drives, or network servers. Many people store smaller data files on diskettes. Unfortunately, diskettes have significant file size limitations, 1.4 megabytes, and are one of the least reliable means of storage. When pressed for time or if other storage media are unavailable, one option is to simply e-mail a backup copy of data to oneself, thereby preserving it temporarily on the server of one's e-mail service.

Spreadsheets typically allow for the creation of multiple worksheets within a single spreadsheet workbook. While engaged in the analysis of a data file, a good practice is to preserve a copy of the original raw data file on one worksheet and then start the data analysis with a copy of the raw data file that is saved to another worksheet within the spreadsheet workbook. For instance, in the spreadsheet workbook in Figure 2.8, the worksheet labeled Working Sheet 1 holds a copy of the data file from which variables are copied and pasted into other worksheets for various statistical tests. This procedure helps to ensure the integrity of the data throughout the data analysis process.

30	0.334638	.00	1.00	.00	2.00	6.00	3.00	3.00	3.00	45.00
31	0.945138	1.00	4.00	255.00	2.00	2.00	4.00	2.00	5.00	37.00
32	0.658431	1.00	8.00	422.00	4.00	4.00	2.00	1.00	6.00	41.00
33	0.233581	.00	3.00	400.00	6.00	8.00	6.00	6.00	6.00	40.00
34	0.148762	1.00	8.00	826.00	2.00	7.00	1.00	1.00	1.00	45.00

Descriptive Stats / Scratch \ **Working Sheet 1** / Raw Data / t-test / One-way ANOVA / Correlation / Chi-Square /

FIGURE 2.8   Spreadsheet Workbook with Multiple Data Files and Data Analysis Worksheets

Summary

This chapter describes multiple methods of bringing data into spreadsheets in preparation for conducting data analysis: the extraction of meaning from numbers. The four levels of measurement of attributes of variables are described. Nominal data indicates kind or type. Ordinal data conveys rank or order in categories within a variable. Interval level variables have attributes with rank order, fixed distance between the attributes or values, and have an arbitrary zero. Ratio level variables have attributes with rank order, a fixed distance between the attributes or values, and have a true zero. This chapter covers data coding and spreadsheet methods of conveying the codes assigned to variable attributes during the process of data entry, including comment windows, text boxes, and codebook sheets. Covered as well are data entry methods, including basic data entry procedures and the creation and use of data entry forms. Described here are several means of downloading data into spreadsheets, including web-based data retrieval, Excel web queries, and data extraction from databases. Described as well are procedures for saving and preserving data prior to and during data analysis.

REVIEW QUESTIONS

1. What are the advantages of collecting data as bits instead of atoms?

2. What is a variable and what is an attribute?

3. What are two examples of nominal, ordinal, interval, and ratio level variables not used in this chapter?

4. What is data coding and why is it important?

5. How do you insert comment boxes and text boxes in a data collection spreadsheet?

6. How do you create data entry forms?

7. How do you retrieve data from the Web using the Excel web query?

8. What is the fundamental principle of data management, once data have been collected?

CHAPTER

3

Selecting Samples

Samples: First Facts

It is virtually impossible to listen to the news during an election year and not hear about samples. Pollsters regularly report on the voting preferences of "a random sample of likely voters." Likewise, news reports of research findings often report that the results are based on subjects randomly selected to participate in the study. All of this leads to the questions, "What is a sample?" and, more particularly, "What are random samples and how are they selected?" A sample is a subset of a population from which inferences about and descriptions of the population under study are made. A population is understood to be the total theoretically specified collection of subjects or cases of interest to the researcher (Healey, 1993). To put an even finer point on the issue, the "study population" is the collection or aggregation of subjects or cases from which the sample will actually be selected.

There are two primary methods of selecting samples: nonprobability or nonrandom sampling and probability or random sampling. Nonprobability sampling relies on available subjects, selected by methods that offer no assurance that each subject in the population has an equal chance of being selected for the sample. Subjects are often selected because the researcher has convenient access to them or because other subjects in a sample know them. The subject selection methods of nonprobability sampling call into question whether the subjects in the sample are actually representative of the population. Nonprobability sampling provides no control for the possibility that bias has shaped the selection of subjects in the sample. The findings from studies that employ nonprobability sampling cannot be generalized to the population from which the sample was drawn. The selection of nonprobability samples with spreadsheets is not addressed in this text because of the fundamental ease with which random samples can be selected from data sets using spreadsheet procedures.

Probability sampling, on the other hand, offers a number of research advantages over nonprobability sampling. Probability sampling methods use some form of random sampling in order to select subjects for the sample from the population of interest. Random sampling enables the selection of a sample of subjects whose characteristics will approximate those of the population from which the sample is drawn. The degree to which a sample is similar to the population is referred to as its representativeness. Additionally, probability sampling ensures that each case or individual in the population has an equal chance of being selected in the sample. Random sampling controls for the possibility of selection bias. Perhaps most importantly, probability sampling makes it possible to generalize findings from the sample to the population. This chapter describes several methods of selecting random samples from data sets using spreadsheets.

Aside from the research rationale for the use of probability samples, there are several other advantages to the employment of random sampling in data analysis applicable to the social services. It is not always necessary or desirable to use all data available on a particular population in order to answer questions of interest about that population. Social service agencies may have databases containing information on thousands of clients from multiple years of service delivery. Health care providers can have datasets composed of tens of thousands of cases. One of the authors of this text once worked for a health care claims administrator that had a dataset containing information on over 400,000 hospitalizations. Advances in the speed and power of personal computers now make it possible to analyze extremely large datasets that were once a challenge to the number-crunching abilities of mainframe computers. However, it is generally not necessary to analyze all the data in a dataset on a particular population in order to make inferences about that population. Instead, one can employ random sampling procedures to select data on a subset of the population of interest and infer from the sample characteristics of the population.

The use of random sampling may be particularly helpful in settings in which client records are paper-based as opposed to electronically stored. If, for instance, one wished to evaluate services delivered to an agency that used paper-based records, a review of all files might represent a particularly onerous and time-consuming task. As an alternative to a complete review of all records, one might elect to select a random sample of case files from which to evaluate service delivery. The selection of a random sample would require the creation of a spreadsheet containing a list of clients served by the agency. This list of clients might be obtained from either the agency's financial database or compiled in the spreadsheet from paper-based records. The dataset listing all the clients or elements from which the sample will be drawn is referred to as the sampling frame. The central point of this discussion is that random sampling, using the following spreadsheet procedures, has utility in data analysis beyond research endeavors. We can now turn our attention to the procedures for generating random samples.

Simple Random Samples

Creating a simple random sample within a spreadsheet is a relatively simple process. The first step is to import or enter into a spreadsheet the population data from which the random sample will be selected. There are a couple of methods for selecting a simple random sample. The first method is to use the RAND function. As defined in Chapter 1, a function is a built-in and predefined formula in a spreadsheet for deriving specific mathematical, logical, informational, or statistical results. The RAND function generates an evenly distributed random number between 0 and 1.

For the purpose of this demonstration, let us assume that we wish to select a random sample from a large client data file (N = 1,000) we have imported into our spreadsheet from our agency's service delivery database. The data are arranged in the spreadsheet with the variable names in the first row. The columns of the spreadsheet contain the variables, and the data for each case are in the rows. We are interested in generating a random number beside each case in this client data file. With a random number beside each case, we will sort the entire list by the column containing the random numbers. This produces a randomly sorted data file. Once we have randomized the cases in this way, we then select the necessary number of cases. For instance, we might want a 10 percent sample, so we select 100 cases. Because the list is now randomized, it does not matter from where in the list we draw our 100 cases. For convenience's sake, we select the top 100 cases.

The steps in this randomization procedure are as follows:

1. Click on "A" at the top of column A. This will select the entire column. Then select in the menu bar Insert, Column. This will insert a new column on the left side of the spreadsheet. Alternatively, simply "right clicking" Column A and choosing Insert from the pop-up menu that appears will insert a column.

2. Once a blank column appears in column A, label cell A1, "Random."

3. Click on the cell in the first column, second row. The cell reference is A2.

4. Again, click on the Insert command in the menu bar. Then click on Function.

5. From the left column of the pop-up window, select All. Then from the right column select RAND and click Finish. This will insert the random number generator function in cell A2.

6. Copy cell A2 with the Copy command under Edit in the menu bar.

7. Select the cells in column A, rows 3–1001 and paste the copied function into them using the Paste command under Edit in the menu bar. Each case now has a random number beside it.

8. Select the entire dataset by clicking the rectangle in the upper left-hand corner of the spreadsheet, to the left of the A at the top of column A and above the 1 labeling row 1.

9. In the menu bar, under Data, select Sort. Make sure to sort on column A (now labeled Random). Sort in either ascending or descending order. This will sort the entire dataset on the random number beside each case. Astute observers may note that once the dataset is sorted, the random numbers are not in sequential order. Once the sort is complete, the random number function generates new random numbers. Rest assured that the dataset is now randomized.

10. Select the top 100 cases. Note that at the bottom of the spreadsheet page there are tabs. Clicking on any of these tabs opens a new page or worksheet in the spreadsheet. Paste the 100 cases into one of these worksheets.

See Figure 3.1 for an illustration of a randomly sorted dataset. Also see the accompanying CD-ROM video animation: "Simple Random Sample."

Systematic Sampling

Systematic sampling is an alternative procedure for selecting a random sample. Rubin and Babbie (2001) and Williams, Unrau, and Grinnell (1998) describe the process of creating a systematic sample in which every kth case is selected. For instance, we may decide to select every fifth case (1/5) from our dataset of 1,000 cases. A systematic sample has no methodological or statistical advantage over the simple random sampling procedure described above. We describe it here because numerous social work research texts refer to the procedure and it is readily done with spreadsheets. Moreover, some researchers prefer and are more familiar with systematic sampling.

To produce a systematic sample we will again start with a 1,000-case data file.

1. Click on "A" at the top of column A. This will select the entire column. Then select in the menu bar Insert, Column. This will insert a new column on the left side of the spreadsheet. Alternatively, simply "right clicking" column A and choosing Insert from the pop-up menu that appears will insert a column.

2. Once a blank column appears in column A, label cell A1 "Random."

3. To produce a systematic sample for every fifth case using a random start (Rubin & Babbie, 2001), insert a random number using the RAND function, as described previously, into cell A2.

4. Reading the random number from left to right, find the first number between 1 and 5. For instance, if the number is 0.19573, we start our sequence with the number 1. We enter the number 1 into cell A2, where our random number generated. As we will select every fifth case, we enter the values 2 through 5 in the four cells below cell A2.

5. Select and copy this 1–5 sequence from cells A2:A6.

6. Select the cells adjacent to the remainder of the dataset and then click Edit, Paste. One important caveat here is that Excel will only allow this pasting process to occur if the area of cells copied and the area into which they are to be pasted are the same size and shape. In other words, if we have 100 cases, we can copy the five-cell sequence and paste it into the cells in column A adjacent to the remaining 95 cases, but it will not allow the pasting of the

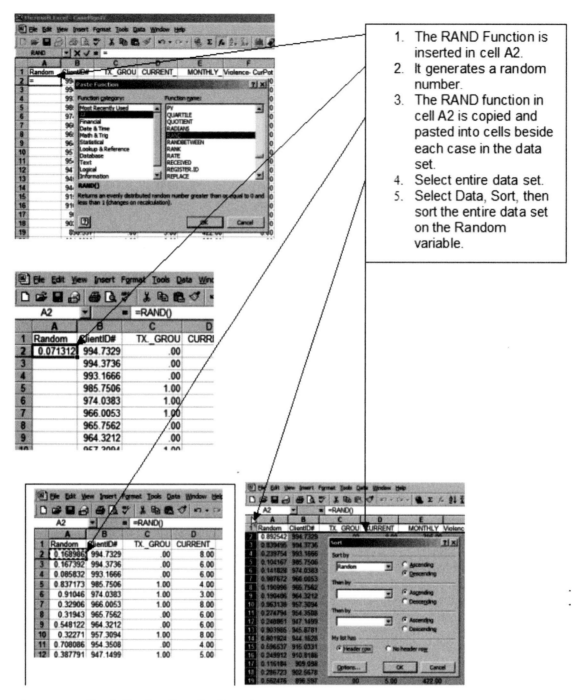

FIGURE 3.1   Simple Random Sampling Procedure

five-cell sequence into 97 rows. The paste area must be some multiple of the copied cell sequence.

7. Next, select the entire dataset by clicking the rectangle in the upper left-hand corner of the spreadsheet, to the left of the A at the top of column A and above the 1 labeling row 1.

8. In the menu bar, under Data, select Sort. Make sure to sort on column A (now labeled Random). Sort in either ascending or descending order. This creates a systematic sorting of the dataset by grouping all the 1s, 2s, and so on together.

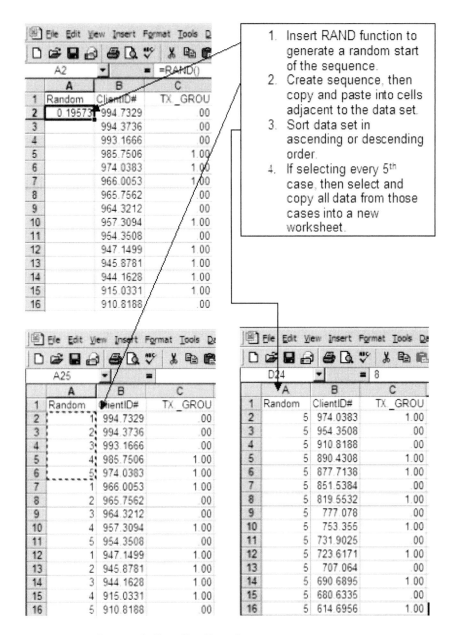

FIGURE 3.2   Systematic Sampling Procedure

9. Our intention was to select one out of five case from the 1,000 cases. We now Select, Copy, and Paste one of the five groups into a new worksheet.

10. A systematically randomly selected sample of 200 cases is now ready for the next steps of the data analysis.

See Figure 3.2 for an illustration of the steps in this process. Also see the accompanying CD-ROM video animation: "Systematic Random Sample."

Stratified Sampling

Another probability sampling method that is widely used and readily produced with a spreadsheet is stratified sampling. Stratified sampling reduces the sampling error through random selection from subsets of the population (Rubin & Babbie, 2001). Stratified sampling is commonly used to ensure the representation of subgroups, or strata, of the population. For example, a state department of children's services decides to conduct face-to-face interviews with a random sample of foster parents in order to assess ways to improve services to children in foster care. Foster parents who are certified by the state to provide therapeutic foster care services comprise a small but significant subgroup of foster parents, approximately 10 percent of all foster parents. Should the researchers in the department of children's service decide to conduct a simple random sampling of foster parents, certified therapeutic foster parents may be over-represented or under-represented in the sample simply due to chance variation in the random sampling process.

Alternatively, the researchers could use stratified random sampling. In this procedure they select all therapeutic foster parents from their foster parent dataset. The researchers would then randomly select a sample from the therapeutic foster parents equal to 10 percent of the overall sample of foster parents. Consequently, the proportion of therapeutic foster parents in the sample would be equal to their representation in the larger group of foster parents.

Stratified random sampling with spreadsheets is accomplished through a series of steps in which one or more subgroups (strata) are filtered from the larger dataset listing all individuals in the population from which the sample will be selected. Again, this listing or dataset is referred to as the sampling frame.

Microsoft Excel has a tool called Auto-filter that is found in the Menu bar under Data, Filter. A filter is a criterion (or set of criteria) that is applied to a dataset in order to select a subset of the dataset. Auto-filter is a quick and easy-to-use tool for filtering a dataset for specified subsets or subgroups. The Auto-filter tool allows one to select a value or word in a specified column and filter the dataset for only cases containing that value or label, the filtering criteria. The filtered dataset displays only the rows that meet the specified criteria. The Auto-filter temporarily hides all the rows containing data not selected in the filtering criteria. We will apply the Auto-filter in creating a stratified random sample by using it to select subgroups in the dataset from which we will then select random samples. Also see the accompanying CD-ROM video animation: "Auto-filter."

To produce a stratified random sample using Auto-filter,

1. Select the first row of the dataset by clicking on row 1 of the dataset. Simply clicking the number 1 on the far left side of the spreadsheet will highlight and select the entire row.

2. From the menu bar, select Data, Filter, Auto-filter. Down arrows will appear in all the cells of the first row of the dataset.

3. Clicking on any of the down arrows reveals a list of all the values, categories, or labels in the selected column. See Figure 3.3.

4. Select the column containing the variable identifying the subgroups from which the stratified random sample will be drawn.

5. Select the value, category, or label for the first subgroup from which a separate random sample is to be drawn. Once selected, only cases from this subgroup will appear in the spreadsheet.

6. In the menu bar, select Insert, Worksheet. This will place a new worksheet in the spreadsheet workbook.

7. Copy this filtered subgroup of cases into a new worksheet. To do this, select the first row, then holding the left

FIGURE 3.3   Auto-Filter Inserted in First Row and Values for Column C Displayed in Dropdown Menu

button of the mouse down, drag the cursor over the numbers of the rows in the data subset now present in the worksheet.

8. Once the entire subgroup is selected, select from the menu bar Edit, Copy, thereby copying the subgroup.

9. Click on the tab for the newly inserted worksheet.

10. Click on cell A1 in the top left-hand corner of the spreadsheet and then select from the menu bar Edit, Paste. This will paste the data for the filtered subgroup into the new worksheet.

11. Click on the tab of the newly created worksheet and type in the name of the subgroup in order to prevent the data in this worksheet from being confused with other data in the workbook.

12. Follow the simple random sample procedures previously described to select a random sample from this filtered subgroup.

13. Return to the worksheet with the original dataset and select the down arrow in the column containing the variable identifying stratified sampling subgroups. Filter the dataset on the name or value for the next subgroup from which a random sample will be drawn. Repeat steps 6 through 12 until random samples are drawn from all subgroups.

14. Once all subgroups have been filtered from the original dataset and randomly sampled, copy and paste all of the subgroup random samples into a single worksheet. The data in this worksheet is the stratified random sample of the original dataset.

Random Assignment

Random assignment is a process of assigning clients, cases, or individuals to two or more groups in order to make comparisons (Neuman & Kreuger, 2003). Technically, random assignment is not in a form of random sampling, although it does utilize some of the same procedures as employed in random sampling. Further, it is based on the same mathematical theory that each case will have an equal and known chance of being assigned to the available groups. Random assignment is used to create equivalent groups for the purpose of making comparisons between the two groups. For instance, random assignment is commonly used in experimental research designs in which subjects are randomly assigned to either an experimental or control group. Random assignment serves to ensure that both groups are equivalent in order to assert that any differences between the two groups at the completion of the experiment are due to the intervention used in the experiment and are not a result of preexisting differences between the two groups.

Random assignment is not only used in highly controlled laboratory experiments but may also be employed in agencies wishing to evaluate the effectiveness of two or more treatment programs or interventions. Each client applying for services might be randomly assigned to a treatment program or intervention. The use of random assignment guards against the possibility of bias in the process by which clients are assigned to treatment programs or interventions. As in the case of laboratory experiments, the equivalent groups that result from random assignment make it possible to rule out selection bias, or more precisely assignment bias, as an explanation for differences, or lack thereof, between treatment programs or interventions at the end of the evaluation period.

There are at least three methods of conducting random assignment with spreadsheets. First, if one already has a database containing the list of individuals to be assigned to groups or interventions, one could simply randomize the list and then divide it into the necessary number of groups. The randomization process, as described previously, requires inserting a column into the database, using the random function to paste a random number beside each case, selecting the entire database, and then sorting the database on the column with the random numbers. In the final step, divide the database into two more groups, copying each group into a new worksheet. Individuals in the database are now randomly assigned to groups.

The second method of random assignment utilizes the Random Number Generator available in the menu bar under Tools, Data Analysis. The Random Number Generator offers several methods for generating distributions of random numbers. For our purposes, we will use the Bernoulli distribution, which generates two possible outcomes similar to coin-flip results. In Figure 3.4 we have inserted a blank column, column A, and labeled it "Random Assignment Group." The Random Number Generator dialog box appears adjacent to column A. We indicated that the number of variables is 1. There are a total of 196 cases in the

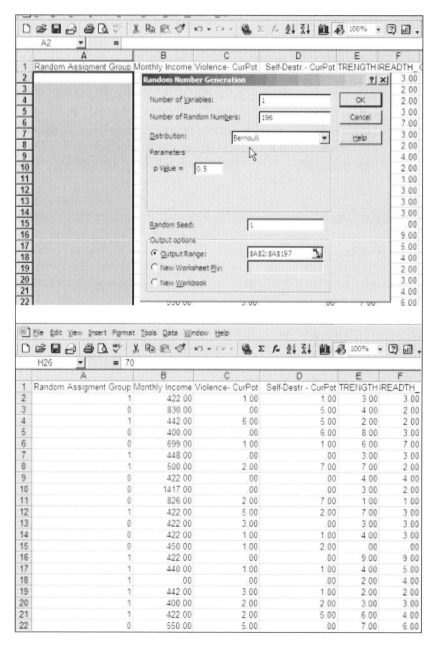

FIGURE 3.4   Random Number Generator Used to Create Random Assignment

dataset, so in the field beside Number of Random Numbers we enter 196. We have selected "Bernoulli" from the drop-down Distribution menu. In order to ensure an equal probability of assignment to one of the two groups we selected a *p* value of 0.5. We used 1 as the Random Seed from which to generate the random numbers. Finally, we specified in the Output Range the cells adjacent to the cases in the database. In Figure 3.4 the randomly assigned values of 1 and 0 appear next to cases in the database. The next step in this process is to select the entire database and sort it on the variable Random Assignment Group. The last step is to then copy and paste each of the groups into a new worksheet. Depending on the purpose of the random assignment, this last step may not be necessary. For a demonstration, see the accompanying CD-ROM video animation: "Random Assignment."

The third method of random assignment assumes that individuals or clients have yet to be entered into a database and in fact may at the time of the creation of the random assignment spreadsheet be unknown to the agency or the researcher. In other words, in this third method we will simply create a spreadsheet with two or more randomly generated numbers. Clients or individuals will then be assigned sequentially to groups as they appear for participation in the experiment or for agency services. This random assignment method may be particularly useful in agency settings in which administrative staff are required to assign clients to interventions or treatment programs. They simply use the spreadsheet with the column of random assignment numbers and enter client data into the spreadsheet as clients appear for services. The steps for creating a random assignment using the random number generator as described on pp. 30–31 are used in this method as well.

Summary

This chapter describes how to use spreadsheets in the selection of random samples and generating random group assignments. A basic rationale for the use of probability sampling is provided. Three methods of probability sampling with spreadsheets are detailed. Sample random sampling using spreadsheets relies primarily on the assignment of a random number to each case using the RAND function and the subsequent sorting of the cases in the spreadsheet all in the random number. Systematic random sampling also uses the Rand function. In this method, the RAND function generates a random number from which to begin the assignment of a sequence of numbers, for instance, 1 to 5, on which to sort the cases and select every fifth case. Stratified random sampling, which ensures the representation of subgroups in the sampling frame, is accomplished by filtering the spreadsheet for the subgroups and then randomly sampling from the subgroups. Random assignment is used to assign individuals or cases to groups in order to ensure group equivalence. Three methods of random assignment are described in this chapter.

REVIEW QUESTIONS

1. What are the differences between nonprobability and probability sampling?

2. What is random sampling and how is it related to probability sampling?

3. How do you create simple random samples, systematic samples, and stratified samples in spreadsheets?

4. What is random assignment and how can the Random Number Generator be used to create a random assignment?

4 Data Cleaning

In the preceding chapters we have discussed the virtues and utility of spreadsheets in data analysis, how to acquire and input data into a spreadsheet, and methods for selecting probability samples from databases. We now turn our attention to procedures for cleaning data that entail the detection and elimination of bad or problematic data in a dataset as well as methods for dealing with missing data.

Social workers and other social service professionals commonly encounter client records and client information in databases with missing, inaccurate, errant, and illegible information. When data are collected from paper-based files or databases, it is not uncommon for these types of data problems to be transcribed or imported into spreadsheet datasets. In some sense, problematic data may be intrinsic to the very nature of social work and social service practice. Data collection and recording are often seen as secondary tasks to the "real" work of the profession. Consequently, time constraints and service delivery priorities may take precedence over accurate and thorough data collection. This reality creates nontrivial challenges for program evaluators, researchers, and administrators attempting to summarize and extract meaning from data riddled with problems.

The validity of any data analysis is dependent on the quality of the data on which the analysis is based. An often-repeated axiom of computer professionals over the last 50 years is, "garbage in, garbage out." In truth, bad data may be worse than no data at all, as it can result in misrepresentation of information and erosion of confidence in the utility of data collection.

Data cleaning is technically not a data analysis function, but is instead a precursor of data analysis intended to detect and eliminate errors made during data entry. The presence of data errors can result in data analysis results that do not make sense, are inconsistent, and undermine the credibility of the findings. Time spent ensuring the integrity and quality of the data prior to the initiation of data analysis is ultimately time saved in the data analytic process. Without proper data cleaning, considerable time must be devoted to addressing overt and subtle inconsistencies, nonsensical findings, and errant representations of information. Data analysis reports derived from problematic data undermine the credibility of both data analysts and the institution or agency they represent.

The subject of data cleaning is predicated on the assumption that whatever problems exist in the data already exist. In other words, the problem has already occurred and the function of data cleaning is to detect the data errors and correct them. Conversely, many data problems can be prevented and the demands of data cleaning diminished with the application of the procedures described in Chapter 2, including clearly specifying data codes, setting up of spreadsheets for ready data entry with visible data codes, and, when possible, the use of data entry forms. The quality of captured data can be further controlled by careful training of agency personnel and research assistants in data entry procedures, careful and accurate use of data codes for the dataset, and data checking to ensure accurate input. Further, data quality can be improved through educating data entry staff, caseworkers, and supervisory personnel about the importance of data quality. More broadly, the design of agency client databases with information and reports germane to the job demands of caseworkers creates an incentive to improve data quality.

Types of Problem Data

There are many types of data entry errors that can result in problematic data. Information on a single individual can be entered into a database more than once, resulting in duplication of information. Personnel responsible for data entry may use invalid codes, miscode information, or simply fail to enter data. The values outside of the expected range of values for a variable may be accidentally entered into a case record. For instance, a 17-and-a-half-year-old (17.5) might have his age recorded as 175. Variations in formatting conventions can produce data errors, especially when working across cultures or internationally. For example, one of the authors worked on a large medical data collection project in rural India. The standard representation of the date in India is to record the day of the month first, followed by month, and then year; February 16th, 2004 would appear as 16/2/04 instead of as 2/16/04, the standard dating convention in the United States. To further complicate the matter, in Japan, the year appears first, then month, and then day of the month (04/02/16). We will address methods for detecting and correcting each of these types of data errors.

Every dataset should be checked for the following:

1. All numeric values are within the expected range of values. Values outside of the expected range of values are referred to as "outliers."
2. There are no duplicate identifiers for clients, subjects, or individuals in the dataset.
3. Ensure that every case has a valid identifier for clients, subjects, or individuals in the dataset.
4. There are no invalid codes in the dataset.
5. Date formats are consistent throughout the dataset.
6. Contingency cleaning has been applied to look for inconsistent or impossible relationships between pairs of variables.
7. Missing data has been located and addressed in a manner appropriate to the intended data analysis.

Procedures for addressing each of these data cleaning procedures are described in the following discussion. Save an original copy of the dataset in a safe place and under a slightly different name before beginning any data cleaning. This precaution serves to preserve the original data should unforeseen circumstances occur during the data cleaning.

Detecting Data Errors

Eyeballing the Data

One of the oldest and perhaps the most tried-and-true methods for detecting data errors is simply eyeballing the data. Spending time examining data in a spreadsheet on a computer screen or in the form of printed output allows the data analyst to become familiar with the data as arranged in rows and columns. Information transferred from multiple case files into a spreadsheet takes on an entirely different appearance. It is no longer dispersed across numerous pages of a case file but instead ordered in rows and columns. It is not uncommon for a data analyst to quickly see anomalies, patterns, missing data, and readily apparent errors in a database once it has been imported or input into a spreadsheet. Eyeballing the data in a spreadsheet is often only the first step in the data cleaning process. It is a means to generate questions about the data, quickly detect readily apparent problems, and to find possible data anomalies requiring further investigation. Eyeballing data in a spreadsheet is not always feasible or advisable with extremely large datasets; however, with small and moderately sized datasets it is a useful initial endeavor.

Auto-Filter

After a preliminary eyeballing of the data, the next step in the detection of data errors should be the examination of all variables in the dataset with the Auto-filter. In Chapter 3, we describe the use of the Auto-filter tool in the creation of stratified random samples. The Auto-filter is also an extremely useful tool in detecting data problems, as it displays in the drop-down boxes of each variable all the attributes or values found in the data of each variable. To activate the Auto-filter, select the first row of a spreadsheet, then from the menu bar choose Data, Filter, Auto-filter. See the accompanying CD-ROM video animation: "Auto-filter—Data Cleaning."

Figure 4.1 displays the use of the Auto-filter to identify an invalid code, "#NULL!" Selection of the invalid code in the dropdown box triggers the Auto-filter to display only those cases that have that particular invalid code in that variable. We will address the issue of what to do with invalid codes and missing data later in this chapter. If the original data is available, one could look up the original value in the data and then substitute it for the invalid code. One could also delete the case from the dataset; however, deletion of cases from a dataset carries its own set of threats to the data analysis that will be addressed later.

The Auto-filter can also be used to quickly identify outliers, values outside of the expected range. For example, in Figure 4.2, scrolling to the bottom of the distribution of values for Age we find 370, a value well outside of anyone's expected life span. Thus the Auto-filter can be used to detect outlier values, values beyond the expected range, on either end of the continuum of values for a particular variable. As in the example of invalid codes, selecting the outlier value in the Auto-filter dropdown box will filter the dataset for that value. Once the specific case with the outlier value is identified, it becomes possible to pursue avenues of inquiry to determine the actual value.

Both invalid codes and outlier values can occur in data secondary to miscoding of information. The Auto-filter will not detect information that is miscoded with a value that is within the expected range of values. For instance, the rating of the strength of a client's support system on a data collection instrument might be 7. If that value is incorrectly entered into the spreadsheet as a 5, Auto-filter will not be able to detect that miscoding of information. Detection of this type of random data entry error is particularly challenging and may not be discovered unless the level of miscoding of information rises to a level that it begins to become evident in descriptive statistics of the data. Descriptive statistics are addressed in Chapter 6.

	File Edit View Insert Format Tools Data Window Help

	A	B	C	D
1	TX_GRC	Cur. Living S	Monthly Incor	Violence- CurF
2	1.00	(All)	422.00	1.00
3	.00	(Top 10...)	830.00	.00
4	1.00	(Custom...)	442.00	6.00
5	.00	1.00	400.00	.00
6	1.00	2.00	699.00	1.00
7	.00	3.00	448.00	.00
		4.00		
8	1.00	5.00	500.00	2.00
9	1.00	6.00	422.00	.00
		7.00		
10	.00	8.00	1417.00	.00
11	1.00	#NULL!	826.00	2.00

B4 = 5

FIGURE 4.1   Auto-Filter Used to Identify Invalid Code

G	H	I	J
READTI ▾	QUALIT ▾	GAFS ▾	AG ▾
3.00	5.00	69	54.00
2.00	4.00	50	55.00
2.00	2.00	41	56.00
3.00	7.00	39	57.00
7.00	6.00	61	58.00
3.00	3.00	60	59.00
2.00	5.00	70	60.00
4.00	5.00	50	61.00
2.00	2.00	60	62.00
1.00	1.00	45	63.00
3.00	8.00	41	64.00
3.00	5.00	51	65.00
3.00	5.00	41	66.00
.00	.00	35	67.00
9.00	9.00	75	68.00
5.00	4.00	45	69.00
			70.00
			78.00
			370.00
			85.00

FIGURE 4.2   Auto-Filter Used to Detect Value
Outside of Expected Range of Values

FIGURE 4.3
Auto-Filter Used
to Detect Violations
of Coding
Conventions

The Auto-filter is useful in finding cases in which there are violations of coding conventions such as date, as previously described. Figure 4.3 shows the Auto-filter dropdown box for the variable Date in which it is evident that some dates have been entered in an alternative format. Again, selecting any value in the dropdown box will filter the dataset for the cases with the selected value. Once a single case or multiple cases are filtered from the dataset, the violations in the coding conventions can be corrected by changing the date format to make it consistent with the rest of the data. Selecting "All" from the dropdown box of the filtered variable restores the dataset to its original unfiltered status.

Duplicate Detection

IF Function Duplicate Detection.   It is not uncommon for social services databases to contain duplicate records for the same individual. A second or third case record for an individual might be entered into an agency client database because the already existing record was not found or recognized when the client presented for services a second or third time. Duplicate case records can also occur as a result of name changes and problems with client identification information such as driver's license, Social Security card, and other forms of identification. Social workers and other social service professionals working on international health-care delivery projects can frequently encounter duplicate case records secondary to the absence of identifying documents, translation errors, and local or cultural variability in naming conventions. The duplicate records can distort data analysis findings, impede service delivery, and create unnecessary complications for both clients and social services professionals. Consequently, methods for detecting and removing duplicate records have utility in both data analysis and services delivery.

Albright, Winston, and Zappe (2003) offer a procedure for detecting duplicate cases using a logical If function, found in the menu bar under Insert, Function, Logical, If. The IF function is a logical test that evaluates whether a condition is true, in which case it returns one value; if the condition is false, it returns another value. In Figure 4.4, the IF function is expressed in the formula =IF(B3=B2,1,0). In essence, the formula means that if the value in cell B3 is equal to the value in cell B2, then paste 1 into the cell containing the formula, but

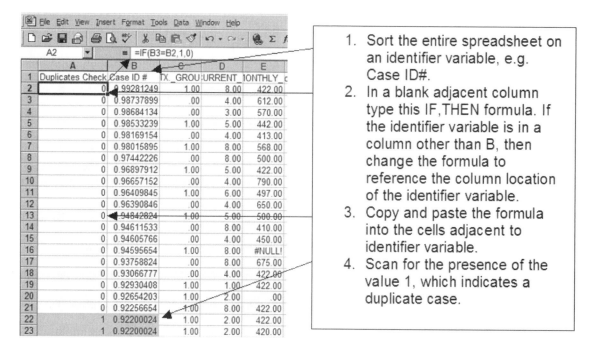

FIGURE 4.4   Duplicate Case Detection Procedure

if the value in cell B3 is not equal to the value in cell B2, then paste 0 into the cell containing the formula. As indicated in Figure 4.4, a column should be inserted into the spreadsheet adjacent to the identifier variable. Next, the entire dataset should be selected and sorted on the identifier variable using Data, Sort in the menu bar. Pasting this IF function, =IF(B3=B2,1,0), into a column adjacent to a dataset that may contain duplicates results in a 1 appearing next to the duplicate values. As is noted in Figure 4.4, if the identifier variable in which the suspected duplicates are located is in a column other than column B, then change the function formula from B to the appropriate column label. Also see the accompanying CD-ROM video animation: "IF Duplicate Detection."

When the dataset is large and duplicates are not readily apparent after completing the duplicate detection procedure, use a SUM formula to determine if the IF function has identified duplicates. If the duplicate detection IF function is in column A and there are 2,500 cases, then in cell A2 we would type the formula =SUM(A3:A2502). Doing this replaces the IF function formula in cell A2 with this SUM function. If the SUM function in cell A2 returns a value greater than 0, then there are duplicates in the dataset. We can then scroll through the entire dataset and delete the duplicate cases that were identified with the duplicate detection IF function.

Pivot Table Duplicate Detection.   An alternative approach to finding duplicate cases in a dataset is to use the Pivot Table data analysis tool to produce a quick frequency count of a case identifier variable. Let us assume that we wish to find duplicate cases in a dataset and that we will examine the client identifier codes to find duplicate cases. We copy the column containing the client identifier codes from the original dataset into a new worksheet. Next, we select the column containing this variable, then select Data, Pivot Table. This will open a dialog window labeled Pivot Table and Pivot Chart Wizard Step 1 of 3. Select in Step 1 Microsoft Excel list or database and Pivot Table, then click Next. It is not necessary in the Pivot Table and Pivot Chart Wizard Step 2 of 3 to specify the range of data, as the column containing the variable has already been selected; click Next. In Pivot Table and Pivot Chart Wizard Step 3 of 3, click the Layout button. The Pivot Table and Pivot Chart Wizard—Layout window appears. Dragging the variable appearing on the right side of this window into the Row area and then dragging the variable again from the right side of the window into the Data area are the next steps in constructing the pivot table frequency distribution. Click on the variable in the Data area and select Count. Now click the OK button. The Pivot Table and Pivot Chart Wizard Step 3 of 3 window appears again. Specify where you want to put the resulting pivot table: in a new worksheet or an existing worksheet. Once the pivot table frequency distribution appears, select all the values in the two columns. From the menu bar, select Data, Sort, then sort the two columns of the pivot table frequency distribution in descending order so duplicate case identifiers will appear at the top of the sorted data. Figure 4.5 illustrates the specific steps of the procedure. Once the duplicate case identifiers are known, the entire dataset can be sorted on the case identifier

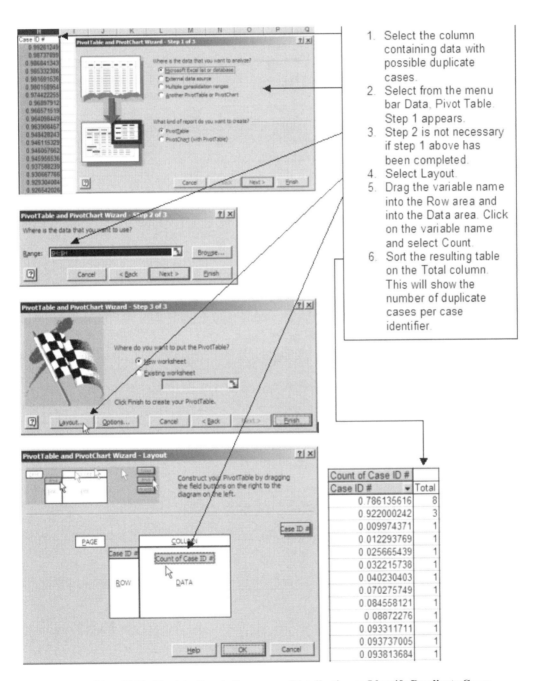

FIGURE 4.5   Pivot Table Used to Create Frequency Distribution to Identify Duplicate Cases

variable and duplicates readily located and removed. Also see the accompanying CD-ROM video animation: "Duplicate Detection—Pivot Table."

Contingency Cleaning

Neuman and Kreuger (2003) describe a data cleaning procedure called contingency cleaning. Contingency cleaning entails looking for logical inconsistencies or impossibilities between two variables. For instance, we might be interested in the relationship between case managers' ratings of their clients' social and occupational functioning and their clients' current potential for violent behavior. We would expect that clients with high ratings of social and occupational functioning would generally not be expected to also have high ratings of potential for violent behavior. Cases with this inconsistent or unlikely set of scores might have data entry errors. Other examples of logical inconsistencies or impossibilities between two variables might include individuals with very low levels of education attainment in professions requiring advanced graduate work or data reporting place of residence as a homeless shelter and indicating an extremely high income level. Contingency cleaning can detect these data anomalies that require further investigation.

We can quickly test for this by using a Pivot Table in which we place the variable Social and Occupational Functioning (Social-OccupFunc) in the Row area, Current Potential for Violence (Violence-CurPot) in the Column area, and count of the variable Violence-CurPot in the Data area (see Figure 4.6). The resulting cross-tabulation table (Pivot Table) shows no cases of high ratings of social and occupational functioning and high potential for violence. However, in the diagonally opposite quadrant we find one case with a social and occupational rating of 1, an extremely low value that would be highly unlikely in the outpatient mental health population from which these data were drawn. This portion of the pivot table is displayed in Figure 4.7. This logically inconsistent value would warrant further investigation to confirm it was not a coding error.

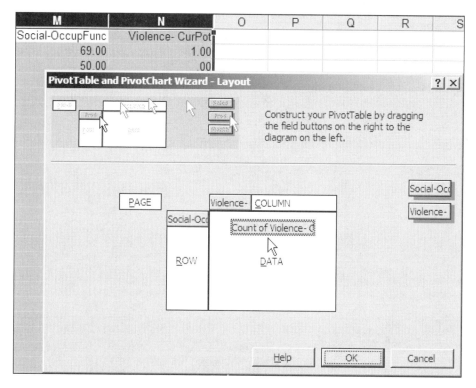

FIGURE 4.6   Pivot Table Used for Contingency Cleaning

Count of Violence- CurPot	Violence- CurPot ▼	
Social-OccupFunc ▼	0	1
1	1	
15	1	
20	2	1
25	1	
27		1
28		
30	2	3
32	1	
35	3	2

FIGURE 4.7   Contingency Cleaning Pivot Table Results

Missing Data: Its Detection and Handling

Missing data are an unfortunate and almost unavoidable reality of collecting data in social service agencies and in social work research. In social service agencies, there are gaps in client records due to haphazard data collection, unavailable information, client unavailability, questions that are not applicable to particular clients, and at times the overriding press of service delivery over data collection. In social work research, missing data may be due to subjects not answering all the questions on a questionnaire, poorly trained research assistants, asking questions not applicable to research subjects, and a wide array of other impediments to complete data collection. At the risk of overstating the case, it is inescapable and inevitable that anyone doing data analysis in the field of social work or social service practice will encounter datasets with missing data. How to detect missing data in a dataset and handle the conundrum of missing data using spreadsheets are the topics to which we now turn our attention.

Detecting Missing Data

There are several simple procedures for detecting missing data in a dataset. In most datasets, one expects that all data is coded into values and the only expected text in the spreadsheet appears in the first row in the form of variable labels. Missing data in such datasets are likely to be represented in one of three ways. There may be blank cells in the dataset. If the dataset has been imported into the spreadsheet from a database or statistical software, there may be inserted text such as #NULL! or N/A in cells to indicate missing data. Finally, some researchers will use 9999 to indicate missing data. The data filtering procedures using Auto-filter, as described previously, are extremely useful in detecting markers of missing data such as #NULL!, N/A, or 9999. One simply examines the Auto-filter dropdown boxes, which display all values and text in the variable. The next step is to filter the variable for a missing data marker and replace it with a blank cell. For this stage of our discussion, we will use a blank cell instead of some other missing data alternative. In the following discussion, we will examine the relative utility of several methods of handling missing data.

There is a useful alternative procedure for detecting both missing data markers and blank cells in a database. Insert a blank column into column A of the dataset. In cell A1, label this new variable as Missing Data. In cell A2 type the formula =SUM(), inserting into the parentheses the range of columns containing data, for example, (B2:Q2). The formula for 16 columns of data would be =SUM(B2:Q2). The formula will return either the sum of all values in that row for the variables from columns B to Q, or it will return an error. An error indicates the presence of data other than a value in one of the columns.

Now copy the formula in cell A2 and paste it into all the cells in column A adjacent to data in the dataset. Next, select the entire dataset and then from the menu bar click on Data, Sort (see Figure 4.8). Select Header row and sort in descending order. This will sort the entire dataset on the new Missing Data variable and bring all the variables with missing data, as indicated by some form of missing data marker, to the top of the spreadsheet. Figure 4.9 displays the results of sorting the spreadsheet on the Missing Data variable. Also see the accompanying CD-ROM video animation: "Missing Data Detection Formula."

As is evident in Figure 4.9, the missing data marker in this dataset is #NULL!. We will use the Find/Replace tool, available in the menu bar under Edit, to find all instances of #NULL! in the dataset and replace them with a blank cell. See Figure 4.10.

The final step in this process is to determine how much data are missing in each case in the dataset. To do this we will click on column B and insert a blank column. Doing this simply moves all data to the right of column A over one column. No information is lost. Once that blank column is inserted into column B, type the variable label "Count" in cell B1. In cell B2, type in the formula =COUNT() and insert into the parentheses the range of columns containing data, using (C2:R2) because the data were moved over one column. The formula for these 16 columns of data would be =COUNT(C2:R2). This formula will return a count of all cells containing values and not text. Copy and paste the formula from cell B2 into all the cells in column B adjacent to data in the dataset. If there was a great deal of missing data in the dataset, it might be necessary to sort the dataset again, this time on the Count variable in ascending order. Doing this will bring the cases with the most missing data and therefore the lowest count to the top of the spreadsheet. This is a good way to assess the quantity of missing data in the dataset before addressing what to do about it, the topic to which we now turn our attention.

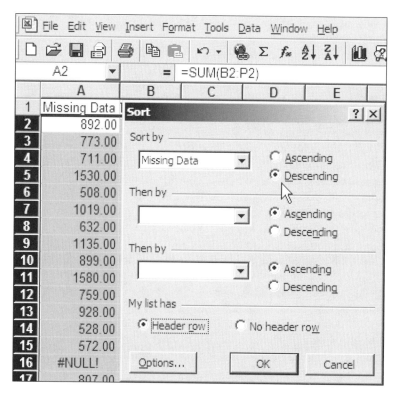

FIGURE 4.8 **Sorting a Dataset on the Missing Data Variable**

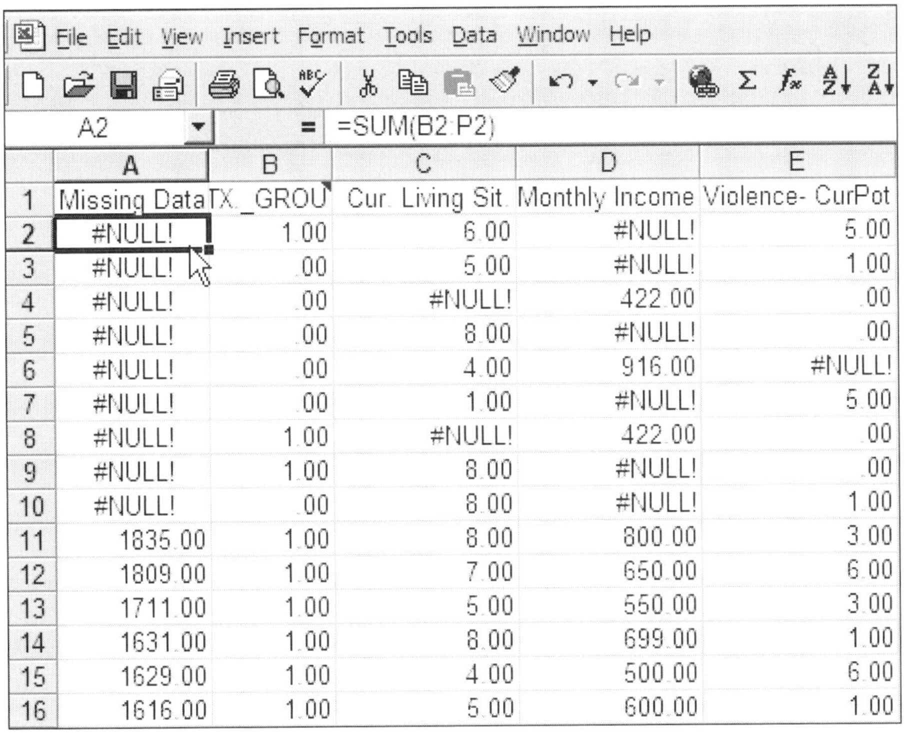

	A	B	C	D	E
1	Missing Data	TX._GROU	Cur. Living Sit.	Monthly Income	Violence- CurPot
2	#NULL!	1.00	6.00	#NULL!	5.00
3	#NULL!	.00	5.00	#NULL!	1.00
4	#NULL!	.00	#NULL!	422.00	.00
5	#NULL!	.00	8.00	#NULL!	.00
6	#NULL!	.00	4.00	916.00	#NULL!
7	#NULL!	.00	1.00	#NULL!	5.00
8	#NULL!	1.00	#NULL!	422.00	.00
9	#NULL!	1.00	8.00	#NULL!	.00
10	#NULL!	.00	8.00	#NULL!	1.00
11	1835.00	1.00	8.00	800.00	3.00
12	1809.00	1.00	7.00	650.00	6.00
13	1711.00	1.00	5.00	550.00	3.00
14	1631.00	1.00	8.00	699.00	1.00
15	1629.00	1.00	4.00	500.00	6.00
16	1616.00	1.00	5.00	600.00	1.00

FIGURE 4.9 Results of Sorting Dataset on the Missing Data Variable

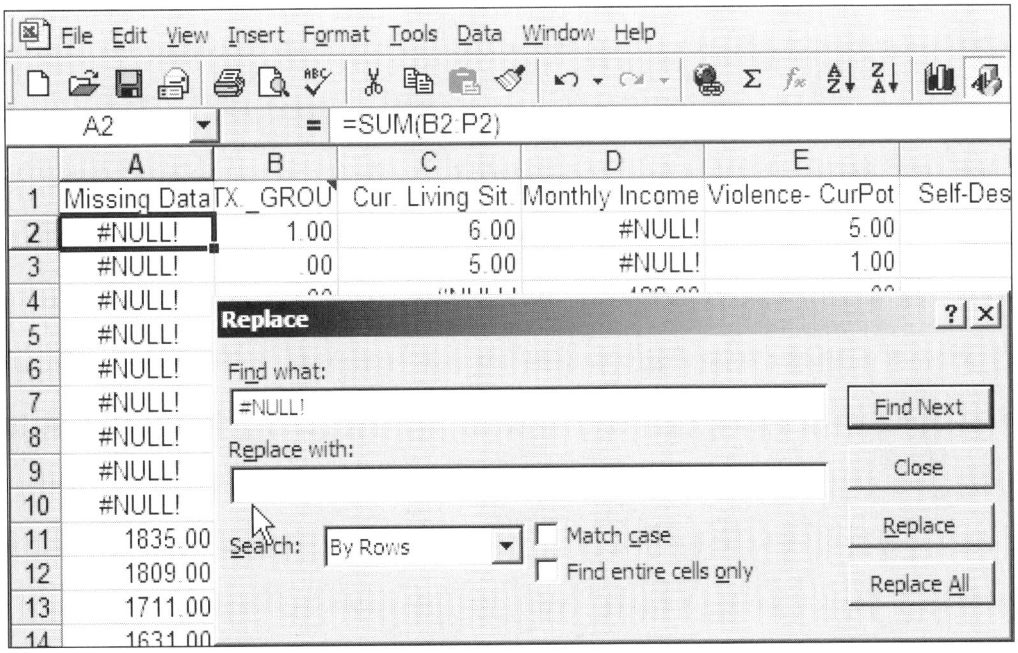

FIGURE 4.10 Find/Replace Tool Used to Replace Missing Data Markers with Blanks

Handling Missing Data

The problem of how to respond to missing data is the subject of considerable debate among researchers and statisticians. Some of the solutions involve rather complex statistical procedures that are beyond the scope of this text. We will first briefly explore the implications of missing data on data analytic procedures in Microsoft Excel. We will then limit our discussion of how to respond to missing data to two methods that can readily be accomplished with standard spreadsheet procedures. These methods are listwise or casewise data deletion and mean substitution.

The first question we need to address is how does Excel handle missing values in its mathematical calculations? Table 4.1 displays two columns of data, one containing missing values and the other with no blanks or missing data between values. The values in the two columns are identical. Beneath these two columns are the descriptive statistics for both sets of data. Descriptive statistics are addressed in Chapter 6, but for now it is sufficient to say that descriptive statistics provide a description and summary of the values in a dataset. Examining Table 4.1 we see there are no differences between the descriptive statistics for the column with missing data and the column without missing data. In other words, the formulas used by Excel for calculating descriptive statistics ignore the presence of missing data in the columns. Good news, right?

If we press our consideration of this issue a little further and examine the correlation between our two columns of identical values we encounter a surprise. Correlation is addressed more completely in Chapter 8, but for right now it is enough to know that correlation a measure of the relationship between two variables. Further, the degree of correlation between two variables is typically expressed in a correlation coefficient that can range from −1 to 1. The closer to either of these values a correlation coefficient is, the stronger the relationship. In this case, because we have two columns of identical numbers we would expect that the correlation coefficient would be a perfect 1. However, as is evident in Table 4.1, Excel calculates the correlation between the two columns as 0.53. So, unlike the calculation of descriptive statistics, Excel includes blank cells (missing values) in its calculation for correlations. Consequently, data analytic caution dictates that for statistical procedures that evaluate the relationship between two or more variables, procedures for addressing missing data should be applied. It is to these procedures the discussion now turns.

Listwise Deletion.   Listwise deletion is a procedure that removes all cases with missing data from variables used in a particular analysis. Most statistical software packages treat listwise deletion as the default method of handling missing data for many statistical procedures (www.utexas.edu/cc/faqs/stat/general/gen25.html). Unfortunately, Excel does not offer listwise deletion as an automated function. In fact, the term *listwise* is not recognized by Excel's Help utility. To address this omission, we suggest the following procedure.

Before beginning this procedure, make sure that all missing data markers have been removed from the dataset and replaced with blank cells, as previously described. To examine the relationship between two or more variables, copy each variable from the original dataset worksheet and paste them into a new worksheet in columns adjacent to each other. Next we want to delete from these variables all rows in which there are blank cells. To do this we again insert a blank column on the left side of the variables and label it "Count." As described previously, we type the formula =COUNT() into cell A2, inserting between the parentheses the cell references for the variables we pasted into this new worksheet. For instance, if there are three variables the formula would read =COUNT(B2:D2). Copy and paste this formula into all cells in column A with data in the adjacent column. Select the entire worksheet and sort it in ascending order on the Count variable. If there are three variables, then any row with a count less than three has missing data as evidenced by blanks and should be deleted before continuing the statistical analysis.

One significant problem with listwise deletion is that deletion of cases reduces the size of the sample and possibly alters the shape of the distribution of values. Sample size affects the power of various statistical procedures to detect differences between groups. Altering the

TABLE 4.1   Excel's Handling of Missing Data

	Missing Data	No Missing Data
	5	5
	2	2
		7
	7	3
		9
	3	2
		4
	9	
	2	
	4	

Missing Data		No Missing Data	
Mean	4.57	Mean	4.57
Standard Error	1.00	Standard Error	1.00
Median	4.00	Median	4.00
Mode	2.00	Mode	2.00
Standard Deviation	2.64	Standard Deviation	2.64
Sample Variance	6.95	Sample Variance	6.95
Kurtosis	–0.45	Kurtosis	–0.45
Skewness	0.80	Skewness	0.80
Range	7.00	Range	7.00
Minimum	2.00	Minimum	2.00
Maximum	9.00	Maximum	9.00
Sum	32.00	Sum	32.00
Count	7.00	Count	7.00

Correlation 0.531494

shape of the distribution of values in a set of variables may compromise their utility, or more precisely, change their ability to meet the assumptions of distribution shape required by many statistical procedures. Without extending this brief statistics lesson further, the point here is that listwise deletion is most appropriate when there are a limited number of cases with missing data to be deleted. The more cases one removes, the less the data from which one wishes to make statistical inferences resembles the original data. Consequently, statistical inferences based on diminished datasets are tenuous, at best. Use listwise deletion with caution.

Mean Substitution.   Mean substitution uses the mean or average value of the variable in place of the missing data in the variable. Its advantage over listwise deletion is that it does not delete cases. The disadvantage is that it reduces the variability in the variable by inserting the mean value where a higher or lower value would likely be found. The more missing data in the variable, the more the variability originally present in the variable is suppressed by mean substitution. Reduced variability affects measurement of correlation between variables and creates other statistical consequences that are beyond the scope of this discussion. It is perhaps sufficient to say that mean substitution, like listwise deletion, should be used with caution. Further, mean substitution can only be used with variables measured at the interval or ratio level of measurement because one can only calculate means for these levels of measurement.

To use mean substitution, copy the variables from the original dataset into a new worksheet. In Figure 4.11 two variables, Age and GAFS-M, appear in columns A and B with blank cells. The mean for the variable GAFS-M is calculated using the Average formula =AVERAGE(A2:A197) that appears in the formula bar. We calculate the mean for each variable copied into the new worksheet that will be used in the analysis. Then select one variable at a time and use the Find/Replace tool described previously. This time, leave

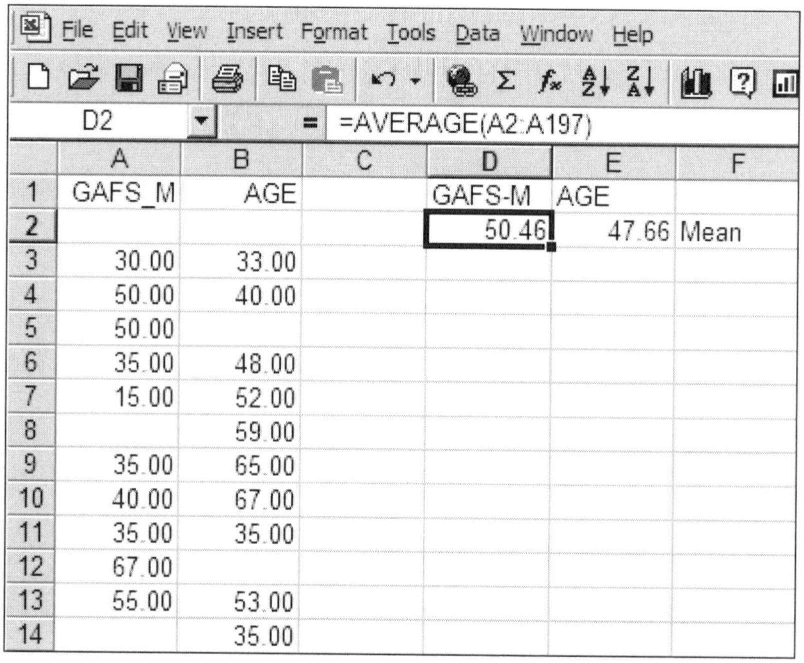

	A	B	C	D	E	F
1	GAFS_M	AGE		GAFS-M	AGE	
2				50.46	47.66	Mean
3	30.00	33.00				
4	50.00	40.00				
5	50.00					
6	35.00	48.00				
7	15.00	52.00				
8		59.00				
9	35.00	65.00				
10	40.00	67.00				
11	35.00	35.00				
12	67.00					
13	55.00	53.00				
14		35.00				

FIGURE 4.11 Mean Calculation for Mean Substitution Procedure

the Find field blank and in the Replace field type in the mean for that variable. Replace all blanks in each of the variables with the mean for the particular variable. Doing this completes the mean substitution procedure and the variables are now ready for the intended statistical analysis.

Summary

In this chapter we address the importance and complexities of data cleaning. The validity of the results found in any data analysis is contingent on the integrity of the data used in the analysis. The training of data collection personnel and close adherence to data collection procedures can in some cases dramatically reduce the extent and necessity of data cleaning. These factors are not always in the control of the data analyst. As a result, data problems can include duplication, invalid codes, miscoded information, values outside of the expected range, variations in formatting conventions, and missing data. Procedures for detecting data errors include eyeballing data, filtering, duplicate detection, and contingency cleaning. Procedures for detecting and handling missing data are discussed, including listwise deletion and mean substitution.

REVIEW QUESTIONS

1. Why is data cleaning important to data analysis?
2. What are the various types of data problems described in this chapter?
3. What types of data problems should every dataset be checked for?
4. What are the three methods of detecting data errors?
5. What is the Auto-filter and how is it used in detecting data errors?
6. How do you detect duplicates in datasets?
7. What is contingency cleaning?
8. How do you detect missing data and what do you do once you find it?

CHAPTER
5 Frequency Distributions and Histograms

Understanding the Distribution of Values

Regardless of the measurement instrument or observation, numerical data collection results in a series of scores or values that have a distribution from lowest possible score to highest possible score. Generally values accumulate nearer to the midpoint of the scale, though not always. These distributions tend to cluster together or disperse to form patterns that provide valuable summary information. Those familiar with statistical analysis will understand that data are most often described based on patterns of central tendency and variability. Each value category will likely include a number of scores or observations. A frequency will be observed for each category. Analyzing and plotting these values can provide insights into the data not realized through observing the raw scores. Understanding the distribution of values and the advantages of spreadsheets in organizing and reporting frequency data is essential for proceeding on to advanced data analytic procedures (Black, 1999).

Normally Distributed Data

When data are said to be normally distributed, the frequency of observed values conforms to a theoretical continuous probability of distribution. That is, the probability of a discrete random variable is a list of probabilities associated with each of its possible values. The horizontal axis of graphed data represents the range of all possible scores for the data. The vertical axis of the graphical representation then represents the probability, or frequency of those values occurring. Scores on the horizontal axis tend to cluster around the mean, forming a symmetrical bell-shaped curve (Vogt, 1999). Probability distributions can be readily demonstrated using spreadsheets. The scores on the horizontal axis may be expressed as raw scores, as in Figure 5.1, but are often also converted to a z-score or standardized score distribution. When score frequencies of values are normally distributed, the measures of central tendency of the variable such as the mean, median, and the mode are the same value.

However, the distribution of values may tend to be skewed to the right such that the greatest number of values orient toward the left or lower horizontal axis values. In this instance of fewer values above the midpoint of the range of values, the values are represented graphically as a positively skewed distribution as seen in Figure 5.2. Most values when positively skewed are less than, or below, the midpoint value.

The distribution of values may also tend to be skewed to the left such that the greatest number of values orients toward the right or higher horizontal axis values. In this instance, values are represented as a negatively skewed distribution as seen in Figure 5.3. Most values when negatively skewed are graphically represented as greater than, or above, the midpoint value.

Evaluating collected numerical information, or numerical data, is generally accomplished in part through the use of tables that demonstrate in some way the distribution of numeric values. The graphical representation of numerical values is also a method used to evaluate distribution. Spreadsheet applications are excellent tools to organize and tabulate data and then convert the data into graphical renderings that aid in the interpretation and understanding of data patterns. Both tables and graphics can organize and represent data

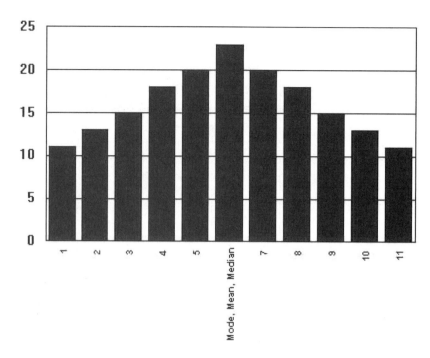

FIGURE 5.1   A Normal Distribution Curve for Categorical Variables

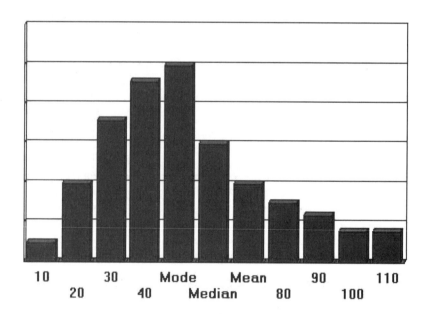

FIGURE 5.2   A Positively Skewed Distribution of Categorical Values

from categorical, ordinal, and continuous scales. These tables and graphics are often used to convey valuable information about the collected data.

Values of the data may have different distributions. These distributions of value need to be understood, so that data trends and descriptive information can be obtained from the distribution. Data analysts, including social workers, can accomplish this quickly by using a spreadsheet for calculating and graphing distributions. We may need to know the numerical information associated with the number of observations that fall into each category determined by a scale's value category to aid in the understanding of the distribution of

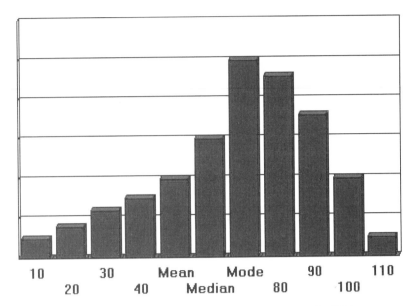

FIGURE 5.3   A Negatively Skewed Distribution of Categorical Values

scores, observations, or subjects occurring in each category. An example might be how many times students in a classroom achieved a score range on a task that resulted in a letter grade of A. The number of times that an observation, or score, occurred within a category of values is said to be the frequency of scores or observations. By counting the number of scores or observations in each category of values, a frequency distribution can be determined for the set of categories of values (Vogt, 1999).

For example, if the frequency of scores represents how many times something occurs, we could look at a classroom of 30 students and observe that 12 students had received a grade of A for the class. So then the frequency of students in the class with an A is 12. We could also calculate the other grade frequencies for a single class, or the number of As for several classes. For example, we might then wish to know how many students with a grade of A are distributed across six available courses of the same subject. By counting the frequency of As observed in each class, we can determine a frequency distribution for the grade of A.

Absolute, Relative, and Cumulative Frequencies

If we also wish to know how many students received a letter grade of A, across all available classes, and our review is exhaustive for all available classes, then we can determine an absolute frequency of students with a grade letter of A. If we identified six classes teaching the same subject on campus, we could determine that of the 180 students in the six classes, only 61 had achieved a final grade of A. Then the absolute number of observations, across all available categories (six classes), sharing the same property (a grade letter of A), is 61 students. The actual number of times that a particular value occurs in the distribution is known as the *absolute frequency* (Vogt, 1999), so the absolute frequency for the property of an A, is 61. However, if we then want to look at the proportion of As given across all classes and all observations of students, including those that did not achieve a grade letter of A, we can determine the proportion of As, 61, against 180 total students. The proportion of times that a particular value, such as the grade of A, occurs in the distribution is known as the relative frequency of the value (Vogt, 1999). In this instance, a relative frequency statement would be that 61 of the 180 students, or slightly more than 1/3 of those taking the course, received a grade of A. This concept may be demonstrated and expanded for cumulative frequencies, as in Figure 5.4 (see the accompanying CD-ROM video animation: "Summing Frequencies").

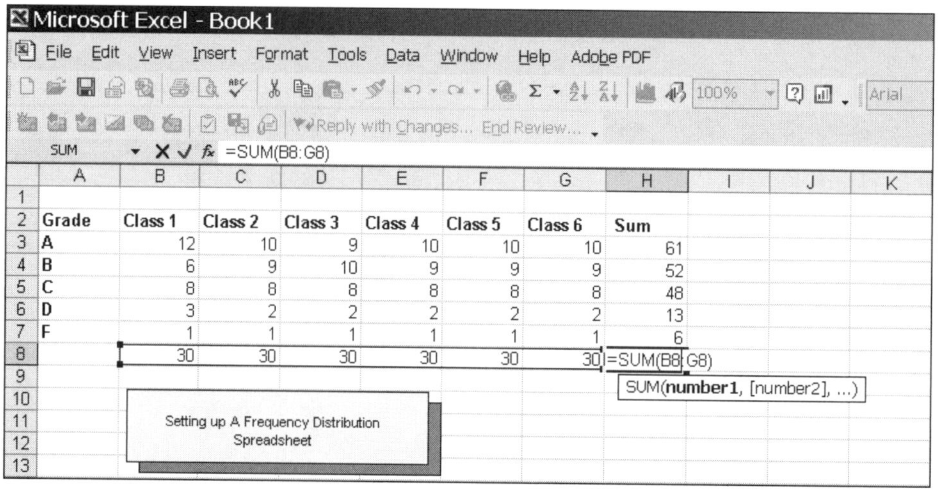

FIGURE 5.4　A Basic Spreadsheet for Summing Frequencies of Classroom Grades

Frequencies in the distribution of values may also be reported as cumulative. A cumulative frequency is based on summing or adding the frequencies observed for each value, or for each class interval in a frequency distribution, that is, the total of frequencies up to and including a specified value or interval. If we wanted to find out how many students received a final grade of less than an A for our six classes, we would need to determine how many students had a grade value of F, how many had a grade value of D, how many had a grade value of C, and how many had a grade value of B of the 180 total students. If we examined the grade books for the six classes and noted that 6 students received a grade of F, 13 students received a grade of D, 48 students received a grade of C, and 52 students received a grade of B, then we can sum or add the frequencies for the values of F, D, C, and B to obtain a cumulative frequency for all grades in six classes that were less than a grade of A. That is, there were 6 students with the lowest value, plus 13 students with the next lowest value, plus 48 students with the middle grade value, and another 52 students with a higher grade value that is less than an A. The cumulative frequency for each grade category that is less than the grade of A for all six classes is 119 students.

Absolute and Cumulative Percentage

Frequencies and frequency distributions can also be summarized and reported as a percentage. The actual percentage of times that an observation within a particular value occurs in the distribution is known as the absolute percentage. All grades in Class 1 (number = 30) would equal 100 percent, whereas the number of grades given that were a B (number = 6) for students in Class 1 are at 20 percent. However, remember that percentages in the distribution of values may also be reported as cumulative. A cumulative percentage is based on summing the percentage observed for each value, or for each class interval in a frequency distribution. In the case of the grades given across six classes, there were 180 student grades given that cumulatively represent 100 percent of the grades. Only 6 students received a failing grade across all six classes. This represents a cumulative percentage for the grade of F of about 3.3 percent of all grades given.

Frequency Distributions

When measuring variables of interest, the concept of numerical scales must be revisited. Raw data may be of nominal, ordinal, interval, or ratio scale and rely on differing types of measurements such as observations, surveys, reports, and so on as discussed in Chapter 2.

The resulting data is unordered and usually drawn from a study sample. Frequency distributions attempt to provide some understanding of the data by organizing information. The data may be generally organized into either a table or graph, or both; then, through visual analysis and evaluation of frequencies, decisions are made about what sorts of summary statistics are needed to further describe the data. To transform raw data into distributions, the data may be counted or grouped into some sort of meaningful categories. Nominally scaled data has no numerical hierarchy and may be arbitrarily ordered into categories. Ordinal data is usually ordered into series or ranks. However, interval scale data has an unknown distance between points and is not therefore considered fixed, but could consist of a single point. Ratio level data tends to have a fixed relationship to true zero and is ordered in fixed intervals (Gravetter & Wallnau, 1999).

However data are organized, it is important to note that scores or data should not belong to more than one class or category, so the categories should be mutually exclusive. No score should be counted more than once. In the example of student grades, we can describe the ordinal or ranked categories of grades (A, B, C, D, and F) by further describing the nominal categories of gender such that a number of male students received a grade letter of A and a number of female students received a grade letter of A. Variables that are not interval or ratio level and that are best ordered into categories are considered discrete variables (or discontinuous variables). Discrete variables are considered to have equality of scale of the categories or counting units. Discrete variables are common to data analysis procedures. Further examples include how many times a juvenile used unacceptable language when visitors are in the home, how many fights break out among students at recess, or the number of students who failed to attend classes on a scheduled class date. The measurement of discrete variables is considered exact so long as counting procedures are very accurate, that is, that the discrete attributes are not counted more than one and are exclusively recorded in reference to a single attribute of a variable.

Variables that have a numerical scale that can be divided and subdivided into an unlimited number of intermediate values, as is assumed to be the case for interval and ratio level scales, are said to be continuous variables. A commonly used example is that of measuring length with a ruler. The ruler can be broken down into yards, feet, inches, fractions of inches, and so on. Measurements of continuous variables are considered to be approximate, as it is theoretically possible to make a more precise measurement than the one available. Continuously measured variables must be ordered into discrete categories or intervals to derive meaning. A unit of measurement must be selected and given a range into which a number of values or observations fall. An example might include measuring the height of all children attending an elementary school and organizing the unit of measurement to determine how many children were of a height designated in inches. For interval and ratio scale data, the categories are numerically defined. The frequency of the distribution is determined by how many observations fall into each category or class (Aron & Aron, 2001).

Graphically representing frequency distributions also depends to some extent on whether the variable of interest is discrete or continuous in scale. For two-dimensional graphs, frequency distributions are plotted on a horizontal axis, or x-axis (values increasing continuously from left to right), referred to as the *abscissa* and organized into categories, classes, or observation or scale intervals. The vertical axis, or y-axis, is referred to as the *ordinate* (scale values or measurements increasing in value from bottom to top). These two axes intersect at their respective low points (frequently, but not always zero). The length of these two axes may vary, but a common convention for plotting frequency distributions is that the vertical axis at the maximum point, or the category with the highest frequency, is approximately three-fourths the size of the horizontal axis. Arbitrary variation from this convention for axis aspect ratio can create different impressions from the same data (Aron & Aron, 2001).

Nominal and ordinal scaled variables are often illustrated on various types of bar graphs. The area of each bar represents the frequency for the defined category. That is, the category is represented by a vertical bar, the height of which is determined by the frequency of the category. There is no convention for order of nominal data categories considered to be equal. Order of the nominal categories is often alphabetical, though they could be ordered by frequency count. The width of the bar is usually set at one unit of the categories or interval represented on the x-axis. In bar graphs, bars are usually depicted separately rather than touching, as categories are not considered continuous in scale. Order of categories for ordinal or ranked data is to place the categories in their naturally occurring ranked order with lowest ranked value near the intersect point of the two axes (Aron & Aron, 2001).

Interval and ratio scaled variables are represented based on equal units of equal size. Generally, bar graphs in which the bars are continuous and the data is considered continuous are referred to as histograms, as compared to bar graphs for categorical data. However, histograms generated in the Excel spreadsheet chart wizard tend to illustrate continuous intervals of scale with a bar that is less than one unit or interval in width. Histograms that are essentially bar graphs may be converted to a continuous line graph representing the highest level of the bar graph as a point rather than a bar. The line then connects the points to represent the data as a frequency polygon, which will be illustrated later. One of the histogram options in Excel represents frequencies as a bar graph and cumulative percent is overlaid with a line represented as a cumulative frequency distribution, as in Figure 5.12 (p. 61). This addition aids in the determination of the number of cases falling above or below a specified point. Cumulative frequency has been converted quickly to cumulative percentage on older and traditional hand-drawn graphs by adding a second percentage-based scale opposite the ordinate or y-axis with scale values set as percents. However, Excel can add a cumulative percentage line easily by making the selection in the Histogram dialog box, as in Figure 5.11 (p. 61).

Production of Frequency Distributions with Spreadsheets

Spreadsheets available in Microsoft Excel have the capacity to produce observed frequencies and frequency distributions using a number of data analytic tools and functions that may then be readily evaluated. To analyze frequency data with spreadsheets, some familiarity is required with the data organization of spreadsheets, data sorting functions, data analysis tools, graphing tools, and pivot table functions of spreadsheets. Most of these topics are described elsewhere in the text, so we will limit our discussion here to frequency distributions.

Producing Frequency Distributions in Excel

To determine the distribution of a frequency, simply enter raw scores into a column of a spreadsheet. When finished, copy the data to extra columns to sort the data in ascending or descending order to visually evaluate the distribution of values. See Figure 5.5. To become familiar with the functions of analyzing frequencies and producing graphics such as histograms, we will use the example of evaluating how class members fared on a midterm examination. To determine frequencies for each value or a group of values, we can use several spreadsheet methods. Let us assume that we have a full classroom of 30 students who scored from 65 to 100 points on an examination of multiple-choice items that were each scored at 5 points.

The frequency distribution of midterm examination data can be examined through use of the data sort function. We may choose to sort the examination scores in ascending or descending order to visually inspect the number of times that students scored in the lower range or upper range of reported scores, as in Figure 5.5 (see the accompanying CD-ROM video animation: "Sorting Frequencies Example One"). In Figure 5.5, column B has already been sorted in ascending order and column C has just been sorted in descending order and remains highlighted.

We can quickly observe that five students scored 100 points and that one student scored 65 points. We can begin to determine the categories of scores in the frequency dis-

	A	B	C	D	E	F
1	Midterm	Midterm	Midterm			
2	Examination =100	Examination =100	Examination =100			
3	85	65	100			
4	95	70	100			
5	90	70	100			
6	90	70	100			
7	100	75	100			
8	85	80	95			
9	95	80	95			
10	100	80	95			
11	80	85	95			
12	90	85	95			
13	100	85	95			
14	95	85	95			
15	90	90	90			
16	100	90	90			
17	70	90	90			
18	80	90	90			
19	90	90	90			
20	95	90	90			
21	70	95	85			
22	85	95	85			
23	80	95	85			
24	95	95	85			
25	95	95	80			
26	75	95	80			
27	100	95	80			
28	65	100	75			
29	70	100	70			
30	85	100	70			
31	95	100	70			
32	90	100	65			
33						

FIGURE 5.5   Visually Evaluating a Frequency Distribution through Sorting

tribution and note that many students did well and scored 95 points. The absolute frequency of 100 points is 5 scores, whereas the absolute frequency of 65 points is 1 score.

As previously discussed, a histogram is essentially a bar graph. The histogram is primarily used to demonstrate the variability of interval or ratio range data that is considered continuous data. Histograms produced in Excel have continuous categories indicated on the horizontal axis of the graph even though the bars themselves do not touch. Histograms representing the frequency of scores for categories or interval of categories are easily produced using several methods (Dretzke & Heilman, 1998).

Using the Frequency Function

The data function dialog box may be accessed either by selecting the function button (*fx*) found on the toolbar with the equation editor window, or by selecting the insert button and dropdown menu on the standard toolbar. By scrolling through the function dialog box, the function for frequency can be selected. A dialog box then opens that requests a range of data or scores in an array and a range of bin categories. Bin categories are user-defined array categories created on the spreadsheet that serve as an array of reference intervals into which the values in the data are grouped. The frequency of each category, including the number of values below the lowest value in the lowest interval and the number of values above the highest value of the highest interval, is returned and visible in the dialog box as seen in Figure 5.6 (see also the accompanying CD-ROM video animation: "Sorting Frequencies Example Two").

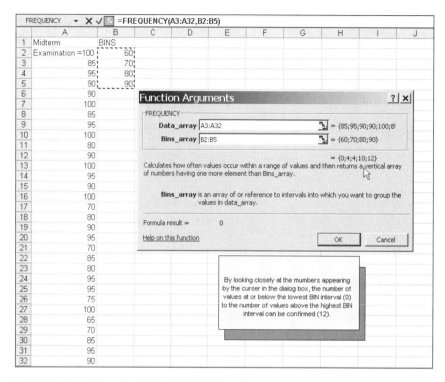

FIGURE 5.6   Using the FREQUENCY Function to Determine a Distribution

Using the Pivot Table Option

A pivot table can be constructed to calculate the frequency distribution of the midterm examination be selecting the Pivot Table and Pivot Chart Report tool located under the Data dropdown menu on the standard Excel toolbar. By selecting the Pivot Table and Pivot Chart Wizard, a sequence of steps or dialog boxes opens to create choices for data analysis and graphical representation. These include selecting the database for analysis, such as the Excel workbook and worksheet, and the range of data. Once the data range is selected, the dialog box includes a selection option to determine whether any tables or charts created should appear in the existing worksheet or a new worksheet. Then by selecting the layout option, a template opens that uses click-and-drag selection of the data with the computer mouse cursor. In this instance only the examination variable should be selected and simply dropped first on the row portion of the pivot template and then reselected and dragged into the data portion of the template so that the icon appears twice. Then the examination data icon in the data section of the template should be selected to ensure that the count of examination scores is selected as in Figure 5.7 (see the accompanying CD-ROM video animation: "Frequencies and Creating a Histogram").

By clicking the OK button, a pivot table of the frequencies of scores occurring for each score value will be calculated. It will indicate the category and the frequency count for each value in the distribution as seen in Figure 5.8.

Producing Histograms Using the Chart Wizard

By proceeding to the chart wizard, selecting and highlighting the pivot table data, and selecting a bar graph, a histogram will be created to represent the frequency of scores for each category, as in Figure 5.9. Though this chart provides a total for each value category, a line indicating the cumulative frequency across categories is not included as the cumulative

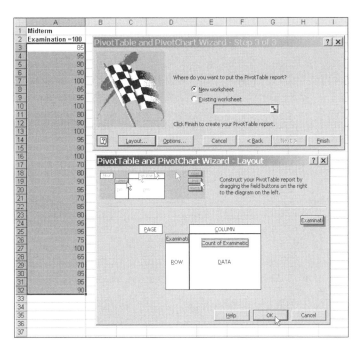

FIGURE 5.7 Pivot Table Layout Template with Drag-and-Drop Data Icons

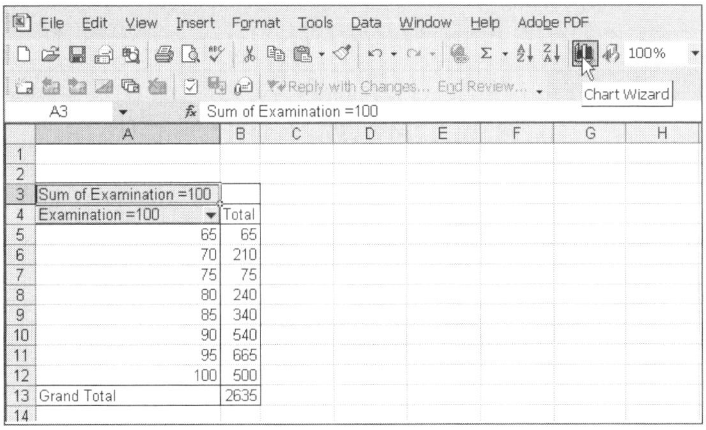

FIGURE 5.8 The Resultant Pivot Table for Midterm Examination Scores

frequency option was not available on the bar graph menu for categorical data. Data categories, however, are assumed to be continuous.

Another option for producing a histogram is to use the Data Analysis pack, which is a useful collection of statistical analytic applications available as an add-on option in the Tools dropdown menu on the standard menu bar in Excel. After selecting the data analysis option, a dialog box containing a list of functions will appear. In this instance a BIN value column is used to set intervals. Select the histogram function after creating a second column with BIN values. After labeling a column as a BIN column, simply input a value into the cells that represents the upper bound limit, or highest numerical value for the array category, of an interval of values preferred to plot a histogram. Enter additional interval values from lowest interval value to highest interval value as in Figure 5.10. Locate the data analysis option on

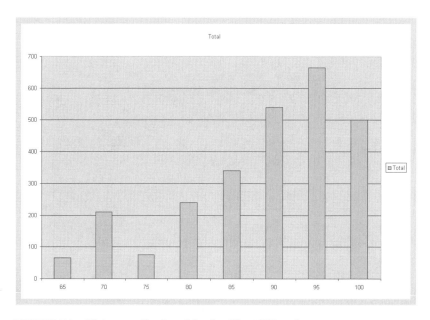

FIGURE 5.9   Histogram Produced by the Chart Wizard

	A	B	C	D	E	F	G
1	Midterm						
2	Examination =100						
3	85			BINS			
4	95			60			
5	90			70			
6	90			80			
7	100			90			
8	85			100			
9	95						
10	100						
11	80						
12	90						
13	100						
14	95						
15	90						
16	100						
17	70						
18	80						
19	90						
20	95						
21	70						
22	85						
23	80						
24	95						
25	95						
26	75						
27	100						
28	65						
29	70						
30	85						
31	95						
32	90						

Data Analysis dialog box:

Analysis Tools

Anova: Single Factor
Anova: Two-Factor With Replication
Anova: Two-Factor Without Replication
Correlation
Covariance
Descriptive Statistics
Exponential Smoothing
F-Test Two-Sample for Variances
Fourier Analysis
Histogram

OK   Cancel   Help

**FIGURE 5.10   Selecting the Histogram Tool from the
Data Analysis Pack**

the Tools dropdown menu. Open the dialog box of available data analytic functions and select the histogram analysis.

By double clicking on the histogram option another dialog box will open. This dialog box will allow for the selection of both the data range or range of scores and the range of intervals included in the BIN labeled column. Options for selecting the cell and column to display the output range, the chart output, and to add a cumulative percentage line are included as seen in Figure 5.11.

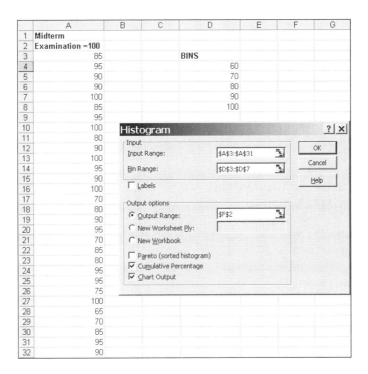

FIGURE 5.11   Making Selections in the Histogram Dialog Box

Figure 5.12 depicts the spreadsheet with the original examination scores, the BIN intervals for data analysis and charting, the histogram data analysis tabular output, and the histogram that includes both frequency categories and a cumulative percentage line. Scores appear in the A column with BINs given in the D column and the derived cumulative frequency percentage given in both the data output table and in the histogram. The score values represent the horizontal axis and the frequencies are represented on the vertical axis of the histogram.

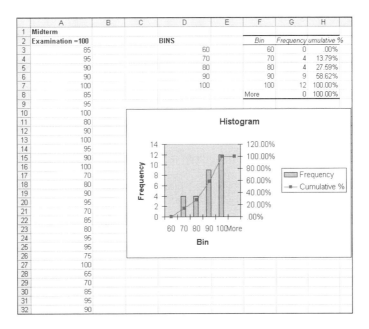

FIGURE 5.12   Tabular and Graphical Output from the Histogram Dialog Box

Summary

As can be seen from the examples given in this chapter, frequency distributions provide a great deal of information that can summarize frequency distributions. We can count and summarize categorical data and determine the range of values within categories. We can also order and describe ranked variables and order continuous variables by increment or interval to provide greater understanding of the distribution. Using spreadsheet graphical representation tools, we can tabulate and recalculate observations or shift the intervals so as to provide a number of graphical display options.

Illustrated and described above are at least three methods of determining the frequency of values occurring in distinct categories. The function menu provides a frequency determination option for the number of observations set by the boundary of user-determined categories or intervals. Pivot table functions can rapidly order spreadsheet data and change the calculation used for the output to provide differing levels of understanding using variable icons that may be dragged and dropped onto a pivot table field for calculation. Furthermore, the data analysis menu included in the statistical add-on packet can deliver specific statistical output to describe data and create a histogram that includes a plotting line for cumulative percentage. These options can be learned quickly and provide methods to create meaningful frequency information using a widely available computing application to perform data analysis using frequency distributions.

REVIEW QUESTIONS

1. What would be an example of a frequency distribution as related to classroom scores on an examination?

2. What is the difference between a normal distribution of values and a skewed distribution, both with respect to the distribution of values and differences in graphical representation?

3. How do bar charts differ from histograms?

4. What are BIN categories used for in Microsoft Excel when generating a histogram?

5. When generating a graph, the abscissa represents what types of values?

6. How is the data sort function in Microsoft Excel used to examine a frequency distribution of values?

7. What are at least three ways of determining the frequency of values occurring in distinct categories that are illustrated and described in this chapter?

6 Descriptive Statistics

Social workers use descriptive statistics to evaluate intervention progress, to describe caseloads, and to describe performance and productivity. Data is collected in case records, program files, grant applications, and a variety of other recording methods that require calculation using common descriptive statistics. Describing information is an important function of deriving meaning from collected data. As in the case of frequencies, the capacity to describe information obtained through data collection depends in part on the level of measurement used to collect the data. Descriptive statistics include procedures that summarize data through summary measures, organization of data, and graphical representation. Descriptive statistics are used only to describe quantitative information and are not concerned with making inferences about a population derived from information for a representative sample of the population. Spreadsheets provide a number of methods for calculating descriptive statistical information. Microsoft Excel can compute descriptive statistical information on one or a number of variables using the add-on data analysis tools pack or the function wizard, as well as by using pivot tables (Patterson, 2000). However, some familiarity with descriptive statistics is needed, especially measures of central tendency and variability, to interpret the spreadsheet output from performing these calculations. Most, if not all, of the statistical terms discussed in this chapter will appear in the output of the descriptive statistics performed by the data analysis tool in Excel.

Measures of Central Tendency

A measure of central tendency attempts to capture the value within a group of numbers that represents the middle or typical value through a statistical summary of the numbers. Common measures or statistics that summarize the typical value, or central tendency, within a group of numbers include the mean, the mode, and the median (Aron & Aron, 2001). The central tendency of a distribution of values is the point in a distribution of scores that corresponds to the typical score in the distribution. Measures of central tendency are not concerned with measuring the dispersion, distribution, or the variation of scores. Several measures of central tendency are available for calculation with spreadsheets and are presented here. These measures do not always agree in value, as the methods to calculate each is different and each has a different result in numerous instances (Gravetter & Wallnau, 1999).

Mean

The *mean* or average value in a group of values is obtained by adding the values of all cases or observations within the group and dividing the total of these values by the number of cases or observations (Vogt, 1999). The mean is used most commonly as the measure for central tendency for interval or ratio scale data (Aron & Aron, 2001). The mean is considered a more powerful measure of central tendency than the mode or median because

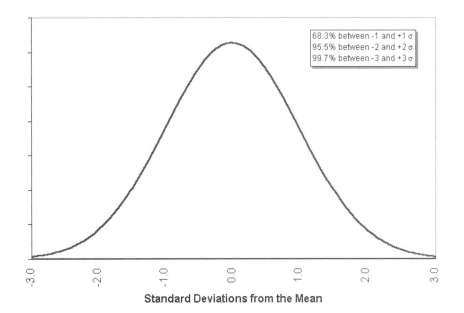

FIGURE 6.1   The Normal Curve Data Distribution: Mean, Median, and Mode = 0.0

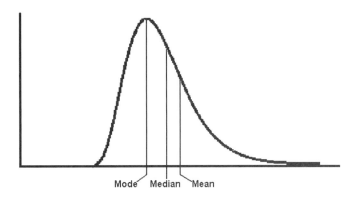

FIGURE 6.2   A Positively Skewed Unimodal Distribution

the mean uses all of the available information in the data. Furthermore, it is relatively simple to calculate. For symmetrically distributed unimodal (with one score, or category, occurring most frequently) data represented on a frequency polygon, the mean, median, and mode are all represented by the same value, as seen in Figure 6.1.

However, for positively (Figure 6.2) or negatively skewed unimodal distributions, measures of central tendency are represented by differing values. Therefore, if we wished to know the average grade achieved by a class of 30 students, and we knew the range of points and scores obtained by each student, we could quickly total the points received by all students and divide this score by 30 students to determine the average number of points received. Then we could compare this number against the course grading scale and note that the average number of points per student fell into the grade range for a grade of B. However, the average score is not necessarily the middle score, or the most commonly occurring score.

Mode

The mode is the most commonly occurring score or most frequent score within a set or group of scores (Vogt, 1999). Categories of scores, such as in the example of grading an examination, are used to determine the mode. For instance, if 8 students out of 30 score an 85 on an examination and this score was the most frequently occurring, then 85 would be the mode. The mode is used most commonly as the measure for central tendency for nominal scale data. If only one score occurs most often within a group of

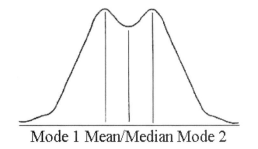

Mode 1 Mean/Median Mode 2

FIGURE 6.3   A Bimodal Distribution

scores, then the distribution is said to be unimodal. If two scores occur more often than other scores within the distribution, then the distribution is considered bimodal as seen in Figure 6.3.

If we were interested in determining the most frequently occurring grade in our class containing 30 students by counting the number of letter grades in each category, we may quickly observe that most students actually achieved a letter grade of A. The most commonly occurring score then differs from the average score for a grade letter of B. The most common score may also differ from the middle score in the set of scores available.

Median

The median is the middle score or measurement in a set of scores that are ranked (Vogt, 1999). The median is the score value that divides a distribution of scores into two equal groups. If there is an even number of scores such that there is no single middle score, the median is obtained through averaging the value of the two middle scores. The median is used most commonly as the measure for central tendency for ordinal scale data and in highly skewed distributions such as income. If we look at the ranked categories of possible letter grades that could be achieved for our class of 30 students, we would determine the grade categories to include A, B, C, D, and F. The median category, or middle score, in this set of possible scores is the grade letter of C. The middle score in many distributions differs from both the most commonly occurring score and the average score. The median score is the score occurring at the 50th percentile in the group. That is, if all the numbers or scores are contained within an array or a distribution, then the 50th percentile is the middle score (Aron & Aron, 2001). If the scores in the array proceed from 0 to 100, then the median score or 50th percentile is 50. However, if the array of scores contains values from 0 to 500, then the median score or 50th percentile is 250.

Measures of central tendency are calculated in different ways, resulting in different values. To understand these differences we need to review the different formulas used to calculate each, as the calculation methods provide differing but valid measures of central tendency. The following examples relate to calculating measures of central tendency for a sample of interest rather than an entire population. Measures of central tendency and measures of dispersion, or spread of score values, are reported in the output of Excel's spreadsheet data analysis tool for descriptive statistics. Some orientation to each term, including information about the formulas used to derive the values of the reported output, is given to aid in the interpretation of results.

Formulas for Measures of Central Tendency

Though this section of the chapter will provide the background information needed to understand the calculation differences for formulas of central tendency, the focus of the chapter is to demonstrate how spreadsheets may be used to find the statistical values described. Understanding calculation procedures is useful in interpreting statistical outputs from spreadsheet calculations.

To begin, let us review the formula for calculating the mathematical mean of a sample of interest. The mathematical mean of a sample distribution is equal to the sum of the frequency associated with each score or class interval of the score values or midpoints of class intervals divided by the total number of cases.

The mathematical mean formula for a sample distribution of scores is (Gravetter & Wallnau, 1999):

$$\text{Mean} = \text{X} = \frac{\Sigma f X}{N}$$

where Σ = the sum of,
         X = either the score values or midpoints of class intervals,
         f = the frequency associated with each score or class interval, and
         N = the total number of cases

The mean can be calculated quickly and separately for any range of data selected using an Excel spreadsheet. The = average function (note that a data range is selected here) can be typed into any available row or column to compute the mean or average for the specified range of data. Additionally, the data can be selected after selecting the mathematical functions icon next to the formula window on the formula toolbar, or from the insert function of the menu bar. These methods also are used for individually calculating any single descriptive statistic manually. The data analysis tool for descriptive statistics can quickly deliver output for most descriptive statistics for single or multiple variables at one time.

Next, let us review the formula for obtaining the median score in a sample distribution in both samples with an odd number of total scores and samples containing an even number of total scores. The median of a range of selected scores can also be calculated using spreadsheet commands or the statistical functions menu in Excel.

The mathematical formulas for the median for a sample distribution are (Montcalm & Royse, 2002):

$$\text{Mdn} = \frac{\text{sample distribution}}{\text{odd population}} = \text{center score}$$

$$\text{Mdn} = \frac{\text{sample distribution}}{\text{even population}} = 2 \text{ center scores, summed and divided by 2}$$

Finally, let us review the formula for obtaining the mode in a sample distribution. The mode can be identified in a number of ways, including by simply sorting and observing the range of scores, but can be calculated using spreadsheet commands or the statistical functions tools menu, which will be described later.

The mathematical formulas for the mode for a sample distribution is (Gravetter & Wallnau, 1999):

$$\text{Mode} = \text{Most Frequent Score}$$

Measures of Dispersion or Variability

A measure of dispersion attempts to demonstrate the spread or variability of scores in a distribution. Common measures or statistics that attempt to summarize dispersion of scores include variance; standard deviation and standard error of the mean, which accounts for dispersion measurement errors based on sampling; *kurtosis,* a measure of variability when scores are not normally distributed; skewness; and range. All of these measures of dispersion can be computed using spreadsheet applications.

Variance

Variance is concerned with the spread or dispersion of scores within a distribution of scores. As the variance of scores increases, the farther the individual cases are from the mean value, or most typical score in the distribution. As the variance of scores decreases, the closer the individual cases are to the mean value. The variance of the distribution of raw scores is most commonly calculated as the average squared deviation from the mean (Gravetter & Wallnau, 1999):

$$\sigma^2 = \frac{\sum X^2 - \frac{(\sum X)^2}{N}}{N}$$

The component parts of this formula are further broken down in most statistical reference texts, if needed for additional background information. To calculate the variance of scores in a distribution we would need to perform the following steps manually:

1. Subtract the mean value from each score to determine that score's deviation.
2. Square each deviation score: X^2.
3. Sum up the squared deviation scores: $\sum X^2$.
4. Divide the sum of the squared deviation scores by the total number of scores in the distribution $\frac{(\sum X)^2}{N}$ and subtract from $\sum X^2$.

Fortunately, the spreadsheet variance function will do this calculation for us.

Standard Deviation

Standard deviation is a statistic that measures the average amount of deviation of scores in a distribution; that is, how much the scores deviate from the mean or average score (Gravetter & Wallnau, 1999). If scores are distributed more widely, then the standard deviation becomes greater. By calculating the square root of the variance of scores, a standard deviation measure can be derived. As the standard deviation value becomes larger, the distribution of scores and the variation in scores are both greater. By adding one standard deviation to the mean score and then subtracting one standard deviation from the mean score in a distribution, the majority of scores will be found to fall between these two measures. If the scores are normally distributed, about 68 percent of all scores will be included. In the case of adding two standard deviations to the mean of the distribution of scores and then subtracting two standard deviations from the mean, about 95 percent of the scores will be found to fall between these two measures. Standard deviation is used to determine the dispersion of scores and identify the portion of the sample that scored within one or more than one standard deviation. Though quite similar, there are two common methods for calculating the standard deviation of a sample from raw scores. Sigma is used for scores from a population, to estimate the score distribution of a parameter on an entire population, whereas a standard deviation is a statistic that estimates the distribution for a sample.

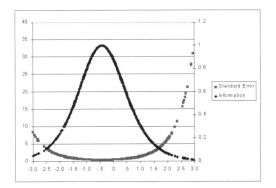

FIGURE 6.4 A Standard Error Plot for a Norm-Referenced Test

Standard Error. Any statistical test or measure can have a standard error. The standard error of a statistic is the standard deviation of the sampling distribution of that statistic. Standard errors are considered important because they reflect how much of a sampling fluctuation a statistic will show. How good an estimate of the population the sample statistic is depends on the sampling, or measurement, error. The standard error of any statistic depends on the sample size (Gravetter & Wallnau, 1999). Larger sample sizes tend to have a smaller standard error or standard error of the mean (S_M). The normal distribution of scores can be compared against the standard error and plotted as in Figure 6.4.

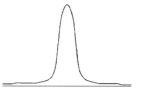

FIGURE 6.5   A Peaked or Leptokurtic Distribution Example

FIGURE 6.6   A Flattened or Platokurtic Distribution Example

Kurtosis

Kurtosis is a measure of the peakedness or flatness of a distribution of scores (Aron & Aron, 2001). Positive kurtosis represents a relatively peaked distribution. Negative kurtosis represents a relatively flat distribution. Normal bell-shaped distributions of scores produce a kurtosis statistic of about zero. A more positive value indicates the possibility of a leptokurtic distribution (Figure 6.5), which has a higher peak than a normal distribution. A negative value indicates a platykurtic distribution (Figure 6.6), which is flatter than a normal distribution.

Skewness

A skewed distribution is considered an asymmetrical distribution; the distribution will likely have a single mode or unimodal distribution, but the distribution is elongated and asymmetrical in relation to the mean (Vogt, 1999). If a distribution is considered positively skewed, then the distribution has an asymmetrical tail that extends upward toward more positive values. A negatively skewed distribution, then, is asymmetrical and extends downward around the mean toward more negative values (Aron & Aron 2001).

Range

The range of scores is another measure of variation of the distribution of scores (Vogt, 1999). The range of scores is the difference between the highest and lowest scores. To derive the range, the lowest value of the scores is subtracted from the highest value. Though the concept of range is easily understood, the measure is sensitive to extreme or outlier scores and may not give an accurate picture of score distribution as per the boxplot in Figure 6.7 used here simply to represent the concept of range of scores. In this figure, the score 65 is the median score; the upper and lower quartiles are represented by the box, scores 65–69 represent the upper quartile of scores, and scores 61–65 represent the lower quartile of scores. In a distribution of frequencies, quartiles are comprised of any three points that divide an ordered distribution in four parts. The whiskers extending from the box represent the distance from the quartile range on either side of the median to the extremes for the set of scores. In this case the upper extreme score is 72 and the lower extreme score is 58.

Maximum and Minimum Scores, Sum, and Count

The maximum score is the largest, or highest, score in the distribution of scores. The minimum score then is the smallest, or lowest, score in the distribution of scores. The sum of scores is the total value of all scores in the distribution. The count of scores is the frequency or number of scores in the distribution of scores (Dretzke & Heilman, 1998).

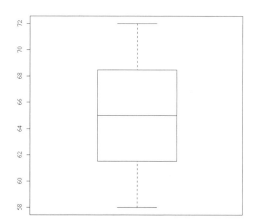

FIGURE 6.7   A Boxplot of Maximum and Minimum Scores and Distribution

Confidence Level

Confidence level is the likelihood, expressed as a percentage, that the results of a statistical analysis are repeatable and not simply due to random chance. That is, if a confidence level for the population mean is calculated at 95 percent, then the data for the sample mean would be consistent 95 percent of the time, with the calculated mean value falling within the high and low range of a calculated confidence interval (Aron & Aron, 2001).

Data Analysis Tools: Descriptive Statistics

To perform descriptive statistics in Excel some familiarity with concepts presented in previous chapters is required. For example, being familiar with how to create new workbooks, new worksheets, and formatting spreadsheet data to use the data analysis and mathematical functions in Excel is essential. Once the data to be described are entered into spreadsheets and the input range (usually including labels) is selected for analysis, then the data analysis functions can be used and descriptive statistics selected. By selecting the descriptive statistics function in the data analysis add-on pack, a dialog box will open to make selections on statistical output preferences to be reported.

For example, suppose that we want to know the descriptive statistical information for a class of students taking a midterm examination. After scoring the examination and entering the data into a spreadsheet, we select Tools and then Data Analysis. From the Data Analysis Tools we select Descriptive Statistics (see Figure 6.8; see also the accompanying CD-ROM video animation: "Descriptive Statistics Example One").

A second dialog box opens to allow selections for calculating Descriptive Statistics (see Figure 6.9). The data range may be input by columns or rows. By selecting labels in

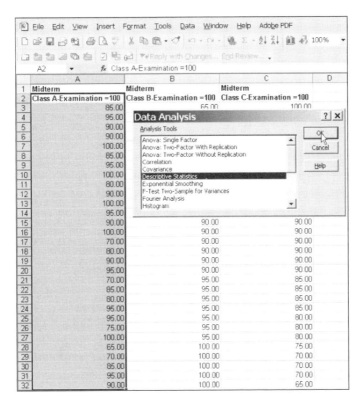

FIGURE 6.8   The Data Analysis Dialog Box

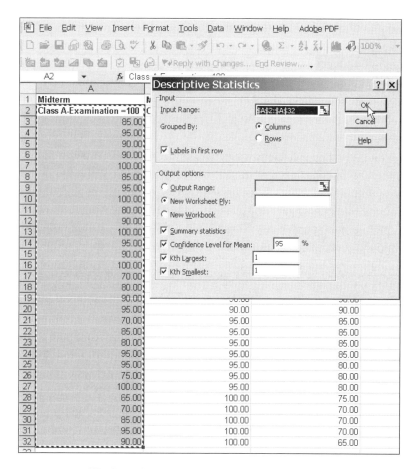

FIGURE 6.9　The Descriptive Statistics Dialog Box

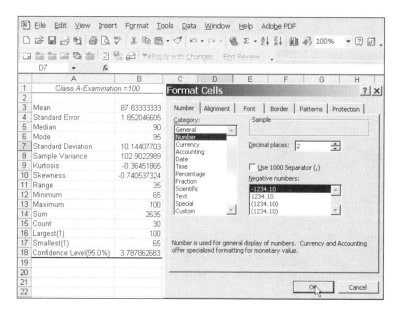

FIGURE 6.10　The Format Cells Dialog Box

	A	B
1	*Class A-Examination =100*	
2		
3	Mean	87.83
4	Standard Error	1.85
5	Median	90.00
6	Mode	95.00
7	Standard Deviation	10.14
8	Sample Variance	102.90
9	Kurtosis	-0.36
10	Skewness	-0.74
11	Range	35.00
12	Minimum	65.00
13	Maximum	100.00
14	Sum	2635.00
15	Count	30.00
16	Largest(1)	100.00
17	Smallest(1)	65.00
18	Confidence Level(95.0%)	3.79

FIGURE 6.11   A Summary Descriptive Statistics Output with Cell Values Formatted Producing Frequency Polygrams

the first row, the output will include labels with numerical output. A choice can be made as to whether output will be entered into a separate worksheet or into the same worksheet. Additional selections can be made for the identification of summary statistics, the confidence level for means, and the lowest and highest case in the distribution.

The output summary of descriptive statistics commonly has multiple decimal spaces and may not be reported as uniform values with a consistent number of decimal spaces. To correct the output information and format for ease of interpretation, simply select the format cells option. This option is available on the standard toolbar. Select and highlight numerical values for cells of interest. Then, from the standard toolbar, select Format, and then Cells. A dialog box with several tabs appears. Select the Number tab and then the Number category. Set the decimal places to 2 for positive numbers and select the OK button to complete formatting of the selected and highlighted cells. The result is a range of numerical values in the output that can be quickly and easily interpreted, as in Figure 6.10.

The final summary includes the descriptive statistical information defined with formulas given in previous examples. Excel can calculate this summary information quickly to answer a variety of daily practice problems for small human service, educational, and other organizations, such as describing case load numerical values, identifying staff performance issues, and evaluating programs and services through descriptive data (see Figure 6.11).

Producing Frequency Polygrams

Though it is covered in Chapter 5, producing frequency polygrams is presented briefly here for review. As mentioned before, a histogram, or frequency polygram, is a graphical representation of a distribution. The X or horizontal axis is composed of raw data sorted into different categories or bins. The Y or vertical axis represents the frequency of occurrence of the raw scores within each category. When discrete or nominal level data is used, fractions do not occur, the values represent the number of subjects, and individual bars are used graphically to represent the number that falls into each category. If, however, the data is of a continuous scale, fractions are possible, such as in the case of measuring length, and a continuous line is drawn from the center of each category to represent a point of value for plotting trend or line graphs.

Let us construct an example of a histogram or frequency polygram with data organized into categories on the horizontal axis to demonstrate the above concepts. A common example might be a supervisor who wants to track the number of case visits made by 50 case managers to residents on an agency caseload for a single month. Most of the case visitation rates fall between 80 and 120 visits. However, we are interested in comparing the frequency of case managers who achieved 90 or below visits, 100 visits, 110 visits, and 120 case visits or more per month.

To evaluate visitation rates we begin by running descriptive statistics in the data analysis tools. We observe quickly that the most frequently occurring rate of visitation is about 86 visits per month. Some case managers are demonstrating much higher visitation rates, though, as the mean is above 95 and the median is at 96. By reviewing the standard deviation we can determine that the majority of our case managers visited a number of cases within the range of about plus or minus 17 cases from an average of 95.31 cases. That means that more than 68 of our case managers were able to visit between 122.94 and 78.94 cases per month as per the summary in Figure 6.12 (see the accompanying CD-ROM video animation, "Descriptive Statistics Example Two").

To gain more information we decide to create a BINS column on our spreadsheet to determine the frequencies of visitation for several categories of interest. In this instance, after setting up intervals in the BINS column, we select Histogram from the data analysis tools.

The data analysis box is then opened. Select the histogram data analysis tool, then the OK button as per Figure 6.13 (see the accompanying CD-ROM video animation: "Descriptive Statistics and Creating a Histogram").

As in Chapter 5, a dialog box opens to permit selection of both an input range and an interval or BIN range for categories or frequencies of interest. Data ranges may be selected along with options to display a sorted histogram, with a cumulative percentage line and chart output on the same or a new worksheet. After making selections, click on the OK button (see Figure 6.14).

A frequency and cumulative percentage output table is created that provides information on the frequency of each interval selected and the cumulative percentage for each interval fre-

	A	B
1	*Cases seen per week*	
2		
3	Mean	95.31
4	Standard Error	2.42
5	Median	96.00
6	Mode	86.00
7	Standard Deviation	16.97
8	Sample Variance	287.97
9	Kurtosis	9.89
10	Skewness	-2.10
11	Range	106.00
12	Minimum	14.00
13	Maximum	120.00
14	Sum	4670.00
15	Count	49.00
16	Largest(1)	120.00
17	Smallest(1)	14.00
18	Confidence Level(95.0%)	4.87

FIGURE 6.12   Descriptive Statistics Output for Case Management Data

quency. A sorted histogram is also displayed with the interval frequencies presented as discrete bars and a cumulative frequency line. Notice that the cumulative percentage line provides little information in this instance, but is inversely associated with the rates of fewer case workers who were able to achieve in excess of 100 case visits for the month of interest as in Figure 6.15.

The histogram serves as a specialized type of bar chart. The histogram that is produced by Excel permits individual data points to be grouped together in classes. The

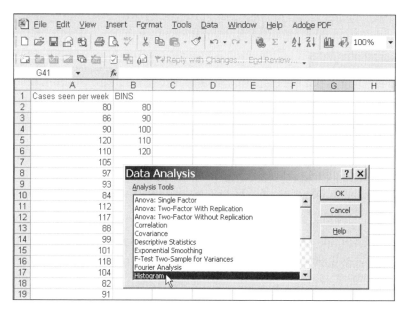

FIGURE 6.13   Data Analysis Dialog Box with Histogram Selected

FIGURE 6.14   The Histogram Dialog Box

viewer can quickly determine the frequency of data occurrence in each class in the dataset. Higher bars on the histogram indicate more points, or greater frequency in a class, and low bars indicate lesser points, or reduced frequency in a class. In the histogram shown in Figure 6.15, the peak is in the 110 to 120 class. In this instance, as the categories have been organized as discrete intervals, the bars have been automatically sorted from most frequently occurring category to least frequently occurring category on the X-axis.

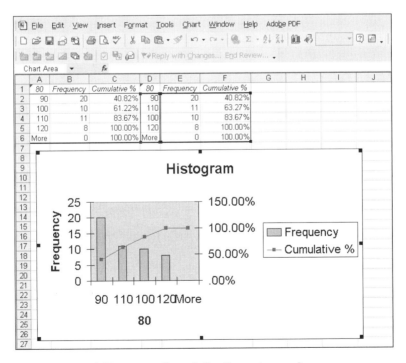

FIGURE 6.15   A Frequency Cumulative Percentage and Histogram Output with Line

The strength of a histogram is that it provides an easy-to-read picture of the location and variation in a dataset. Again, however, histograms have two weaknesses as alluded to in Chapter 5:

- Histograms can be manipulated to show different pictures. When too few or too many bars are used, the histogram can be misleading.
- Histograms can also obscure the time differences among datasets.

However, the original data is quickly accessible and linked to the data within the spreadsheet workbook for clarification.

Summary

Descriptive statistics and the frequency polygram, or histogram, can provide a great deal of aggregate information about a set of scores or raw data. Measures of central tendency and variability describe the shape of the data and provide important information about the characteristics of the sample. Through the use of spreadsheets, we are able to perform many simultaneous statistical tests at once and to know our confidence level in the summary information reported in the output. Spreadsheets have the capacity to work with both discrete and continuous information. The descriptive statistics reported in the output summary can determine the portion of the sample of the score distribution that is not affected by the standard error of the mean, and for which the summary information is valid.

Highly typical situations such as the analysis of classroom score distribution and the level of productivity of case managers in supervision have served as examples to strengthen our understanding of the importance and relevance of descriptive statistics. Though descriptive statistics are considered among the most basic of methods to analyze and evaluate data, they are a part of our everyday lives. We are aware of descriptive statistics as a part of sporting events, surveys and polling information, financial planning and budgeting, case studies and demographics, and, as in the example, as a routine function of educational settings. Spreadsheets can perform descriptive data analytic functions with a minimum of training (Patterson, 2000).

REVIEW QUESTIONS

1. How do measures of central tendency differ when distributions are not symmetrical?

2. Describe at least three measures of variability or dispersion.

3. What are standard deviation scores used for?

4. What is the difference between a platykurtic and leptokurtic distribution of values?

5. What tools are available in Excel to calculate descriptive statistics?

6. Can you give an example of a human service agency informational need that would require descriptive statistics?

7. The median score in a distribution is located at what percentile of the distribution?

7 Statistical Inference and Hypothesis Testing

Statistical inference and hypothesis testing is concerned with some very practical questions that are of interest to those evaluating practice interventions or programs. These questions include: (a) What does my data tell me about my study sample? (b) Can I draw any conclusions from the data? and (c) Are the findings from the sample useful or sufficient to generalize to my service population or to the general population? Spreadsheets can be developed to assist with the evaluation of hypotheses made about a service population sample and the generalizations that can be derived from the conclusions made about the hypotheses that are of interest to social service providers.

Spreadsheets are extremely useful tools for evaluating programs or practice through the use of representative samples (please see Chapter 3 for a thorough discussion of sampling issues). For instance, how is your service group or population of interest performing when compared to other service providers, to other service populations, or to the general population? By comparing your clients or program recipients to established norms for a service population and setting criteria for meeting standards or for meeting a research inquiry, you can begin to make comparisons and describe and make inferences about your service group. Social service providers are increasingly pressed to demonstrate effectiveness of programs and interventions in order to meet legislative or departmental mandates, to maintain service funding, and to demonstrate advanced service capabilities to third party payer and referral sources. Evidence-based practice has become a generally accepted practice goal with increasing emphasis placed on the service organization and the practitioner to demonstrate in aggregate that services and interventions are reaching the standards expected by regulatory authorities.

The concepts of distributions of sample scores as compared to a normal distribution of expected scores are of critical importance to service providers. The essential questions are: (a) How does the distribution of scores from my sample differ from the expected distribution of scores? and (b) How is my sample different? There is an established social research and evaluation tradition of setting the criteria for a research inquiry in advance for a sample of service recipients and then analyzing a representative sample to determine if the study participants have met the proposed criteria through hypothesis testing.

However, there is an interaction of sample representativeness, sample size, the distribution of score means, and score variation that can effect the statistical validity of hypothesis testing so that mistaken assumptions about the sample may be made. This chapter will present these issues and demonstrate their interaction through a spreadsheet application that can educate the novice evaluator with respect to sample size issues and can also be replicated with data from the reader's own samples to yield useful information about the sample's capacity to make correct inferences.

Normal Distributions

A normal distribution is a theoretical construct based on the concept that all possible values of a continuous probability distribution can be plotted on the horizontal or X-axis of a graph, while the probability of each value occurring can be plotted on a vertical or Y-axis of a graph. These values or scores tend to concentrate or cluster near the mean value, or other central tendency measure, of all scores. This pattern is referred to as a bell curve. This curve has also been referred to as a normal curve of distribution, a unimodal curve, or a symmetrical curve. Scores in such a normal distribution are also often presented as z-scores.

A z-score is a standardized score that is represented as a normal distribution by converting scores to a standard score. The z-score is used to compare different groups of scores that are sometimes produced or assessed on differing scales or metrics. The z-score has a mean of 0.00 and a standard deviation of 1.00. By using z-scores we can compare an individual's scores from two or more differing assessments, or the same assessment given at different points in time. The different assessments, such as performance examinations, may have differing means and standard deviations. The general formula for comparing how far two scores varied from the mean on assessments taken at different times and with different scores may be accomplished through use of the following formula. To compare scores, simply take each score and subtract it from the mean of all scores for an administration of an assessment. Then divide this result by the standard deviation of scores for that administration. Do the same procedure for the alternate score from a second administration and compare the difference in standard deviation units represented by 1.00.

If we consider producing standard scores, or z-scores, for each distribution of an assessment score for a sample, or for different samples to be compared, then we may realize a series of normal distributions for each administration of an assessment. This occurs as the mean value of scores on the vertical axis may be different for different distributions. The standard deviation of values on the horizontal axis may also be different for different distributions. This creates a range of possible normal distributions for every value combination of each mean and each standard deviation.

Whenever a number is used to describe some characteristic of a variable of interest, or a characteristic of a group of data, it is referred to as a statistic. When a sample is taken from a population of sufficient size or is randomly drawn, the sampling distribution or summary description of a given variable in a sample tends to produce a normally represented distribution of scores. Therefore, the concept of a normal distribution is often used as the basis for making a statistical inference from a sample. The range of normal distributions possible for an infinite number of samples drawn from a population is often referred to as the Gaussian distribution.

Let us try an example of data analysis with a spreadsheet to evaluate whether a distribution of values is normally distributed. By setting up a simple three-column worksheet, we can begin with three statistical or numerical values that we might have derived from some earlier work. For example, we might provide a questionnaire with a scale of 100 to a set of clients to determine the degree to which they may be satisfied with an agency service. We might arrive at a survey completed by 40 available clients with the following values, derived by performing some simple descriptive statistics discussed earlier in the text.

Sample size = 40

Survey mean score = 50

Standard deviation = 7.45

Graphing scale interval width = 5 points

(Note: an interval of five points into which a number of scores fall and their frequency can be represented for each five-point interval in a graph.)

Then we may want to determine graphically whether the sample scores are normally distributed, or if the distribution is skewed. A skewed distribution is one in which the distribution of scores produces a nonsymmetrical distribution that is considered to be not usually representative of the population of survey respondents. We can quickly set up a simple spreadsheet as seen in Figure 7.1. This spreadsheet has used an interval midpoint, or a midpoint value, for each five points of value in the scale to demonstrate a normal probability distribution to be compared to a distribution of scores. Although a frequency count for each

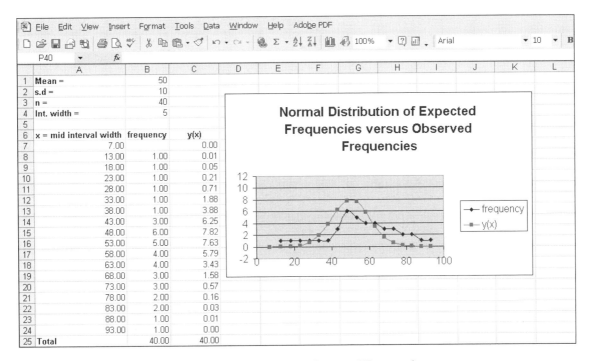

FIGURE 7.1   Spreadsheet of Normal Distribution versus Observed Frequencies

value could be calculated, this would potentially produce up to 100 categories of values. Therefore, a midpoint value is used as a method to smooth the distribution curve to make visual interpretation simpler. The spreadsheet in Figure 7.1 establishes a column for the chosen five-point scale in column A. Column B contains the frequency for all observed scores falling within the interval of five points. Finally, column C includes values that would be expected for score frequencies if the scores were normally distributed in a bell curve. To obtain these values, we create a formula in column C where the cell is in the same row for the first midpoint interval used to record frequencies. For graphing purposes you may wish to include an additional score interval midpoint for the intervals falling below and above the first observed frequency. At this first cell in column C (in this case cell C7), insert the formula =B$4*B$3*NORMDIST(A7.B$1.B$2,0) to create the values for expected frequencies, or frequencies that might be predicted in column C. Copy this formula for all cells below the first cell entered where there is a corresponding interval midpoint value in column A. That is, we set up an Excel formula that will provide the expected normally distributed frequencies to be compared to the observed frequencies. Then, in the Excel chart wizard, we may plot the two line graphs or curves by selecting the data from all three columns and choosing the scatterplot XY graph with the smoothed line option for the best display (Tufte, 1983). The resultant spreadsheet and graph, when labeled, should appear as in Figure 7.1 (see the accompanying CD-ROM video animation: "Normal Distribution"). You may compare your sample of survey respondents to the expected normal distribution of survey responses.

Probability Distributions

Probability is frequently explained through the analogy of flipping a coin (Weinbach & Grinnel, 2001). For example, if one flips a coin one time, there is an equal probability that the coin will land on heads as there is that the coin will land on tails. The likelihood of either event is about 50 percent. If we flip the coin a few times, the coin will land on heads some of the time and on tails some of the time. At first, there will likely be a noticeable difference.

Perhaps in a series of trials where we flip the coin 10 times, the coin lands on heads only two times, and on tails eight times. Then, in a series of 100 successive trials, we notice that although any series of 10 coin flips may not have an even number of heads and tails, this is not the case when we review all of the trials, in aggregate. At the end of 100 or so trials, we may notice that some trials have greater differences and others have minimal differences, and that overall there are more trials with minimal differences. Eventually, if we plot these trials of 10 coin flips from an extreme of one head and nine tails, to the other extreme of nine heads and one tail, a curve of probability begins to form with a greater number of coin flip trials falling somewhere in the middle of these extremes. That is, the likelihood of a trial yielding any particular combination of heads or tails can be determined by the distribution of many coin flip trials. This curved distribution becomes a normal curve or normal probability distribution, as continuous trials tend to smooth out the differences between previous trials.

A probability distribution, then, is a construct that refers to the probability, or likelihood, of each outcome occurring among all possible outcomes within a distribution. This construct of the range of all possible probabilities and outcomes is often referred to as the "empirical probability distribution" of obtaining a result. However, the construct of a probability distribution can also refer to the likelihood of getting a specific result within a large number of trials or opportunities to obtain the result (Black, 1999). This likelihood of obtaining the specific result is often referred to a "theoretical probability distribution." This theoretical probability distribution can be compared to the empirical probability distribution by using a number of test statistics depending on the level of numerical scale of the data or scores. That is, there may be a difference between the expected or theoretical distribution and the distribution obtained empirically or from the actual scores.

For example, a statistic or a statistical test, such as chi-square or another of several tests, might be used to compare observed versus expected frequencies for a score or result occurring for a categorical, nominal, or ordinal scale, or variable numerical data based on relative frequencies. The presence of continuous level data, such as interval or ratio scale, however, may require a statistic that reports probabilities in terms of odds, or percentages of likelihood.

Suppose our community agency is considering proposing a program to reduce placement disruption for children in foster care. We are interested in learning for which children the program will be most effective. The community agency does not have the long-term resources to expend on children for whom the program is not effective. We are undertaking a study to determine the effectiveness of the proposed program. To properly test the proposed program we need a random sample of children in foster care. If the sample is overly representative of the children who respond best to the program, our data may be misleading and cause the agency to expend future resources on children who do not respond well. If, however, children who respond poorly to the program are overly represented in our sample of those, the community agency may mistakenly assume that the intervention is not effective and not invest the resources to help those children who might respond to the program.

Previous research suggests that children scoring within a certain range of scores on a standardized assessment will likely benefit from the program. We have reviewed the scores and descriptive statistics of the community agency's children clients who are being considered for foster care placement and determined that the assessment scores for these children are comparable to the established norms for the assessment used nationally. We need to know whether our selecting any child at random for the evaluation project will have an expected probability of meeting the assessment score criteria needed to respond or not respond to the program. In order to answer this and similar questions, and ensure that our evaluation sample fits the study's need with respect to answering the research question, we will likely want to know if our sample has a probability distribution that is similar to the population to be generalized. We would likely plot the scores of the sample and compare these to a plot of expected scores or to a normal distribution of scores.

Skewness

Skewness refers to the possibility that scores may not distribute in a normal curve distribution, but may distribute unevenly such that there is a bunching-up effect on one side of the measure of central tendency. There would also be a corresponding thinning out of scores on the other side of the measure of central tendency. The direction of the thinning scores determines the direction of skew in the distribution (left and negatively skewed, or right and positively skewed). There is also a greater variability of scores relative to the degree of skewness in the distribution (Montcalm & Royse, 2002). A normal distribution is visually represented as a bell-shaped curve that is symmetrical on both sides of the mean, whereas a skewed distribution tails off in one direction while maintaining the majority of scores on one side of the mean and is represented as nonsymmetrical.

A number of computer applications such as spreadsheet applications generate a measure or index of skewness as a descriptive statistic for a range of values in a distribution, as seen in Chapter 6. For this descriptive statistic, positive values refer to a positive skew where the tail in the distribution is in the direction of the positive values in the distribution and negative values refer to a negative skew where the tail in the distribution is in the direction of the negative values in the distribution (Weinbach & Grinnell, 2001). In Figure 7.1, observed scores are not normally distributed and are unimodal; that is, the distribution has only one curve, has only one number representing the most frequently occurring score(s), and has a slightly positive skew to the distribution curve.

Understanding Hypothesis Testing

A hypothesis is a statement that is testable regarding the relationship between or among variables that a researcher intends to study (Vogt, 1999). In the case of social services practice we might want to test whether one intervention is more effective than another, whether a service team is performing substantially better on some measurable goal, or even whether our program is achieving the desired outcome. The hypothesis may be presented in response to the research question. The hypothesis is set up as an operationally defined restatement of the research question that has specific criteria with a test condition for the criteria. The restated hypothesis is then evaluated with a statistical procedure to determine if the test condition holds true, to determine whether the evaluator should accept the assumption of no change in the relationship between or among variables, or to confirm that sufficient change has occurred. If the chosen test condition or statistical value holds true by demonstrating a sufficient, or greater than would be expected by chance, change in the relationship between or among variables, then a theory or an experimental prediction will have been confirmed. Usually, hypothesis testing occurs as an either/or proposition: either the "alternative hypothesis" will be confirmed and thus confirm an outcome of a measurable difference or change, or it will confirm the study's null hypothesis. A null hypothesis is a statement that there will be no difference or change between a sample exposed to an intervention condition and a sample that is not. A null hypothesis that holds true suggests no effect or change for a condition or intervention. There may be change or effect, but to an insufficient degree to reject chance as the reason for the change. By convention, hypotheses are usually stated such that the condition of no change or the null hypothesis is the expected outcome. Hypotheses are often stated in one or more pairs or sets of alternative and null hypotheses that are mutually exclusive.

For example, suppose that we would like to compare whether a Web-based information technology application that provides timely case data to child protective service workers will have the desired effect of reducing placement disruptions for foster children. We would like to test this research question in a district where federal guidelines for placements have been difficult to adhere to. We could hypothesize that one year of the information technology use along with the requisite training would serve to substantially reduce the number of placement disruptions. Our null hypothesis might be that there would be no significant differences in placement disruptions at the end of twelve months of information technology service for a representative sample of trained caseworkers when compared to another representative sample of case workers who did not receive training or access to the data. An alternative hypothesis would assert that there would be a measurable and significant difference between the two samples that would not be considered to be due to chance alone.

The comparison could be made by selecting and computing a test statistic and determining statistical significance based on the probability that the observed values could have been due to chance or random error. A decision then must be made about which of the two hypotheses, the null hypothesis or the alternative hypothesis, is true. However, a significant finding by a test statistic may also be in error. Therefore, a deductive or decision-making model for assessing the risk of error and a number of methods to determine where such an error may occur have also been developed to confirm the accuracy of hypothesis testing, as seen in Table 7.1.

Hypothesis tests of significance may be stated, and organized, so that the critical region is specified as a region where the significance level (discussed later in this chapter) must be confirmed in order for the null hypothesis to be rejected and for the alternate hypothesis, also referred to as the experimental condition hypothesis, to be accepted. That critical region is the area under the normal curve where most of the scores must fall based on the alpha level and confidence levels that were set. These scores may fall in an area on one side of the normal distribution, or in two areas on either side of the normal distribution. Hypotheses then may be stated as either one-tailed or two-tailed hypotheses.

The scores that represent the difference between group means may be expected to fall entirely in a critical region above the mean of the normal distribution or in a critical region entirely below the mean of the normal distribution. In either of these cases, the alternative hypothesis may be stated as a one-tailed hypothesis. For example, a one-tailed hypothesis with scores expected to fall above the mean of the normal distribution might be stated as: "There will a significant improvement in emotional functioning after six weeks of participation in the agency support group," whereas a two-tailed alternative hypothesis may be stated as: "There will be a significant difference in emotional functioning after six weeks of participation in the agency support group."

If the possibility of making a "type one error" (a true null hypothesis is rejected) is located in one tail or area of a normal probability distribution and a directional prediction is preferred, then a one-tailed hypothesis would be stated. A two-tailed hypothesis is considered less stringent than a one-tailed test. The statistical functions for most spreadsheet data analytic programs report both the one-tailed and two-tailed critical region values in the results summaries of the tests.

Assume that we would like to compare two small group samples of agency clients who had endured a local natural disaster about six months earlier to see which group was functioning with less residual emotional disturbance. The sample members participated in different types of intervention following the crisis. One group requested and received traditional mental health services, including brief cognitive behavioral therapy, while the other group preferred less formal intervention but agreed to participate in one or two sessions of critical

TABLE 7.1   Hypothesis Testing Decision Table

	Null Hypothesis (True):	Alternate Hypothesis (True):
Null Hypothesis (True):	Correctly retaining the null hypothesis	Type I (alpha) error: Incorrectly rejecting the null hypothesis when true
Alternate Hypothesis (True):	Type II (beta) error: Incorrectly accepting the null hypothesis as true	Correctly rejecting the null hypothesis

incident stress debriefing. The two groups are assumed to be equal as they were randomly selected from larger groups of services recipients. All sample members were contacted and asked to complete a Beck Depression Inventory to assess their current functioning at 20 weeks following the disaster. The groups were hypothesized to have no significant differences in functioning. The null hypothesis, then, is that there is no statistically significant difference between the two groups; the mean difference in scores is zero as the group means are not statistically different. An alternate hypothesis is that the two groups will have statistically significant differences in group means when compared using a t-test for independent samples and using alpha at .05 as the criterion for demonstrating a significant difference in group means and in functioning as rated on the scores from the Beck Depression Inventory.

To evaluate the functioning of the two groups, we begin by setting up a spreadsheet to test the differences between the levels of emotional disturbance of the two groups. We are interested in determining if there is a difference in the average level of depression between the groups. To do that we use the following steps:

1. The Beck Depression Inventory scores for each group are input into two columns. We use a column heading to distinguish the two groups.

2. The two sets of scores may be sorted within columns, using the Excel sort function on the toolbar to visually evaluate differences between sample scores.

3. Visually inspect the data to determine any trends in terms of frequency of interest, and if the data appears to be similarly distributed; then, calculate descriptive statistics for each group.

4. Select the scores from one group at a time while completing steps 5–8.

5. Select the Tools on the Excel menu bar, and select the data analysis function.

6. From the data analysis window, select Descriptive Statistics. Select the data input range for the group, grouped by columns, and for the output to be reported on a new spreadsheet. Then check the boxes for summary statistics and the confidence level for the mean of the group selected. The confidence level represents the level or degree to which the evaluator or researcher is confident of a prediction. If an alpha level of .05 is selected, and the statistical result is found to be significant, then alpha of .05 may be subtracted from 1.00 and multiplied by 100 to derive the confidence level of 95 percent. We may then select an alpha level at .05 to determine a confidence level of at least 95 percent.

7. Press the OK button.

8. Descriptive statistics for the group selected will appear on a new worksheet with the summary statistics labels. These may be recopied to the main page and values pasted into columns to represent each group, as in Figure 7.2.

9. Select the Tools menu again and select the data analysis function. In the data analysis window, locate and select the statistical analysis procedure for t-test: two samples assuming equal variances. (We are assuming that our group samples were drawn randomly from a larger pool of survey respondents.)

10. Select the variable ranges for Group 1 and Group 2 and enter these ranges into the t-test function window. You may enter a hypothesis such as a mean difference of zero, which suggests that we would expect that there is no difference between the group means. We may select an alternate value if preferred, for example, if we expect the two groups to have some known weight or difference between them and expect them to be not equal by some known estimate prior to testing the null hypothesis. In most instances a mean difference of zero will be selected. Leave the labels box unchecked and note that alpha is preset to .05 and output options are preset to report results in a new worksheet, unless other preferences are made.

11. Press the OK button.

	A	B	C	D	E	F
1	Hypothesis Testing	For: u_1-u_2	Summary Statistics for:	Group I	Group 2	
2	The difference between	two sample means	Mean	10.25	11.80	
3	Group I: CBT @ 20 wks	Group 2: CISD @ 20 wks	Standard Error	1.18	1.20	
4	Raw Data: BDI Scores	Raw Data: BDI Scores	Median	8.50	11.00	
5	3		3 Mode	8.00	9.00	
6	4		5 Standard Deviation	5.27	5.35	
7	5		6 Sample Variance	27.78	28.59	
8	5		7 Kurtosis	-0.59	-0.02	
9	6		8 Skewness	0.67	0.59	
10	7		9 Range	18.00	20.00	
11	7		9 Minimum	3.00	3.00	
12	8		9 Maximum	21.00	23.00	
13	8		10 Sum	205.00	236.00	
14	8		11 Count	20.00	20.00	
15	9		11 t-Test: Two-Sample Assuming Equal Variances			Ho: mean u_1-u_2 = 0
16	10		13	Variable 1	Variable 2	Alpha = 0.5
17	11		13 Mean	10.25	11.80	
18	12		13 Variance	27.78	28.59	
19	12		14 Observations	20.00	20.00	
20	16		14 Pooled Variance	28.18		
21	16		18 Hypothesized Mean Differei	0.00		
22	18		18 df	38.00		
23	19		22 t Stat	-0.92		
24	21		23 P(T<=t) one-tail	0.18		
25			t Critical one-tail	1.69		
26			P(T<=t) two-tail	0.36		
27			t Critical two-tail	2.02		

FIGURE 7.2   Hypothesis Test for a Two-Group Comparison of Means Using a t-Test

12. T-test statistics for the comparison of means differences for the two groups will appear on a new worksheet with the summary statistics labels. These may also be recopied to the main page and values pasted into columns to represent each group or variable, as in Figure 7.2.

A completed hypothesis test for a two-group comparison of means using a t-test function may look similar to Figure 7.2 when completed (see the accompanying CD-ROM video animation: "Hypothesis Testing").

Statistical Significance

Statistical tests, of which there are many, assist in the determination of likelihood that research results are not due to random error or chance. If a statistical test is employed and the result obtained from a variable or several variables is smaller than would be expected by chance alone, then it is said to be significant. Significance is determined in part by the p-value selected for the research study.

p-Value

The probability value, or p-value, is an estimate of probability that the obtained value for an outcome of a statistical test would have been due to chance or random error. It is less than 5 percent, if the statistical result indicated significance at the .05 level. However, the significance level could have been alternatively set at .01; if the p-value for an outcome of a statistical test was found to be .01 or less, then the likelihood that this result would have then been due to chance or random error is less than 1 percent. The smaller the value for "p," the greater the likelihood that the obtained result could have been due to chance.

Though the p-value is the actual probability level for the test, it is determined by the associated number reported with it, which is known as the alpha level. Alpha level is chosen by the researcher and is an estimate of making a Type I error and rejecting a null hypothesis of no difference that is actually true. In other words, the alpha level is selected as the "significance level" for the test statistic (Vogt, 1999). The p-value and alpha level are reported in the spreadsheet in Figure 7.2. In this instance, there was no reported significant difference in the functioning of the two groups of service recipients after six months as compared to initial responses to a Beck Depression Inventory. Both the p-value and the critical regions of one- and two-tailed hypotheses of a difference in group means is given in the t-test results summary.

There is no rule with respect to selecting an appropriate p-value or alpha level for a statistical test. However, the choice of alpha level has an effect on the statistical power of the statistical test. Statistical power is concerned with the capacity of the selected test or procedure to detect associations or differences between variables when actually present and rejecting the null hypothesis of no difference when false. The higher the criteria for the alpha level, the higher the power needed to detect the statistical difference in most, but not all, instances. By the same token, the power of a statistical test to reliably identify an association between variables is affected by both the sample size and the amount of variance or standard deviation of scores for the sample. We will demonstrate the effect that sample size has on the power of a statistical test later on in a spreadsheet example. For now, let us assume as we plan our research study that estimates of a sample mean may be obtained from similar published research data. We can also determine an estimate of the standard error of the mean to determine the expected degree of variation from a sample. A sampling error may occur whereby the sample does not accurately reflect characteristics of the population that the sample was drawn from. Standard error is a measure of estimating the degree to which the sample statistic or test result serves as an accurate estimate of the sample population.

Given that we may draw any number of possible samples from a population, there is a likelihood of drawing a sample from which the members score in the expected mean score range, or within the normal distribution for the population. There is also a possibility of drawing a sample from which the members will perform, or score, closer to the distribution associated for an expected sample error range of value, making inferences from the sample to the population inaccurate. These two sample distributions may have a limited area of shared association. If there is too much variation between the score distributions for expected versus observed scores, then a less powerful statistical test may not be able to detect an association or effect size (explanation follows) if the association exists. In the spreadsheet example in Figure 7.1 (p. 77), the expected distribution includes the observed distribution of scores near the sample mean, but this is not always the case.

Type I and Type II Errors

When determining the significance level for a set of hypotheses related to a research question, it is possible to make errors about the accuracy of the statistical finding. Two types of errors are possible, commonly known as Type I and Type II errors. Type I errors are associated with drawing a false conclusion that a relationship exists between two variables where none exists. Type I errors are known as alpha errors. Type II errors are concerned with denying a legitimate effect that does exist. This is done by failing to reject a null hypothesis. Type II errors are known as beta errors.

Spreadsheets can also be formatted to provide a decision as to whether to reject or accept the null hypothesis (Dretzke & Heilman, 1998). The critical value necessary under the normal curve to reject the null hypothesis for a one-tailed test is plus or minus 1.645 and for a two-tailed test is plus or minus 1.96. For many hypothesis tests that are compared to the normal probability distribution, there will be limited difficulty in making the decision to accept or reject the null hypothesis. However, there are Web-based resources for formatting pages that are exceptions (Pinto, 2001).

Effect Size and Sample Size Estimation

Understanding the material that follows on effect size and sample size estimation may be considered somewhat advanced and require more than one reading. However, practice level research is often of limited usefulness with respect to making meaningful inferences because the samples chosen for a study are too small to reliably detect even a modest association even if one is actually present. Yet selecting large samples is often expensive and burdensome. The following material addresses the question of how to use spreadsheets to estimate an appropriate sample size for your evaluation or research effort. The material becomes more readily understandable if the spreadsheet templates are constructed as discussed and different sample size, power, or alpha levels are used to make estimates.

Effect size refers to an alternate method to measure significance of an association between variables that is thought to be more practical or realistic than that of the p-value of a test statistic. The effect size is an estimation of the difference between an average subject in a sample who received an intervention and an average subject in a sample who did not receive the intervention. An effect size can be thought of as a standardized difference; an effect size, which is denoted by the symbol "d," is the mean difference between groups in standard score form. An effect size may also be thought of as the ratio of the difference between the means to the standard deviation (Vogt, 1999). In a series of procedures designed to evaluate the necessary sample size needed to have sufficient power to assure the detection of an effect size, this method estimates the degree to which the null hypothesis is false. Effect size is an alternative way, thought by many to be more reliable, of evaluating the effect of an intervention or presence of change resulting from an intervention. The sample's size may not be sufficient in some instances for a reliable finding using a statistical test even if the result is a significant p-value or alpha level. In other instances, there may be insufficient power (beta), due to the statistical test selected, or the sample size to be confident of a significant finding. An effect size is based on determining a difference between the mean of the control group and experimental group using an alternate calculation. The concept is to calculate the difference between an average subject who received an intervention and one who did not. The resultant "d" or "delta" difference is evaluated much like a correlation as a measure of association and has a determination between the numerical values of 0.00 and 1.00. As the "d" value approaches 1.00, the effect size is considered to be greater. The conventional values of effect size are (Welkowitz, Ewen, & Cohen, 1982):

1. Small effect size, d = .20
2. Medium effect size, d = .50
3. Large effect size, d = .80

There are several ways to calculate effect size. The most commonly used, though, is the basic formula proposed by Glass and others (Glass, 1976; Glass, McGraw, & Smith, 1981):

$$\frac{\text{Mean of control group} - \text{Mean of treatment group}}{\text{Standard deviation of the control group}}$$

However, this formula does not do justice to the complexities involved in controlling for statistical and measurement differences between the two or more groups to be compared if they occur in different types of research projects that are being compared without similar research controls. This formula is given to provide only a basic orientation to the concept of evaluating effect size. The group values can be obtained from a spreadsheet comparison of the difference between two groups as the values are given in the descriptive statistical summary. To evaluate an effect size for an intervention through use of a spreadsheet, however, we need to know the following:

- The outcome measures being used
- The number of subjects, the mean, and the standard deviation values for the treatment group and the control group

- The raw score differences
- The standardized differences

LaMorte (1999) has proposed an innovative spreadsheet sample size estimator based on deriving reference values for specified alpha and beta criteria; this can be used for calculating sample estimates needed to obtain a satisfactory effect size for two group comparison studies. The formula for obtaining these reference values (LaMorte, 1999) is given as

$$\left(\frac{Z \times 1 - \text{alpha}}{2 + 1 - \text{beta}}\right)^2$$

This formula produces values that may be placed into a spreadsheet cell in Excel and referenced in spreadsheet formulas to calculate needed sample estimates, as may be seen on the online demonstration located at www.bumc.bu.edu/Departments/PageMain.asp?Department ID=287&Page=2120.

Values derived from the above formula for alpha = .10 and beta = .05, .01, .02, and .05 are reported, respectively, as "10.8," "8.6," "6.2," and "2.7." Values derived from the formula for alpha = .01 and beta = .05, .01, .02, and .05 are reported, respectively, as "13," "10.5," "7.8," and "3.8." Values derived from the formula for alpha = .02 and beta = .05, .01, .02, and .05 are reported as "15.8," "13," "10," and "5.4." Finally, values derived from the formula for alpha = .01 and beta = .05, .01, .02, and .05 are reported as "17.8," "14.9," "11.7," and "6.6" (LaMorte, 1999).

These values may be ordered into a table or placed separately into reference cells or formulas and used to calculate a number of common sample size estimates for two group comparisons, as in the online example. The group mean and standard deviation may be modified to accommodate differing samples for the two group comparison of sample size estimates for either differences in group means or differences in proportions.

To set up a spreadsheet to perform a two-group comparison to evaluate differences in group means, follow these steps.

1. Consider the level of power (1-beta) or confidence level (1-alpha) that you would like to achieve in the group comparison. Then, format the spreadsheet to determine the sample size needed for each group to ensure the statistical power needed to detect an adequate effect size.

2. Paste in a reference table of the values needed for confidence and power levels of interest.

3. Format rows for group 1 and group 2 to include the mean and standard deviations for each group derived from original scores, from reference data on scale values for an assessment instrument, or from another source.

4. Set up a location to calculate the difference in means for the groups by using this formula:

$$\frac{\text{ABS (cell value for mean of sample group 2 } - \text{ cell value for mean of sample group 1)}}{\text{cell value of the mean of sample group 1} \times 100}$$

5. Set up a table to calculate sample size estimates for each alpha level and beta level of interest.

6. Set up a cell location in the table at the intercept of columns for the p-value and power levels of interest. Then, in each cell, format a formula that will include the reference value for the confidence level pasted into the spreadsheet earlier.

7. Use the formula

$$\frac{[(\text{mean of sample group 1})^2 + (\text{mean of sample group 2})^2]}{(\text{mean of sample group 1} - \text{mean of sample group 2})^2} \times \text{cell value for the p-value and power of interest}$$

In the following example, the formula for spreadsheet cell E36 would be written as: =(($B$27^2 + $B$30^2)* J5)/($A$27–$A$30)^2. The cell value in J5 is the reference value given for power 80 percent at alpha .10 from the z-score formula previously given.

8. This two-group comparison template can translate the values of means and standard deviations for each group to various sample sizes needed for the p-value and power levels associated with the included reference values.

To set up a different spreadsheet to perform a two-group comparison to evaluate differences in proportional frequencies, simply modify this template by following these steps.

1. Again, consider the level of power (1-beta) or confidence level (1-alpha) that you would like to achieve in the group comparison. Then format the spreadsheet to determine the sample size needed for each group to ensure the statistical power needed to detect an adequate effect size.

2. Begin by pasting in a reference table of the values needed for confidence and power levels of interest.

3. Format rows for group 1 and group 2 to include the proportion with and proportion without for each group derived from original scores, from reference data on scale values for an assessment instrument, or from another source.

4. Set up a table to calculate sample size estimates for each alpha level and beta level of interest.

5. Set up a cell location in the table at the intercept of columns for the p-value and power levels of interest. Then, in each cell, format a formula that will include the reference value for the confidence level pasted into the spreadsheet earlier.

6. Use the formula

$$\frac{[(\text{proportion with of sample group } 1 \times \text{proportion without of sample group } 1) + (\text{proportion with of sample group } 2 \times \text{proportion without of sample group } 2)] \times \text{reference value for a p-value and power level of interest}}{(\text{proportion with of sample group } 1 - \text{the proportion with of sample group } 2)^2}$$

Use these steps for determining the difference in proportions or frequency and the earlier steps for differences in group means.

In the next two figures are adaptations of the sample size estimator that was previously referred to for sample size differences in group means. In Figure 7.3 (see the accompanying CD-ROM video animation: "Sample Size") is an example of two groups with means of 25 and 20, respectively, as might be seen for two groups whose scores are compared on a standardized depression assessment scale. However, in this example the standard deviation is large at 15. Notice that as a result of the expected variance being high, a larger sample is needed to detect an effect or association between the scores for the two groups.

Figure 7.4 is a second example of the two groups with the respective means of 25 and 20. However, in this second example the standard deviation is moderate at 10. Notice that as a result of the expected variance being less, a smaller sample is needed to detect an effect or association between the scores for the two groups. The sample size needed is nearly half of the first example, as the association between the two groups will be more readily detected with less expected variation, as represented by smaller standard deviation for the two groups. Therefore, we might expect that our need for a larger sample size will increase as we increase the p-value expectation for alpha (e.g., from .05 to .01), as we strive to

	A	B	D	E	F	G	H	I	J
21									
22	Sample Sizes for Difference in Group Means (2 Groups)					Table: (z1-a/2+z1-b)sq.			
23	Expected Values							beta (1-b)	
24						alpha (1-a)	0.05	0.1	0.2
25	*Sample Group 1*					0.1	10.8	8.6	6.2
26	Mean	Stan. Dev				0.05	13	10.5	7.8
27	25	15				0.02	15.8	13	10
28	Sample Group 2					0.01	17.8	14.9	11.7
29	Mean	Stan. Dev							
30	22	15							
31									
32	Difference in means	12.00 %							
33									
34	alpha level	Power							
35	("p" value)	95%	90%	80%					
36	0.10	540.00	430.00	310.00					
37	0.05	650.00	525.00	390.00					
38	0.02	790.00	650.00	500.00					
39	0.01	890.00	745.00	585.00					

FIGURE 7.3 A Sample Size Estimator for Group Comparison with High Group Variance

	A	B	D	E	F	G	H	I	J
21									
22	Sample Sizes for Difference in Group Means (2 Groups)					Table: (z1-a/2+z1-b)sq.			
23	Expected Values							beta (1-b)	
24						alpha (1-a)	0.05	0.1	0.2
25	*Sample Group 1*					0.1	10.8	8.6	6.2
26	Mean	Stan. Dev				0.05	13	10.5	7.8
27	25	10				0.02	15.8	13	10
28	Sample Group 2					0.01	17.8	14.9	11.7
29	Mean	Stan. Dev							
30	22	10							
31									
32	Difference in means	12.00 %							
33									
34	alpha level	Power							
35	("p" value)	95%	90%	80%					
36	0.10	240.00	191.11	137.78					
37	0.05	288.89	233.33	173.33					
38	0.02	351.11	288.89	222.22					
39	0.01	395.56	331.11	260.00					

FIGURE 7.4 A Sample Size Estimator for Group Comparison with Moderate Group Variance

increase statistical power to detect an adequate effect size (e.g., from 80 percent to 95 percent), and as we note higher levels of variation in our sample scores as represented by higher standard deviations (e.g., from s.d. = 10 to s.d. = 15).

From these examples we can clearly see the interrelationship between alpha and power, as well as the effect of sample size on effect size and the determination of a relationship between variables. Furthermore, we can evaluate these aspects of evaluating a sample change or an intervention for effectiveness and statistical conclusion validity by using fairly simply constructed spreadsheet templates. For the purposes of practice evaluation and program effectiveness studies, the optimum sample size, power, and alpha level can be determined as part of the planning effort for the study. These can more readily ensure that the evaluative effort will correctly detect an association between variables that is actually present. This will reduce the risk of making inferences from a sample to a population that may be in error.

Likewise, the proportion of the expected sample mean to the standard deviation is also a factor in determining sample size. In Figures 7.3 and 7.4, the group means are set at 25 and 20, respectively, with standard deviations of 10 or 15. However, if the proportion of the standard deviation to the group mean is smaller, a smaller sample size will suffice. For samples with large means that are as much as 10 times the expected standard deviation for the sample, a dramatically smaller sample size may be well able to detect an association between variables of interest, or a smaller effect size.

There are a number of additional online templates for differing power and effect size estimates that use Excel programming script and may be generally located by using the following search terms on the Web: .xls, spreadsheet, effect size, power, and sample size. Many are available for free download; others may be viewed and used as guides. However, depending on the need, some spreadsheets that perform sample size calculations are included in costly Excel add-on programs and provide some additional advanced functions.

Statistical power is the third determinant of obtaining an adequate effect size when employing a statistical test to evaluate the success or degree of change from an intervention when comparing a control and an experimental group. Statistical power refers to the capacity of the selected statistical test to identify or detect a relationship between variables; it is the power of the test to correctly reject the null hypothesis when it is false. The power estimate of a statistical test is determined by subtracting beta from 1.00, or the probability of making a Type II error from 1.00. Beta in this instance refers to beta error, or the error involved in failing to reject a null hypothesis that is false. The often accepted convention for most studies using statistical tests is a power estimate of at least .80. Power estimates can be included in spreadsheet calculations to assist in the determination of sample size required for a statistical test to determine a relationship between variables, such as an effect size, with some degree of confidence that rejecting the null hypothesis is the correct decision.

Summary

As we have seen, spreadsheets have a number of useful applications with respect to making inferences and evaluating hypotheses about research questions or to determine associations between variables of interest. Spreadsheets can be formatted to illustrate the distribution of values against a normal probability distribution to enhance the visual understanding of the characteristics of the sample. Spreadsheets can be designed to evaluate hypotheses for two or more group comparisons and display summary descriptive statistics as well as information on whether to reject or accept the null hypothesis, as in Figure 7.2 (p. 82). However, if there is concern about the statistical decision's validity due to its sample size, adequate statistical power to detect an effect size if present, or about the inferences made from a sample due to sample error or sample variation, spreadsheets can be used to evaluate sample and power needs before conducting an experiment or evaluation. Furthermore, spreadsheets can be used as training tools to improve practice and understanding for those needing to master data analysis concepts such as sample size considerations by using similar models as the examples depicted in Figures 7.3 and 7.4. The relationship between alpha, power, and sample size can be varied so that planning in the evaluation of an intervention can occur prior to implementation. Then, if an intervention effect or a finding of an association between two or more variables is made, the evaluator can have greater confidence in the statistical conclusion validity of the sample's distribution of scores and any inferences to be made from sample data, including decisions to accept or reject the null hypothesis.

REVIEW QUESTIONS

1. Explain how sample size, sample representativeness, score variation, and distribution of score means affect statistical conclusion validity.

2. What is the purpose of converting raw scores to z-standard scores?

3. Give an example of a probability distribution.

4. Define the critical region under a normal probability distribution.

5. What is the p-value in statistical testing?

6. Define the effect size as a measure of significance of association between variables, and give an example.

7. How does sample size affect the power of a statistical test to determine an association between variables?

8 Bivariate Statistics

Bivariate statistics may be created along with graphical representations that illustrate findings using available spreadsheet programs. Statistical procedures used to describe the relationship between two variables are considered bivariate statistics. The primary focus of the analysis of associated or bivariate variables is on the extent to which they co-vary, or vary together (Welkowitz, Ewen, & Cohen, 1982).

Bivariate statistical analysis should be differentiated from multivariate statistical analysis. Multivariate analysis is more complex and deals with three or more variables. In the case of bivariate statistical analysis, we are primarily concerned with the association between two variables. In the case of multivariate analysis, often referred to as an elaboration model or a contingency control model, a relationship between an independent and a dependent variable is analyzed while holding a third variable constant. Multivariate analysis will be explained in more detail in Chapter 11.

In the instance of bivariate analysis we are concerned with measures of association that describe the nature of the relationship between two variables. In the ideal relationship between variables, a change in one variable is associated with a change in the second variable. Bivariate statistics attempt to ascertain the strength of association between two variables. Most measures of association indicate a perfect positive relationship by 1.00 and a perfect negative relationship by –1.00. The closer the value of the measure is to –1.00 or 1.00, the stronger the relationship. The closer the value is to zero, the weaker the relationship (Weinbach & Grinnell, 2001).

Hypotheses to be tested by use of bivariate and other statistical test procedures are stated in two forms. To review, the first form is that the test will reveal no statistical relationship or difference between two variables of interest. The second form specifies the relationship or association expected if the hypothesis of no association or relationship is proven false. These are referred to as the null hypothesis and the alternative or research hypothesis (Montcalm & Royse, 2002).

The null hypothesis is usually stated as follows:

- There is no relationship between two variables in the population, or
- There is no difference between a sample statistic and a population statistic.

The alternative or research hypothesis is usually stated as follows:

- There is a difference or relationship between variable X and Y.

Chi-Square Test of Independence

The chi-square test of independence is essentially a nonparametric analysis test of statistical significance for bivariate data that is in a tabular form such as cross-tabs or cross-breaks tabulation. The most typical hypothesis tested with chi-square is whether two different samples of nominal or categorical data are different from expected values if there was no relationship between them in some characteristic or aspect of their behavior. In other words, we hope to generalize from our samples that the populations from which our samples are drawn are also different in the same behavior or characteristic. Like other tests of statistical significance, chi-square lets you know the degree of confidence you can have in accepting or rejecting a hypothesis.

As chi-square is a nonparametric test, it does not require the sample data to be more or less normally distributed, though it does rely on the assumption that the variable is normally distributed in the population from which the sample is drawn (Vogt, 1999). The chi-square test has the following requirements:

- The sample must be randomly drawn from the population.
- Data must be reported in raw frequencies.
- Measured variables must be independent.
- Values or categories on independent and dependent variables must be mutually exclusive and exhaustive.
- Observed frequencies cannot be too small.
- Fisher's exact text (or another appropriate goodness of fit test) may be used when cell frequencies are less than five.

To calculate chi-square, data is presented in a tabular form of rows and columns of categorical level data. The cells of the table are compared for differences in observed (O) versus expected (E) frequencies; the difference between the observed and expected frequency in each cell is calculated. The expected frequency calculation is a simple probability statement of probability, or the expected possible frequencies that may fall into each cell value of columns and rows. For example, 100 observations across 5 available cells in one row, assuming independence of observations, would result in an expectation of 20 frequencies for each of the 5 cells. The formula for expected frequency for a cell is (Column Total × Row Total) / Grand Total. The difference between observed and expected values is determined by subtracting expected scores from observed scores. Then the mathematical square of that difference is calculated, and then the product of this squared difference is divided by the difference itself. The chi-square test formula can be expressed as: $(O - E)^2/E$. However, in Excel the subtraction occurs automatically within the chi-square statistical function as the data ranges for observed and expected values are entered into the dialog box.

Chi-square is considered an approximate test of the probability of getting the frequencies you've actually observed if the null hypothesis is true. It is based on the expectation that within any category, sample frequencies are normally distributed about the expected population value. Frequencies cannot be negative, so the distribution cannot be normal when the expected population values are close to zero. Sample frequencies cannot be much below the expected frequency, though they can be much above it and create an asymmetric distribution. When expected frequencies are large enough, there is no problem with the assumption of a normal distribution, but the smaller the number of expected frequencies, the less valid are the results of the chi-square test. Expected frequencies are derived from observed frequencies. If there are cells in a bivariate table that show low, raw observed frequencies of five or below, then expected frequencies may also be too low for chi-square to be appropriately used. Because the mathematical formulas used in chi-square use division, no cell in a bivariate table should have an observed raw frequency of zero.

Therefore, the following minimum frequency thresholds should be obeyed:

- For a 1 × 2 or 2 × 2 table, expected frequencies in each cell should be at least five.
- For a 2 × 3 table, expected frequencies should be at least two.
- For a 2 × 4 or 3 × 3 or larger table, if all expected frequencies but one are at least five, and if the one small cell is at least one, chi-square is still a good approximation.

Chi-square interpretation also depends on degrees of freedom (*df*), the number of values free to vary when computing a statistic. Degrees generally tell us how much data was used to calculate a statistic, and this value is usually one less than the number of variables. In general, the greater the degrees of freedom (i.e., the more values or categories on the independent and dependent variables), the more lenient the minimum expected frequencies threshold.

Observed Frequencies

Observed frequencies are the actual data in the chi-square tabulation. These are compared to expected frequencies. The expected frequencies are those that would be expected if the independent variable had no effect. If there is a difference between observed and expected frequencies, then a relationship between the variables being tested is thought to be present.

Expected Frequencies

Expected frequencies are the frequencies that would be predicted in a chi-square tabulation if the marginal total of frequencies is known and the variables being tested are assumed to be independent. If the expected frequencies were significantly different from the observed or actual frequencies, then a relationship between the variables being tested would be assumed.

Chi-Square Value

The chi-square statistical test is used as a test of independence of two variables, and is also used as a goodness of fit test. The test may be converted to one of a number of similar measures of association. These include phi coefficient, Cramer's V, and contingency coefficient. Results of the chi-square value are reported as the squared difference between observed and expected (bivariate) frequencies, which is then divided by the value for the expected frequencies. Degrees of freedom (df) are also usually reported, as is the significance level (p) of the test result.

p-Value

The probability value that a statistical test result could have been produced by either chance or random error is known as the p-value of the test. We refer to a relationship between variables as statistically significant when the probability that it is explained by chance is at or below a point such as $p < .05$ (a 95% probability that the result is not due to chance) or $p < .10$ (a 90% probability that the result is not due to chance). We identify in advance of the statistical test how low that we are willing to risk refuting chance as a plausible rival hypothesis. The p-value is also known as the significance level, or the degree of likelihood that an observed, empirical relationship could be attributable to sampling error.

Chi-Square in Microsoft Excel

Suppose that you are performing a class assignment by surveying the color preference of automobiles purchased by a convenience sample of 30 respondents over a one-hour interval at a local public location. You are interested in comparing only three color preferences. Under these conditions, using three variables and a single choice of color preference, we might expect that approximately 10 people would select each of the three offered color choices if there were no difference in color preference. The colors for selecting a preference, in this instance, are red, white, and blue. You have hypothesized that red cars are preferred over other color choices, even though we would expect that there would be no difference in purchase based on color preference.

To perform a simple chi-square test to compare observed versus expected frequencies, you could perform the following sequence of steps to obtain a significance value for chi-square:

1. Begin by entering the observed results on one row and the expected results on a second row on the Excel spreadsheet. Then place the cursor at the cell and highlight the cell you wish to have the significance test for chi-square appear in and select the cell by clicking the mouse button. Next, move the cursor to the Function Wizard (*fx*) button and select the function dropdown menu as per Figure 8.1 (see the accompanying CD-ROM video animation: "Chi-Square Example One").

2. A dialog box will appear. Select the Statistical category from the category section of the box and CHITEST on the function section. After making those two selections, select OK at the bottom of the dialog box as in Figure 8.2

3. Then, enter the cell range for the observed data in the Actual range box. This may be done by either typing the cell locations, such as B2:D2, or by moving the cursor to the beginning of the set of scores you wish to use and selecting and dragging the cursor across them. The same procedure can be used for the expected results in the Expected range box. Once you have entered the range for both variables, all that remains is to select OK at the bottom of the dialog box, as in Figure 8.3.

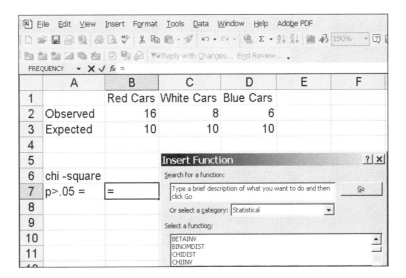

FIGURE 8.1 Setting up Observed and Expected Values and Selecting a Cell for a p-Value

FIGURE 8.2 Performing the Chi-Square Significance Test

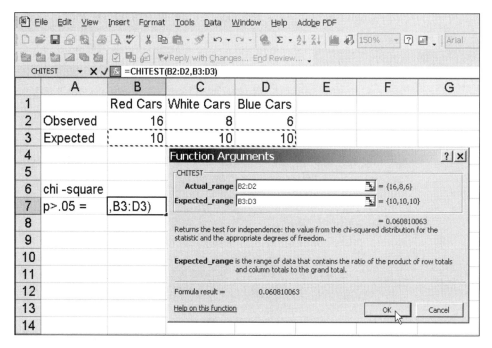

FIGURE 8.3 Inputting Function Arguments for Actual versus Expected Range of Values

4. The significance test for chi-square goodness of fit will then appear in the cell previously selected for the significance level as in Figure 8.4.

5. To find the actual chi-square value, again select the function button and open the dialog box for functions. This time, select the statistical function for CHIINV; by selecting and clicking on the OK button, the chi-square will be calculated as in Figure 8.5.

6. By selecting OK, the p-value appears, which is 0.060810063 as in Figure 8.6.

7. To find the chi-square value, use the CHIINV function as in Figure 8.7.

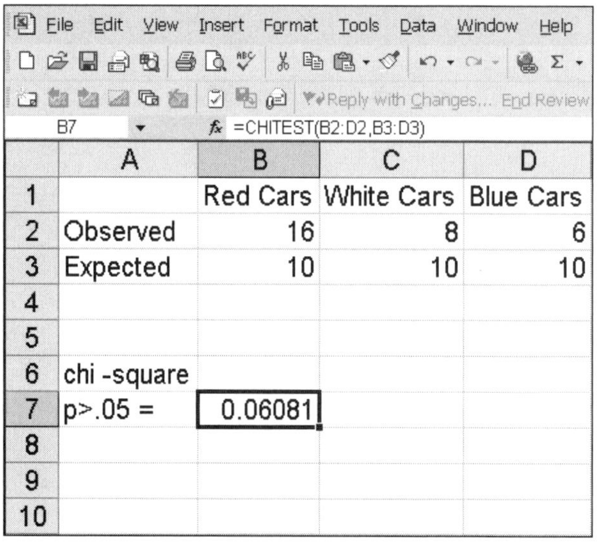

**FIGURE 8.4 The Significance or p-Value
for Chi-Square**

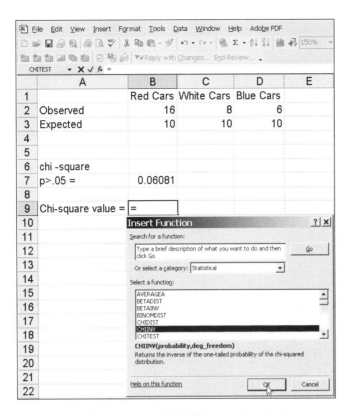

FIGURE 8.5   Selecting the CHIINV Test to Provide the
Chi-Square Value

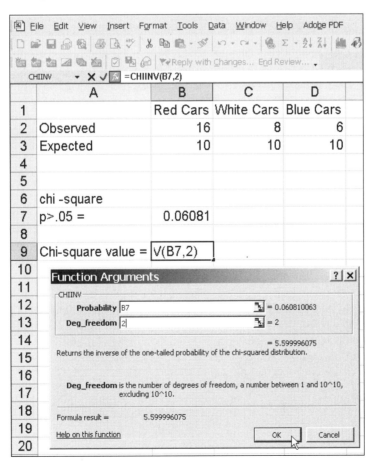

FIGURE 8.6   Obtaining a Chi-Square Value

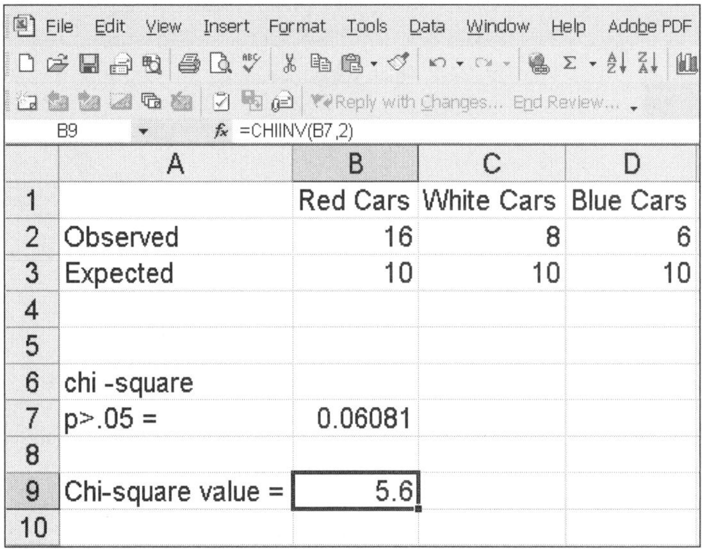

**FIGURE 8.7   The CHIINV Function Has Calculated the
Chi-Square Value**

8. When the CHIINV box appears, enter 0.060810063 for the probability value, then 2 for the degrees of freedom. Degrees of freedom = (number of columns – 1) × (number of rows – 1), or in this case, 2. The chi-square equals 5.5999996075.

As the chi-square value of 5.6 was not found to be significant due to the probability of 0.06 being higher than the p > .05 level needed, you would have to accept the null hypothesis of no difference, or that for the sample of respondents, there was no significant difference between expected and observed preference for car color.

However, a more complex chi-square test situation could occur if two or more variables were compared across a number of conditions—where there are two or three rows, or more, of data for each variable to be compared. This situation would call for the calculation of expected frequencies to correspond with each cell of data listing observed frequencies in each variable or condition.

For example, suppose that a clinical practitioner is comparing the demographic makeup of attendees of two loss support groups in two different service locations. The practitioner has observed that there are fewer attendees in both groups in the 20 to 40 years range, with more attendees noted in the 40 to 60 years range and the greatest number of attendees in the greater than 60 years age range. However, the practitioner would like to know if the response rates for the two groups are statistically equivalent or different. The observed attendance or enrollment rates are recorded on a spreadsheet for both loss groups. However, because we have three conditions for attendees based on age grouping, we need to calculate the expected frequency of attendance for each age range or row of data, and for each loss group. For example, these two loss support groups may be differentiated for intervention condition by labeling each as loss support support group 1.00 and loss support support group 2.00.

To determine the expected frequencies for each cell value of observed frequencies, we will need to apply the formula:

$$\frac{\text{sum of row values for age category} \times \text{sum of column values}}{\text{total of all observations}}$$

This formula will need to be replicated for each cell representing observed values, and the value derived from the formula in each case will need to be entered into a table on the spreadsheet with the same number of rows and columns that will represent expected frequencies.

Once the expected frequency values are known for all corresponding cells of observed values, the chi-square test for significance of difference between the two loss support group attendees can be run using Excel. The sequence is the same as in the previous example when running the function for CHITEST. However, in this instance, we will select the range of all observed values represented in multiple rows and columns of cells for variable one in the CHITEST function dialogue window and the range of all expected values represented in multiple rows and columns of cells for variable two in the CHITEST function dialog window. (This procedure has been illustrated in the CD-Rom video animation, "Chi-Square Example Two.")

t-Test

A t-test determines whether the difference between two group means is statistically significant. The t-test is also used as a test statistic in other statistical procedures, such as correlation and regression coefficients. There are several different types and formulas of t-test. These include t-tests for one sample and t-tests for comparing groups that are either independent or correlated in some way.

In order to understand t-test and other bivariate test output we need to review the types of errors to statistical conclusions and the hypothesis testing conventions for comparing differences in sample means. You may recall that a null hypothesis is established for statistical testing results to predict a condition of no change, no effect, or no significant difference in means for samples compared. There are two types of statistical conclusion errors possible for hypotheses, which are referred to as Type I and II errors. A Type I error rejects a null hypothesis that is really true (with tests of difference, this means that you say there was a difference between the groups when there really was not a difference). The probability of making a Type I error is the alpha level you choose. If you set your probability (alpha level) at $p < .05$, then there is a 5% chance that you will make a Type I error. You can reduce the chance of making a Type I error by setting a smaller alpha level ($p < .01$). The problem with this is that as you lower the chance of making a Type I error, you increase the chance of making a Type II error. A Type II error fails to reject a null hypothesis that is false (with tests of differences, this means that you say there was no difference between the groups when there really was one).

Hypotheses can be stated as either nondirectional or directional in nature. A nondirectional hypothesis is referred to as two-tailed, meaning that there will be a significant difference in means as plotted under a normal distribution curve or similar distribution, such as the t-distribution or F-distribution. Hypotheses are further formulated as pairs of predictions of statistical test outcomes that are mutually exclusive and exhaustive; either one or the other hypothesis will be considered true based on the statistical result. For two-tailed, or nondirectional hypotheses, the null hypothesis (H0) is usually stated as there is no statistically significant difference between the mean of one sample and the mean of another. The alternative hypothesis (HA) is usually stated as there is a statistically significant difference between the mean of one sample and the mean of another.

In the case of directional hypotheses, or one-tailed hypotheses, the null hypothesis identifies the direction of the predicted statistically significant finding. The null hypothesis (H0) is usually stated as the mean of sample 1 will not be either statistically higher or statistically lower than the sample mean of sample 2. The alternative hypothesis (HA) is usually stated as the mean of sample 1 will be either statistically higher or statistically lower than the sample mean of sample 2. Understanding these conventions is useful in interpreting the spreadsheet output for statistical tests of mean comparisons.

One-Sample t-Test

A one-sample t-test attempts to compare the sample mean to a standard score of a normally distributed population mean. That is, the one-sample t-test attempts to compare the sample to a known population by converting the sample mean to a common metric score for comparison to the population parameter. T-distributions differ based on the degrees of freedom, which shape to some extent the curve of a statistical probability distribution. When the degrees of freedom are infinite, the t-distribution is the same as a standard normal distribution. When the values of degrees of freedom are small, the tails of the distribution stretch out farther before approaching the abscissa or x-axis of a graphed distribution, producing an arclike shape that may not be completely symmetrical.

If we are interested in comparing the mean of our sample to the known mean of an attribute in the general population, then a one-sample t-test can be performed in Excel. For example, if we are looking at a survey item from a sample of 10 individuals who ranked an attribute from 0 to 100, and we know that the average ranking among respondents in the population is 60, then we can compare our sample to the population as in Figure 8.8 (see the accompanying CD-ROM video animation: "t-test Paired 2 Sample for Means").

Then the variable ranges, hypothesized mean difference, and alpha level are selected in the t-test dialog box as in Figure 8.9. This results in the statistical output, which includes

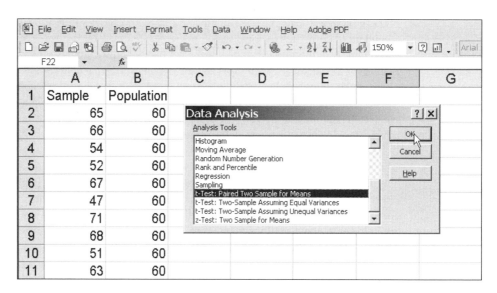

FIGURE 8.8   Set up a Comparison Column of the Population Mean and Use Paired t-Test

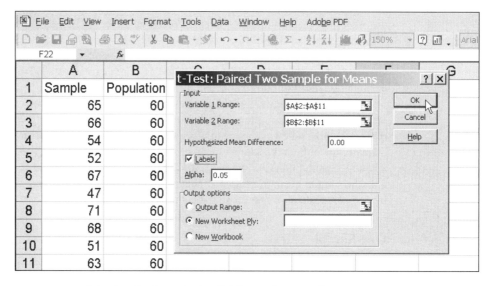

FIGURE 8.9   Selecting the Data, Alpha (0.05), and Mean Difference Test for Two Variables

	A	B	C
1	Sample (one sample t-test)	Population	
2	65	60	
3	66	60	
4	54	60	
5	52	60	
6	67	60	
7	47	60	
8	71	60	
9	68	60	
10	51	60	
11	63	60	
12			
13	t-Test: Paired Two Sample for Means		
14			
15		*65*	*60*
16	Mean	59.89	60.00
17	Variance	78.61	0.00
18	Observations	9.00	9.00
19	Pearson Correlation		
20	Hypothesized Mean Difference	0.00	
21	df	8.00	
22	t Stat	-0.04	
23	P(T<=t) one-tail	0.49	
24	t Critical one-tail	1.86	
25	P(T<=t) two-tail	0.97	
26	t Critical two-tail	2.31	

FIGURE 8.10 Output for the t-Test: One Sample Compared to a Population Mean

the mean, variance, and observation values, as well as correlation values where appropriate, hypothesized mean difference, degrees of freedom, the value of the t-statistic, and significance and critical values for both one-tail and two-tail hypotheses as seen in Figure 8.10.

The output provides information on the number of observations of different values of the sample compared to the known population mean. A Pearson's correlation indicating a measure of association between the two variables is not returned in this instance, as there is no variance in the population mean values. The hypothesized population mean is the value that we are testing against to determine a difference between the sample and the population mean. The degrees of freedom (*df*) is 8.00, as the number of scores in the sample of 10 minus 1 for each test (–2) results in 8. The t-statistic value is given as –0.04. The P, or p-value, for the t-test is not significant for both a one-tail and two-tail hypothesis of mean difference, with the critical regions under the normal curve given for each hypothesis (Dretzke & Heilman, 1998).

t-Test for Two Independent Samples

The independent samples t-test is used for evaluating the difference in the sample means of two groups that are independently drawn from a population. This t-test is used when cases are randomly selected and the selection does not affect the likelihood of any other case being drawn. The two sample groups do not have to be of equal or near equal size to compare differences in sample means. To use Excel's independent sample t-test tool, you must first arrange your data into two columns or rows representing data for the two groups being compared.

Suppose that you would like to compare the differences between two groups that are assumed to be not associated with one another. For example, you are tutoring two groups of students for a statistics examination. You have been using different methods to assist each group and would like to know which is more effective. Group 1 has been tutored in a classroom. Group 2 is tutored over the Internet using chatroom discussion and e-mail assignments. You have given the two groups of 10 students a practice examination worth 50 points. As the two classes are of the same size and study materials have been similar, we opt to assume that our two groups have equal variances as in Figures 8.11 through Figure 8.13 (see the accompanying CD-ROM video animation: "t-test Paired 2 Sample Equal Variances").

Then the variable ranges, hypothesized mean difference, and alpha level are selected in the test dialog box as in Figure 8.12.

This results in the statistical output to include the mean, variance, and observation values, as well as pooled variance, hypothesized mean difference, degrees of freedom, the value of the t-statistic, and significance and critical values for both one-tail and two-tail hypotheses as seen in Figure 8.13.

	A	B	C	D	E	F
1	Group 1-class	Group 2- web				
2	47	42				
3	40	45				
4	36	40				
5	48	38				
6	50	41				
7	43	50				
8	32	47				
9	48	34				
10	49	45				
11	38	46				
12						

Data Analysis

Analysis Tools

Histogram
Moving Average
Random Number Generation
Rank and Percentile
Regression
Sampling
t-Test: Paired Two Sample for Means
t-Test: Two-Sample Assuming Equal Variances
t-Test: Two-Sample Assuming Unequal Variances
z-Test: Two Sample for Means

OK   Cancel   Help

FIGURE 8.11   Selecting the t-Test: Two Samples Assuming Equal Variances

	A	B	C	D	E	F	G
1	Group 1-class	Group 2- web					
2	47	42					
3	40	45					
4	36	40					
5	48	38					
6	50	41					
7	43	50					
8	32	47					
9	48	34					
10	49	45					
11	38	46					

t-Test: Two-Sample Assuming Equal Varian...

Input

Variable 1 Range: $A$2:$A$11
Variable 2 Range: $B$2:$B$11

Hypothesized Mean Difference: 0.00
☑ Labels
Alpha: 0.05

Output options
○ Output Range:
● New Worksheet Ply:
○ New Workbook

OK   Cancel   Help

FIGURE 8.12   Selecting the Data, Alpha (.05), and Mean Difference Test for Two Variables

	A	B	C
1	Group 1-class	Group 2- web	
2	47	42	
3	40	45	
4	36	40	
5	48	38	
6	50	41	
7	43	50	
8	32	47	
9	48	34	
10	49	45	
11	38	46	
12			
13	t-Test: Two-Sample Assuming Equal Variances		
14			
15		*47.00*	*42.00*
16	Mean	42.67	42.89
17	Variance	42.25	25.11
18	Observations	9.00	9.00
19	Pooled Variance	33.68	
20	Hypothesized Mean Difference	0.00	
21	df	16.00	
22	t Stat	-0.08	
23	P(T<=t) one-tail	0.47	
24	t Critical one-tail	1.75	
25	P(T<=t) two-tail	0.94	
26	t Critical two-tail	2.12	

FIGURE 8.13   Two Samples Assuming Equal Variances

The output provides information on the number of observations of different values, the mean for each administration, and the variance for each. A pooled variance provides a measure of score dispersion. The hypothesized mean is the value that we are testing against to determine a difference in two independent group means. The degrees of freedom (df) is 16, as the number of scores in each sample minus 1 for each test (–2) results in 8 per sample.

The t-statistic value is given as –0.08. The P, or p-value, for the t-test is significant for both a one-tail and two-tail hypothesis of mean difference, with the critical regions under the normal curve given for each hypothesis. There is no statistically significant difference between the test means for the two tutored study groups.

Paired Samples t-Test (Dependent)

The paired samples t-test is used for evaluating the difference in the sample means of two groups that are thought to be correlated in some way. This t-test is often referred to as a dependent t-test, or matched groups t-test. The test is used for two related samples that are measured once, or one sample that is measured twice.

In the case of paired samples t-tests a relationship between the first sample and the second sample is assumed. For instance, if the group members take a pretest inventory of awareness of local driving while intoxicated laws that is scaled from 1 to 10, and then take the posttest of the same items and scale after an educational seminar of drinking while intoxicated laws, the paired sample t-test is useful to compare differences in means. If the same instrument is given at pretest and posttest, our results may look similar to the data in Figure 8.14. The data is first entered in to an Excel spreadsheet for the two measures. Then, the data analysis tool pack is selected from the Tool dropdown menu. The data analysis dialog box opens to permit the selection of t-tests including the option for the t-test: Paired Two Sample for Means, as per Figure 8.14.

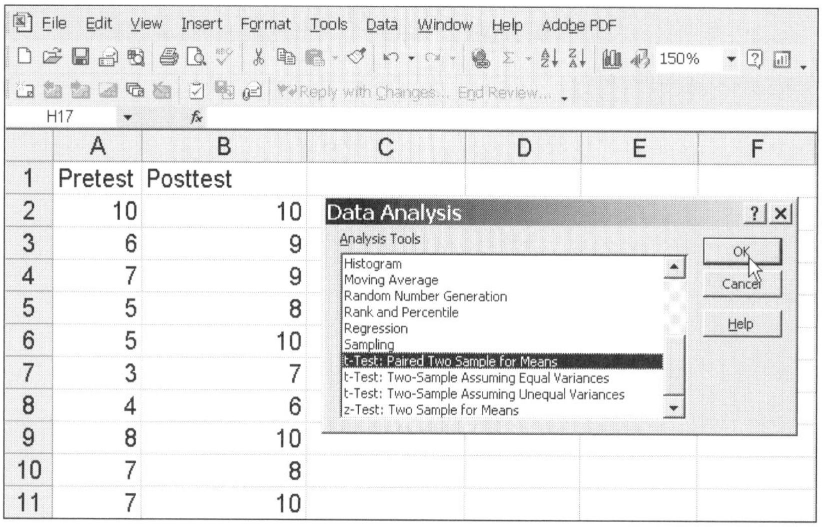

FIGURE 8.14   Selecting the t-Test: Paired Two Sample for Means

Then the variable ranges, hypothesized mean difference, and alpha level are selected in the test dialog box as in Figure 8.15. This results in the statistical output to include the mean, variance, and observation values, as well as correlation values where appropriate, hypothesized mean difference, degrees of freedom, the value of the t-statistic, and significance and critical values for both one-tail and two-tail hypotheses as seen in Figure 8.16.

The output provides information on the number of observations of different values, the mean for each administration, and the variance for each. A Pearson's correlation indicates a measure of association between the two variables. The hypothesized mean is the value that we are testing against to determine a difference in group means. The degrees of freedom (*df*) is 8, as the number of scores in the sample of 10 minus 1 for each test, or (–2), results in 8. The t-statistic value is given as –6.93. The P, or p-value, for the t-test is significant for both a one-tail and two-tail hypothesis of mean difference, with the critical regions under the normal curve given for each hypothesis.

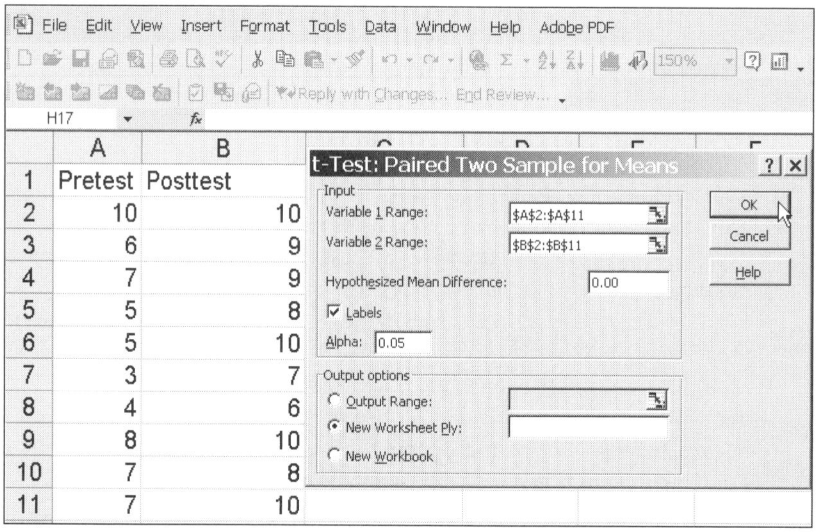

FIGURE 8.15   Selecting the Data, Alpha (.05), and Mean Difference Test for Two Variables

	A	B	C
1	Pretest	Posttest	
2		10	10
3		6	9
4		7	9
5		5	8
6		5	10
7		3	7
8		4	6
9		8	10
10		7	8
11		7	10
12			
13	t-Test: Paired Two Sample for Means		
14			
15		10.00	10.00
16	Mean	5.78	8.56
17	Variance	2.69	2.03
18	Observations	9.00	9.00
19	Pearson Correlation	0.70	
20	Hypothesized Mean Difference	0.00	
21	df	8.00	
22	t Stat	-6.93	
23	P(T<=t) one-tail	0.00	
24	t Critical one-tail	1.86	
25	P(T<=t) two-tail	0.00	
26	t Critical two-tail	2.31	

FIGURE 8.16   Output for the t-Test: Paired Two Sample for Means

ANOVA

Analysis of variance is used to test hypotheses about differences between two or more means. The t-test based on the standard error of the difference between two means can only be used to test differences between two means. When there are more than two means, it is possible to compare each mean with the other means using t-tests. However, conducting multiple t-tests can lead to severe inflation of the Type I error rate. Analysis of variance (ANOVA) can be used to test differences among several means for significance without increasing the Type I error rate.

Frequently when we attempt to compare means between groups we have more than two samples. When we have several samples and we would like to know if there is evidence that our samples may have been taken from different populations, we use ANOVA to help answer the question. The samples are assumed to be randomly drawn. The populations from which the samples are drawn are assumed to have the same standard deviation. Each sample size must be at least 5, with the total of all samples at least 15 if the populations from which the samples are drawn are known to have normal distributions of the variables being compared. If the populations are roughly equivalent, sample sizes must be at least 40. Standard deviations are considered to be close enough for the samples if the ratio of the largest sample standard deviation to the smallest is less than two.

One-Way Between-Groups

The ratio of the mean squared of the between-group variance to the mean squared within-group variance is used by applying an F test and critical values of F to carry out a one-way between-groups ANOVA. We are interested in conducting an evaluation of depressed mood among three sample groups of 10 respondents who have completed a Beck Depression Inventory to assess level of depressed mood. Our null hypothesis is that there will be no significant difference in the variance of group scores and that all groups are experiencing equivalent levels of depressed mood. An alternative hypothesis, then, would be that the variance of group scores would be significant and suggest that some groups have respondents that are more depressed than others. Though we expect some variations within each group, we need to know if the variations between the three groups are greater than the within-group variance.

We begin our analysis by entering the screening inventory scores for group members of each group onto a spreadsheet. Then from the Tools menu we select the dialog box for data analysis tools and further select the ANOVA: Single Factor test, selecting OK to bring up the test dialog box as in Figure 8.17 (see the accompanying CD-ROM video animation: "ANOVA Single Factor").

Then the variable input range, grouping method, alpha level, and output range for the spreadsheet are selected as in Figure 8.18.

This results in the statistical output to include a summary of count, sum, average, and variance of groups, as well as an ANOVA table of source of variation (between groups, or within groups), sum of squares, degrees of freedom, mean squared, F value, significance or p-value, and F critical value as seen in Figure 8.19.

The Summary table shows the counts, means, and variances for the data. The ANOVA table shows the results of the completely randomized analysis of variance. In this set of data, because the calculated F = 15.18 is greater than the tabled F, Fcrit = 3.35, we reject the null hypothesis that the three groups scored equally. An additional post hoc test can be performed to determine which pair or pairs of means caused rejection of the null hypothesis.

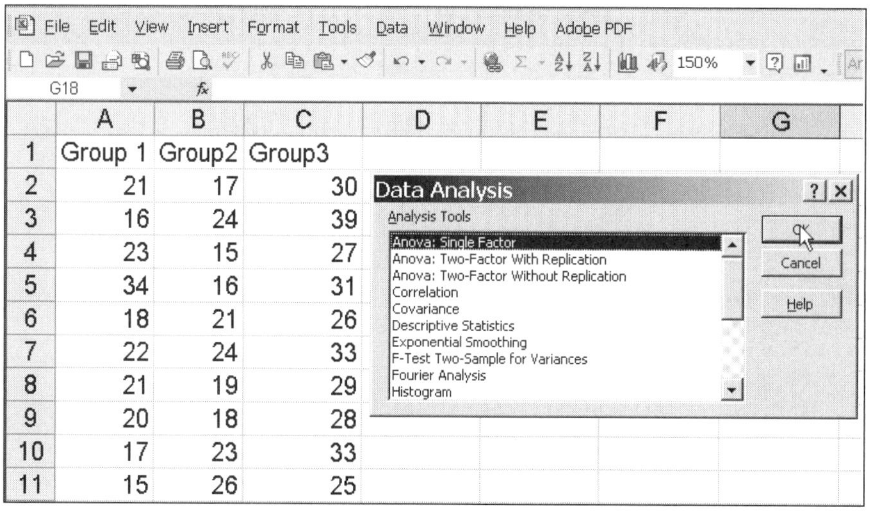

FIGURE 8.17   Selecting the ANOVA: Single Factor Test

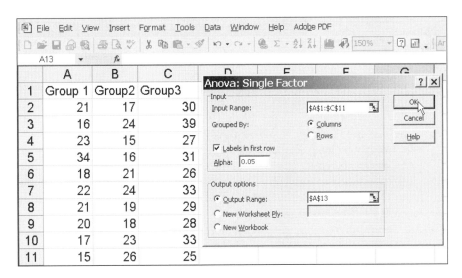

FIGURE 8.18 Selecting the Data Range, Alpha Level, and Output Range for ANOVA

	A	B	C	D	E	F	G
1	Group 1		Group2	Group3			
2		21	17	30			
3		16	24	39			
4		23	15	27			
5		34	16	31			
6		18	21	26			
7		22	24	33			
8		21	19	29			
9		20	18	28			
10		17	23	33			
11		15	26	25			
12							
13	Anova: Single Factor						
14							

FIGURE 8.19 The Summary Table and the ANOVA Results Table

Two-Way Between-Groups

Groups may have more than one sample of data for analysis. For example, if we have three groups of respondents that are involved in more than one trial of an intervention, then we would need to evaluate the variance of three groups under two conditions. This would require that we evaluate whether the variance between the groups and between the two trials or test conditions were greater than the variance within the samples of three groups and the samples under the two trial conditions. This level of analysis is referred to as a two-way between-groups analysis of variance.

For instance, if we had an interest in evaluating three groups of adolescents from different cultural backgrounds who were having aggressive outbursts and had participated in two trials of aggression replacement therapy for six weeks each, we might use this analysis. Let us further suppose that each day of their trial interventions, our participants had completed an anger assessment instrument for the day that determined their self-report of anger on a 1 to 10 scale. Later, these scores were averaged to give a measure of average anger over the first and second trials of the intervention. We might set up our spreadsheet data as in Figure 8.20 (see the accompanying CD-ROM video animation: "ANOVA Two Factor with Replication").

Then the variable input range, grouping method, alpha level, and output range for the spreadsheet are selected as in Figure 8.21.

This results in the statistical output to include a summary of count, sum, average, and variance of groups as well as for all trials or conditions, and an ANOVA table of source of variation (sample, columns, interaction, and within), sum of squares, degrees of freedom, mean squared, F value, significance, or p-value, and F critical value as seen in Figure 8.22.

The Summary table shows the counts, means, and variances for the data. The ANOVA table shows the source of the variation with total variation partitioned into sample variation (trials 1 and 2), column variation (group), interaction variation (trial × group interaction), and within-groups variation. In this set of data, because the calculated F value, F = 3.84, is greater than the tabled F, or Fcrit = 3.40, column variance or between-group differences for the three groups is found to be significant. This is not true for either of the trial conditions or the interaction of trials and groups. Therefore we reject the null hypothesis that the three groups scored equally, but accept the null hypothesis that there was no significant difference between first and second trials for the groups and no significant difference between groups based on the interaction of group membership and trials.

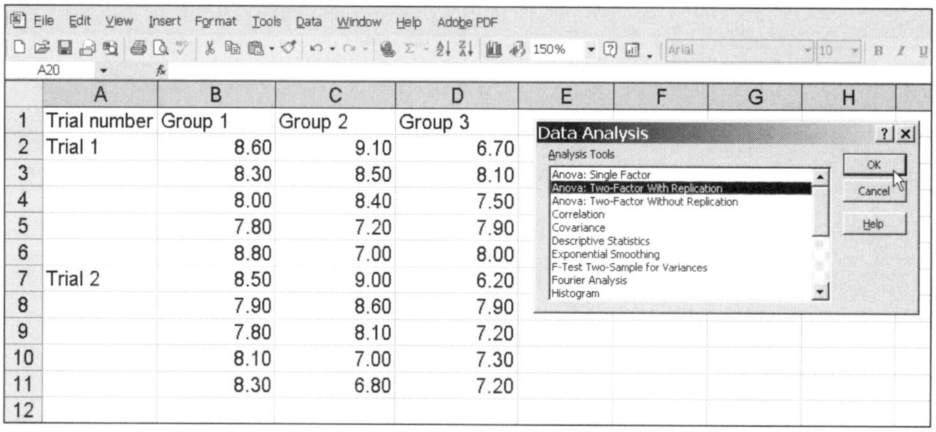

FIGURE 8.20   Selecting the ANOVA: Two Factor with Replication Test

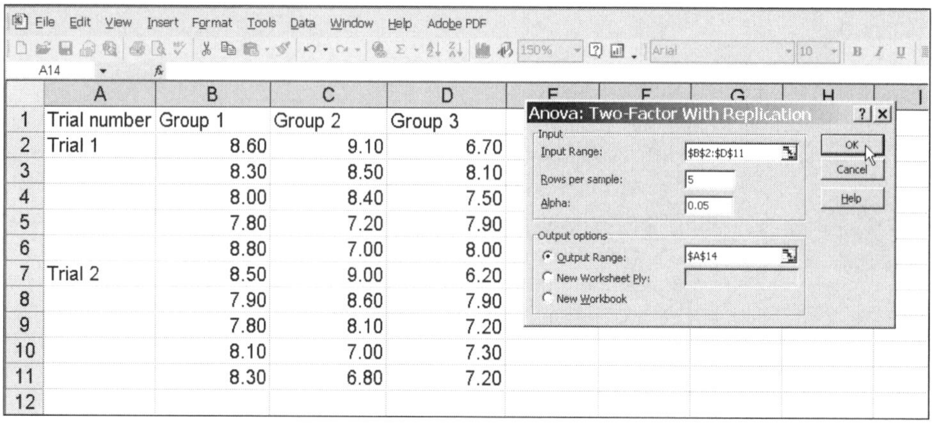

FIGURE 8.21   Selecting the Data Range, Alpha Level, and Output Range for ANOVA

	A	B	C	D	E	F	G
1	Trial number	Group 1	Group 2	Group 3			
2	Trial 1	8.60	9.10	6.70			
3		8.30	8.50	8.10			
4		8.00	8.40	7.50			
5		7.80	7.20	7.90			
6		8.80	7.00	8.00			
7	Trial 2	8.50	9.00	6.20			
8		7.90	8.60	7.90			
9		7.80	8.10	7.20			
10		8.10	7.00	7.30			
11		8.30	6.80	7.20			
12							
13	Anova: Two-Factor With Replication						
14							
15	SUMMARY	Group 1	Group 2	Group 3	Total		
16	Trial 1						
17	Count	5.00	5.00	5.00	15.00		
18	Sum	41.50	40.20	38.20	119.90		
19	Average	8.30	8.04	7.64	7.99		
20	Variance	0.17	0.81	0.33	0.45		
21							
22	Trial 2						
23	Count	5.00	5.00	5.00	15.00		
24	Sum	40.60	39.50	35.80	115.90		
25	Average	8.12	7.90	7.16	7.73		
26	Variance	0.08	0.94	0.37	0.58		
27							
28	Total						
29	Count	10.00	10.00	10.00			
30	Sum	82.10	79.70	74.00			
31	Average	8.21	7.97	7.40			
32	Variance	0.12	0.78	0.38			
33							
34							
35	ANOVA						
36	Source of Variation	SS	df	MS	F	P-value	F crit
37	Sample	0.53	1.00	0.53	1.18	0.29	4.26
38	Columns	3.46	2.00	1.73	3.84	0.04	3.40
39	Interaction	0.17	2.00	0.09	0.19	0.83	3.40
40	Within	10.82	24.00	0.45			
41							
42	Total	14.99	29.00				

FIGURE 8.22   The Summary Table and the ANOVA Results Table

Post Hoc Tests of Means

There are a number of post hoc tests that can be run to determine which means are responsible for a significant ANOVA. Though they are not part of the data analysis or functions pack of Excel, they can be templated if used frequently; a spreadsheet can be designed to perform the calculations. Examples of these are available in some research texts. Here is a brief listing of the most commonly used:

   1. *Levene's Test:* Levene's test (Levene, 1960) is used to test if k samples have equal variances. Equal variance across samples is called homogeneity of variances. Some statistical tests, for example, the analysis of variance, assume that variances are equal across groups or samples. The Levene test can be used to verify that assumption. Levene's test is more robust in determining equal variances in data where the normality assumption has not been met.

   2. *Bartlett's Test:* Bartlett's test (Snedecor & Cochran, 1989) is used to test if k samples have equal variances. Equal variances across samples is called homogeneity of variances. Some statistical tests, for example, the analysis of variance, assume that variances are equal across groups or samples. The Bartlett test can be used to verify that assumption. Bartlett's test is a common method of determining equal variances where there is certainty that the normality assumption has been met.

3. *Duncan's Test:* A Duncan's test or Duncan's Multiple Range test is performed after an ANOVA has been conducted to determine which group means are significantly different from one another (Black, 1999).

4. *Tukey's b Test:* When completing an ANOVA to determine the difference between group means, the ANOVA will indicate that some group means may be significantly different from other group means. A post hoc comparison test such as Tukey's HSD or Tukey's b test is performed to determine which group means are significantly different (Black, 1999).

Summary

Bivariate statistics are concerned with the comparison of differences between two or more variables. In the case of chi-square, the comparison is between frequencies observed and expected. For various t-tests, the comparison of difference between sample means or between a sample and a population can be used to determine the efficacy of an intervention, or to compare samples through a common metric of the t-distribution. ANOVA, then, permits comparison of multiple groups for differences in means and evaluates the interaction as well as main effects of two or more variables using the F distribution. All of these functions may be rapidly produced with minimal effort from data formatted into spreadsheets.

REVIEW QUESTIONS

1. Give two or more examples of how bivariate statistics differ from multivariate statistics.

2. Write out at least two examples of a null and an alternate hypothesis for a bivariate statistical example.

3. What does chi-square test for and with what levels of data is it used?

4. What does a t-test demonstrate and with what levels of data is it used?

5. State an example of a null hypothesis for a two-tailed, nondirectional hypothesis.

6. Explain how to calculate a t-test using Microsoft Excel spreadsheets.

7. What is ANOVA used to test for?

CHAPTER

9

Pivot Tables

In several of the preceding chapters we have described how to use pivot tables in several data analytic procedures. This chapter focuses on the use of data tables in data summarization and reporting. Data tables are a means to collapse and summarize data in order to understand the relationship between two or more variables displayed in the table. These tables are sometimes referred to as contingency tables or cross-tabulation tables. For reasons described below, Excel refers to them as pivot tables. In this chapter, we describe the flexibility, utility, and application of pivot tables in the production of data tables. Pivot tables are one of Excel's most powerful features. They are robust data analysis tools that are both user-friendly and interactive. They are extremely useful for summarizing large amounts of data, evaluating outcomes, and examining trends. Information summarized in pivot tables can be quickly converted into charts and graphs displaying the summarized information in the table.

Basic Steps for Creating a Pivot Table

Let us review the basic steps in creating a pivot table. This discussion will provide the foundation for the remainder of this chapter, in which we explore the multiple data analysis capabilities of pivot tables. We will use data from a study that evaluated intensive case management in a community mental health center as a means to reduce rates of rehospitalization of individuals classified as being severely and persistently mentally ill (Patterson & Lee, 1998). The four variables of interest are treatment group, rehospitalization, diagnostic category, and social and occupational functioning (GAFS-M). We begin the process of creating a pivot table by selecting the variables of interest as displayed in Figure 9.1. From the menu bar we select Data, PivotTable, and PivotChart Report. Figure 9.2 illustrates the next three steps of the process. In Step 1, select the source of the data for analysis. In this case, the data are in a spreadsheet. As is evident in the Step 1 window, it is possible to incorporate data from other sources, including databases, other pivot tables, and pivot charts. In Step 2, provide the range of the data. The range of data consists of the columns and rows

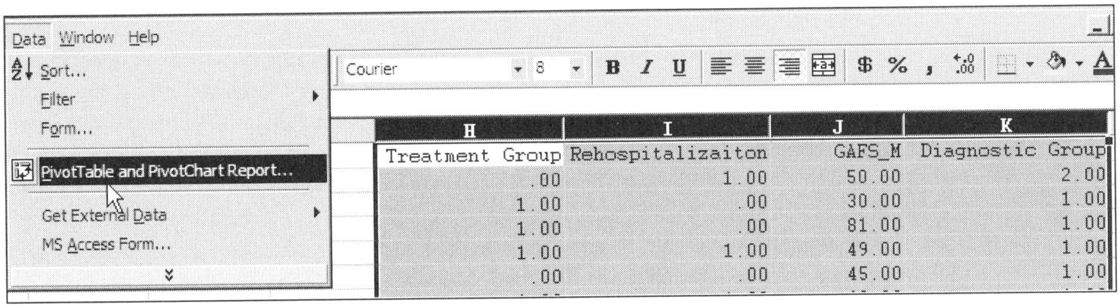

FIGURE 9.1   The First Steps in Creating a Pivot Table, Selecting the Data, and Opening
PivotTable and PivotChart Report

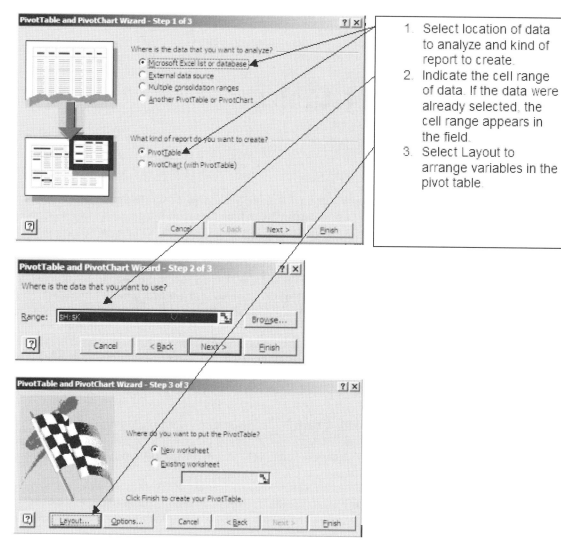

FIGURE 9.2   The Preliminary Steps to Creating a Pivot Table

containing the variables intended for summarization in the cross-tabulation table. If the range of the data is selected before opening the PivotTable Wizard as we have done here, this data range will appear in the Range box. The variables specified in the data range need to be in adjoining columns. In other words, a variable in column A and column D cannot be selected for the data range. If the variables are not adjoining, insert a column beside one of the variables, then cut or copy the second variable and paste it into the newly inserted column. If the data range is not selected prior to starting the PivotTable Wizard, then in Step 2, click the icon to the right of the Range box. The Step 2 window will disappear and the spreadsheet containing the data becomes visible. Select the columns and rows (range) containing data intended for summarization in the table. Click the Range icon and the Step 2 window reappears. Click Next and the Step 3 window appears. Click the Layout button to open the PivotTable and PivotChart Wizard–Layout window, displayed in Figure 9.3. Also see the accompanying CD-ROM video animation: "Basic PivotTable Steps."

The name "pivot table" is derived from the fact that variables in the table may be readily repositioned, or pivoted, to modify the composition of the table. In the PivotTable and PivotChart Wizard–Layout window, drag the field buttons (variable names) on the right side of the window into the diagram, indicating whether the variable is to be in a row or a column in the table. Drag the field button (variable name) to be summarized into the Data sec-

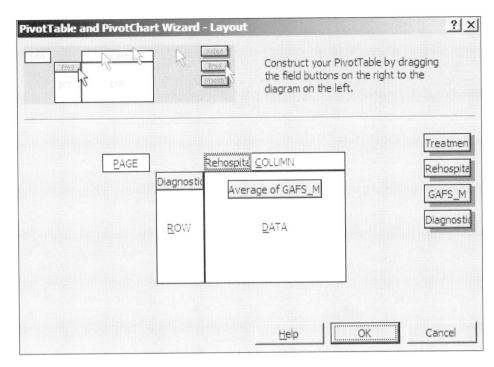

FIGURE 9.3   PivotTable Layout Window

tion of the diagram. In Figure 9.3 we have placed the variable Rehospitalization in the Column area. Rehospitalization is a dichotomous nominal level variable with 0 and 1 indicating the absence or presence of an episode of rehospitalization. Placing this dichotomous variable in the Column area means that the pivot table will have two columns. In the Row area we place the variable Diagnostic Group, though in Figure 9.3 it appears as Diagnostic. This nominal level variable has four categories and as such it will create four rows in the table. Together these two variables will create two columns and four rows: a two-by-four, eight-cell table.

The type of data or level of measurement for each of the variables typically determines the layout of a pivot table. Categorical or nominal data can only be summarized in the data field as a count. Continuous data such as interval and ratio data, which represent some quantity, are generally not appropriate for column or row fields, but instead they are more appropriately summarized in the data field.

As is evident in Figure 9.3, we placed the variable GAFS_M in the Data area of the pivot table. GAFS_M is an interval level variable used as a measure of social and occupational functioning. It has a possible range of 1–100. Note that the field button is labeled Average of GAFS_M. After dragging the GAFS_M variable into the Data area, we clicked on the GAFS_M field button and the PivotTable Field dialog window appeared (see Figure 9.4). The PivotTable Field dialog window offers numerous ways of summarizing data. Here we have selected Average because we want to compare the average level of social and occupational functioning across the four diagnostic groups for individuals who were rehospitalized versus those who were not. The research question we are asking is whether there is a difference in social and occupational functioning across diagnostic groups for individuals who experienced rehospitalization compared to those who did not.

Once we have arranged the layout of our intended pivot table, we click OK and return to the dialog window for Step 3 (see Figure 9.2). In the Step 3 dialog window we specify the intended location of the resultant pivot table in either a new worksheet or in an existing worksheet. If the existing worksheet option is selected, click the Range icon and then indicate where in the existing worksheet to place the table. Table 9.1 displays the resulting pivot

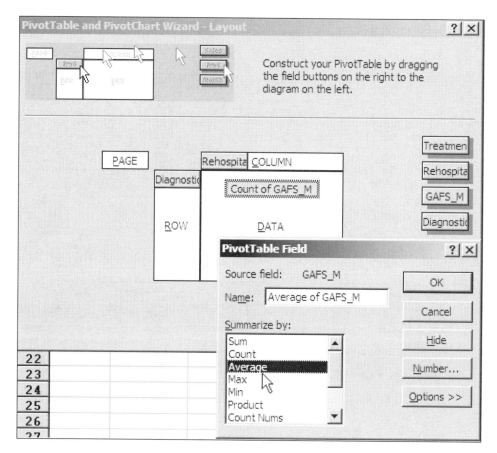

FIGURE 9.4   PivotTable Field Dialog Window

TABLE 9.1   Pivot Table of Social and Occupational Functioning by Episode of Rehospitalization and Diagnostic Group

Average of GAFS_M		Rehospitalization	
Diagnostic Group	*0*	*1*	*Grand Total*
1	52.79	48.66	49.42
2	63.80	50.50	52.05
3	61.00	53.00	54.00
4	61.00	54.92	55.79
Grand Total	55.28	49.73	50.64

table. Note the differences in average level of social and occupational functioning between individuals who were rehospitalized versus those who were not across the four diagnostic groups.

Expanding the Pivot Table Analysis

We can use the versatility of pivot tables to expand our understanding of the data displayed in Table 9.1. Although we can see the average level of social and occupational functioning of the groups of individuals represented in each of the eight cells, we do not know the frequency count for each of the cells. In other words, we do not know if the mean value dis-

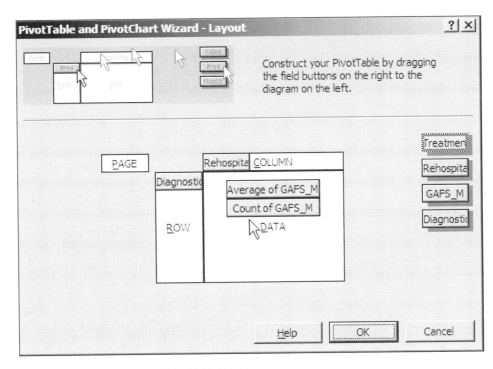

FIGURE 9.5   Added to the Pivot Table Design

**TABLE 9.2   Pivot Table of Social and Occupational Functioning by Episode
of Rehospitalization and Diagnostic Group with Cell Frequency Count Added**

Diagnostic Group	Data	Rehospitalization		
		0	*1*	*Grand Total*
1	Average of GAFS_M	52.79	48.66	49.42
	Count of GAFS_M	24.00	107.00	131.00
2	Average of GAFS_M	63.80	50.50	52.05
	Count of GAFS_M	5.00	38.00	43.00
3	Average of GAFS_M	61.00	53.00	54.00
	Count of GAFS_M	1.00	7.00	8.00
4	Average of GAFS_M	61.00	54.92	55.79
	Count of GAFS_M	2.00	12.00	14.00
Total Average of GAFS_M		55.28	49.73	50.64
Total Count of GAFS_M		32.00	164.00	196.00

played in any one of the eight cells represents a single individual or numerous individuals. To answer this question we add an additional data summarization element (count) to the pivot table design. See Figure 9.5 and the resulting modified pivot table in Table 9.2. Table 9.2 gives us a much richer understanding of the data than Table 9.1. It is clear from the data in Table 9.2 that rehospitalization was much more common than the alternative. It is also evident that individuals in diagnostic categories 3 and 4 were relatively uncommon in this sample.

Adding an Additional Variable

In Table 9.2 we see the three variables we placed in our pivot table: GAFS_M, Rehospital-ization, and Diagnostic Group. When we selected the data for the pivot table we included a fourth variable, Treatment Group. To push our exploration of these data, we can add Treatment Group to the pivot table. Doing this will provide us with a more discrete and refined understanding of the relationship between the four variables. More specifically, we would like to examine the relationship between treatment group, rehospitalization, and social and occupational functioning. We will leave Diagnostic Group in the table to provide an even more magnified view of the data.

We add the new variable by right-clicking on our existing pivot table and selecting Wizard. This causes PivotTable and PivotChart Wizard–Step 3 to appear. We select Layout. In the Layout window, we drag Treatment into the Row area and place it above the variable Diagnostic. Doing this tells the PivotTable Wizard to divide the table rows by the two categories of the Treatment Group variable, 1 and 0, where 1 equals intensive case management and 0 equals standard case management. See Figure 9.6. Also see the accompanying CD-ROM video animation: "Pivot Table Added Variable."

Adding this new variable to the pivot table layout produces Table 9.3. Note that instead of the original eight cells of information displayed in Table 9.1, Table 9.3 has 16, making it possible to see the average level of social and occupational functioning by rehospitalization, treatment group, and diagnostic group.

The Grand Total column allows us to make comparisons across rows. The Total and Grand Total rows are of particular utility for comparing mean level of social and occupational functioning between treatment groups and across rehospitalization. There are four mean values in bold in Table 9.3 that warrant further consideration, 45, 46.71, 55.61, and 53.14. In the row labeled 0 Total we see the value 45, which represents one or more individuals in Diagnostic Group 1, receiving standard case management and experiencing no episode of rehospitalization. Clinically, it might be expected that a low level of social and occupational functioning paired with an absence of intensive case management would result in at least one episode of rehospitalization. We will return to a deeper evaluation of this value later.

The highest mean value is 55.61, representing individuals in the intensive case management group who did not experience an episode of rehospitalization. This finding may

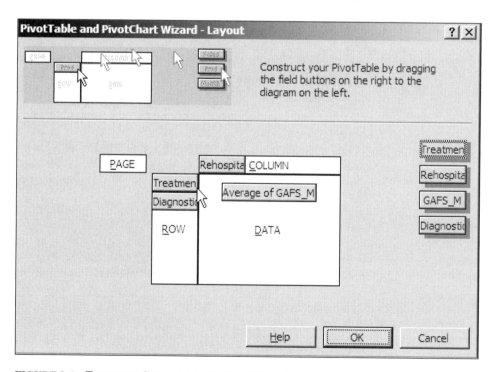

FIGURE 9.6   Treatment Group Added to Pivot Table Layout

TABLE 9.3   Pivot Table of Social and Occupational Functioning by Episode of Rehospitalization and Diagnostic Group with Treatment Group Added

Average of GAFS_M		Rehospitalization		
Treatment Group	*Diagnostic Group*	*0*	*1*	*Grand Total*
0	1	45.00	46.04	46.02
	2		46.81	46.81
	3		52.00	52.00
	4		47.50	47.50
0 Total		**45.00**	**46.71**	46.69
1	1	53.13	50.96	51.59
	2	63.80	58.50	60.06
	3	61.00	55.50	57.33
	4	61.00	62.33	62.00
1 Total		**55.61**	**53.14**	53.85
Grand Total		55.28	49.73	50.64

support the hypothesis that individuals receiving intensive case management would have a higher level of social and occupational functioning and avoid rehospitalization. Of course from a statistical perspective what we do not know is if the differences between the four values of 45, 46.71, 55.61, and 53.14 are greater than would be expected by chance. In other words, we do not know if these differences are statistically significant. To test that we might use a one-way ANOVA, as described in Chapter 8. For our present purposes we will continue to explore the utility of the pivot table in understanding these data.

Drilling Down

Our understanding of these data would be improved if we knew the frequency counts of the 16 cells of Table 9.3. Knowing the frequency counts of the cells would tell us, for instance, if the value 45 representing the social and occupational functioning of the non-rehospitalized in standard case management was a single individual or a group of individuals in a single diagnostic category. In other words, does this value represent a very unique group in our dataset or simply a single individual?

There are two ways we can answer this question and other questions about specific values in a pivot table. First, we could return to the Layout window and add Count of GAFS_M to our pivot table layout. Doing this would produce a pivot table with a cell beneath each mean value containing a frequency count. The resultant table would display a great deal of specific information about the dataset; however, it might be overly complex and difficult to read.

The alternative means of determining the frequency count for any cell in a pivot table is to employ a feature of the Excel pivot table called drilldown. Clicking on any value in a pivot table will automatically open a new worksheet containing all the data represented by the value clicked on in the pivot table. This is a rather remarkable feature. It allows us to see all the data for all the cases represented by a particular value in the pivot table. For instance, Figure 9.7 illustrates how if we click on the value 55.61, which represents individuals in the intensive case management group who did not experience an episode of rehospitalization, a new worksheet with all the data for these individuals appears. We can then use a Count formula to determine the number of individuals in this group. Using the drilldown feature on the value 45 discussed previously, we find this is a single individual and does not represent a larger subgroup in the sample represented in the dataset. Also see the accompanying CD-ROM video animation: "Pivot Table Drilling Down."

The Excel pivot table drilldown feature allows one to look beneath the values on the surface of the pivot table to see and conduct subgroup analysis of the underlying data. As is

Average of GAFS_M		Rehospitalizaiton		
Treatment Group	Diagnostic Group	0	1	Grand Total
0	1	45.00	46.04	46.02
	2		46.81	46.81
	3		52.00	52.00
	4		47.50	47.50
0 Total		45.00	46.71	46.69
1	1	53.13	50.96	51.59
	2	63.80	58.50	60.06
	3	61.00	55.50	57.33
	4	61.00	62.33	62.00
1 Total		55.61	53.14	53.85
Grand Total		55.28	49.73	50.64

Clicking a value in a pivot table drills down to the underlying data and displays that data in a new worksheet.

Treatment Group	Rehospitalizaiton	GAFS_M	Diagnostic Group
1	0	60	1
1	0	30	1
1	0	81	1
1	0	60	1
1	0	63	1
1	0	60	1
1	0	32	1
1	0	41	1
1	0	35	1
1	0	67	1
1	0	69	1
1	0	60	1
1	0	51	1
1	0	48	1
1	0	50	1
1	0	35	1
1	0	85	1
1	0	80	1
1	0	27	1
1	0	40	1
1	0	50	1
1	0	68	1
1	0	30	1
1	0	75	2
1	0	61	2
1	0	63	2
1	0	55	2
1	0	65	2
1	0	61	3
1	0	61	4
1	0	61	4

FIGURE 9.7   Pivot Table DrillDown Results

demonstrated above, one can quickly determine the size and composition of cases represented by a single value in the pivot table. Outlier values can readily be found. The size of subgroups can be determined. The drilldown data can be sorted and described. This is a powerful tool with which to explore parts of a dataset and to address questions that emerge in that exploration.

Data Display Options

The Layout window offers several options for the format of data within the pivot table. In Figure 9.8 we opened the PivotTable Field dialog box by clicking on the variable Rehospitalization in the Data area. In the PivotTable Field, we select Options and the Show data as

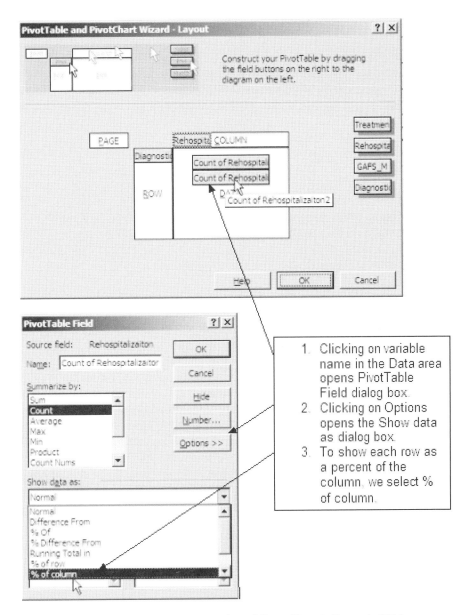

FIGURE 9.8 Changing the Representation of Count Data to Percent of Column

dialog box opens to reveal an array of data display options. We select "% of column" to show each row as a percentage of the column. Table 9.4 contains the resulting pivot table. In this table, for each diagnostic group there is a frequency count for each category of rehospitalization, 0 = no and 1 = yes. The cell below each frequency count displays its relative percentage for the column. In order to read and comprehend the table, the rule to remember is that one makes comparisons in the opposite direction of the percentage calculation (Neuman & Kreuger, 2003). Therefore, for each diagnostic group, we can examine the relative frequency of rehospitalization verses nonrehospitalization. Inspecting Table 9.4, we can conclude that individuals who did not experience rehospitalization were most commonly diagnosed in diagnostic category 1, whereas individuals experiencing rehospitalization were more frequently diagnosed in diagnostic categories 1 and 2. It is also evident from the frequency count labeled as Total Count of Rehospitalization that hospitalization was a common occurrence in this sample. Also see the accompanying CD-ROM video animation: "Pivot Table Percentages."

TABLE 9.4   Frequency Count and Percentage Displayed

| Diagnostic Group | Data | Rehospitalization | | |
		0	1	Grand Total
1	Count of Rehospitalization	24.00	107.00	131.00
	Count of Rehospitalization2	0.75	0.65	0.67
2	Count of Rehospitalization	5.00	38.00	43.00
	Count of Rehospitalization2	0.16	0.23	0.22
3	Count of Rehospitalization	1.00	7.00	8.00
	Count of Rehospitalization2	0.03	0.04	0.04
4	Count of Rehospitalization	2.00	12.00	14.00
	Count of Rehospitalization2	0.06	0.07	0.07
Total Count of Rehospitalization		32.00	164.00	196.00
Total Count of Rehospitalization2		1	1	1

The versatility of the PivotTable Field dialog box makes it possible to compose pivot tables displaying basic descriptive statistics for interval and ratio level data segmented by row and column categories. In Figure 9.9 we selected count, average (mean), and standard deviation for GAFS_M in order to create a pivot table allowing us to compare treatment groups across levels of medication compliance. Table 9.5 displays the results of these pivot table composition decisions. This provides us with a high level of detail by which to explore the relationship between these three variables. Two cells contain an error message, #DIV/0!, which indicates that the standard deviation formula could not be calculated. The frequency count for each of these two cells was 1, thereby precluding the possibility of computing a standard deviation. The level of detailed information in Table 9.5 is further amplified by the fact that we can use the drilldown function of the pivot table to see the data underneath the descriptive statistics. The three cells containing data on individuals in treatment group 1 and with a rating of 9 on medication compliance have a relatively high mean

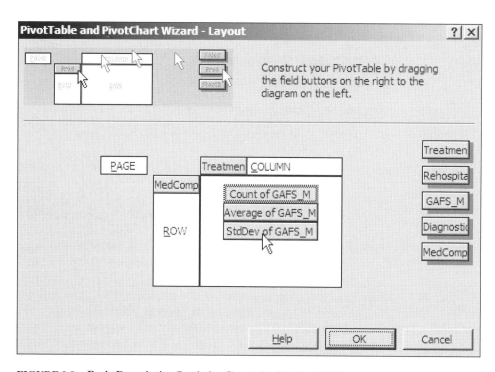

FIGURE 9.9   Basic Descriptive Statistics Created with PivotTable

TABLE 9.5 **Pivot Table with Basic Descriptive Statistics**

| MedCompliance | Data | Treatment Group | | |
		0	1	Grand Total
0	Count of GAFS_M	3.00	5.00	8.00
	Average of GAFS_M	46.00	47.40	46.88
	StdDev of GAFS_M	25.06	8.56	14.89
1	Count of GAFS_M	5.00	1.00	6.00
	Average of GAFS_M	26.00	41.00	28.50
	StdDev of GAFS_M	11.94	#DIV/0!	12.31
2	Count of GAFS_M	6.00	3.00	9.00
	Average of GAFS_M	32.83	45.00	36.89
	StdDev of GAFS_M	9.81	10.00	11.05
3	Count of GAFS_M	12.00	1.00	13.00
	Average of GAFS_M	37.50	51.00	38.54
	StdDev of GAFS_M	10.98	#DIV/0!	11.16
4	Count of GAFS_M	7.00	6.00	13.00
	Average of GAFS_M	47.14	49.67	48.31
	StdDev of GAFS_M	7.56	14.49	10.85
5	Count of GAFS_M	6.00	13.00	19.00
	Average of GAFS_M	47.50	47.54	47.53
	StdDev of GAFS_M	18.10	11.26	13.25
6	Count of GAFS_M	9.00	12.00	21.00
	Average of GAFS_M	51.33	52.83	52.19
	StdDev of GAFS_M	14.35	10.77	12.11
7	Count of GAFS_M	12.00	12.00	24.00
	Average of GAFS_M	49.17	62.67	55.92
	StdDev of GAFS_M	9.00	8.35	10.94
8	Count of GAFS_M	12.00	27.00	39.00
	Average of GAFS_M	53.50	53.33	53.38
	StdDev of GAFS_M	12.48	16.32	15.08
9	Count of GAFS_M	16.00	28.00	44.00
	Average of GAFS_M	55.31	57.50	56.70
	StdDev of GAFS_M	12.45	20.64	17.96
Total Count of GAFS_M		88.00	108.00	196.00
Total Average of GAFS_M		46.69	53.85	50.64
Total StdDev of GAFS_M		14.59	15.62	15.54

GAFS_M score (57.50); with a large standard deviation of 20.64, this suggests considerable variability in the GAFS_M scores for that group. This anomaly might merit further exploration and the use of the drilldown function to see the underlying data. This is but one example of how detailed pivot tables with embedded descriptive statistics empower data analysts to make comparisons and examine the relationships between variables that are generally not possible in standard statistical software packages.

Creating Charts and Graphs

The creation of charts and graphs from pivot tables is a remarkably easy task. They can be generated either through the PivotTable and PivotChart Wizard or from an existing pivot table. We will describe both ways.

To create a chart or graph through the PivotTable and PivotChart Wizard, select Pivot-Chart (with PivotTable) in the Step 1 window, in response to the question, "What kind of report do you want to create?" See Figure 9.2 (p. 110) for a review of Step 1. In the Layout window, we construct our pivot table from which the chart or graph will be generated. The basic steps are displayed in Figure 9.10. The PivotTable and PivotChart Wizard automatically generates a pivot table accompanying the pivot chart. In Step 3, we specify a location for this pivot table. Also see the accompanying CD-ROM video animation: "Pivot Chart Creation."

In Figure 9.11 we see the pivot chart produced from the steps illustrated in Figure 9.10. Two things that require comment are immediately apparent in Figure 9.11. First, the PivotTable toolbar is present in the lower right-hand corner. The toolbar provides a number of shortcuts for modifying pivot tables and pivot charts, including the Chart Wizard for modifying the chart format and type. The second noteworthy observation about the chart in Figure 9.11 is that it is not an optimal representation of the relationship between level of medication compliance displayed on the x-axis, the two treatment groups represented by the stacked bars, and GAFS_M. One significant problem with the representation is that the stacked columns make it difficult to compare the two groups across levels of medication compliance. Consequently, we need to modify the pivot chart. To do this we click on the Chart Wizard, displayed in Figure 9.11, and select the Clustered Column option. In Step 2 of the Chart Wizard, we title the chart and then click Finish. Figure 9.12 displays Step 1 of the Chart Wizard and the final chart. Note how in this version it is much easier to compare the social and occupational functioning of the two treatment groups across levels of medication compliance. With the exception of the cases in the lowest level of medication compliance, there is a notable positive relationship between social and occupational functioning and medication compliance for both treatment groups. One final point: the data displayed in Figure 9.12 is the same data presented in Table 9.5, excluding frequency count and stan-

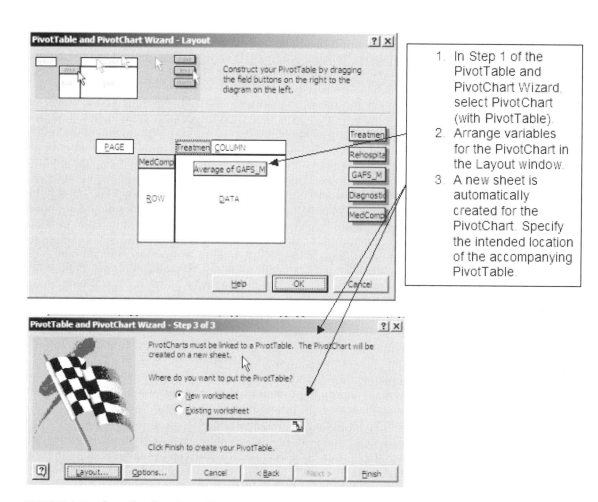

FIGURE 9.10   Steps for Creating a Pivot Chart

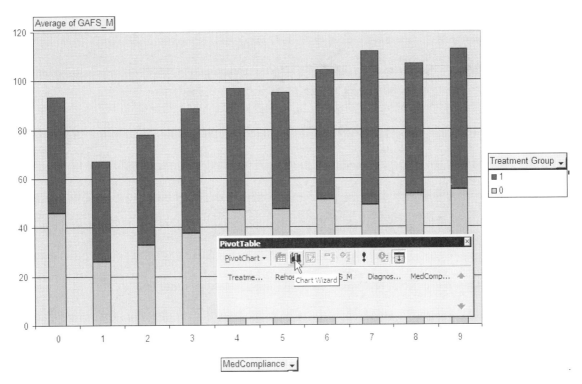

FIGURE 9.11   PivotTable ToolBar Visible on Pivot Chart Needing Revision

dard deviation. The pivot chart makes the relationship between the variables much more evident.

To create a pivot chart from an existing pivot table, right click on the pivot table and from the menu window that appears select PivotChart. A pivot chart is immediately created in a new worksheet. Changes to the pivot chart are made in one of three ways. The first option is to right click on the chart and in the menu window that appears, select Chart Type. The Chart Type dialog window offers a wide range of charts and graphs. The choices include column, bar, area, and pie charts, among others. The second option is to select Chart from the menu bar. When a worksheet contains a chart, the Chart dropdown menu appears in the Excel menu bar. This Chart dropdown menu contains options for chart type and chart options. The Chart Options menu item is a particularly useful resource for modifying the appearance of the chart, including the addition of titles and legends. The third option for changing a pivot chart is to click on the Chart Wizard icon in the menu bar. This is a small, colorful chart that appears in the standard menu bar. Clicking on the Chart Wizard icon opens the Chart Wizard, which is a set of four steps for changing the chart type, data, format, and location of a pivot chart. Each of the three methods of modifying pivot charts described here makes it possible to quickly modify and enhance a chart generated from a pivot table.

Summary

In this chapter we discuss the use of data tables, specifically pivot tables, in the summarization, reporting, and graphing of data. We demonstrate the use of pivot tables to collapse large quantities of data and to explore the relationships between variables. We present the basic steps for creating a pivot table and demonstrate several methods of expanding the analysis of data through a variety of pivot table options including adding additional variables, drilling down in the data, and expanding the information displayed in data tables. Methods for creating pivot charts and graphs are detailed in this chapter as well.

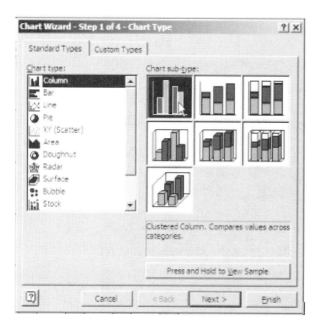

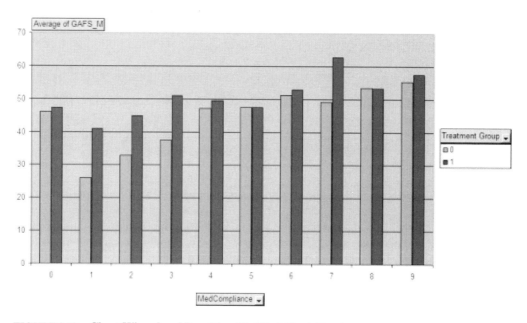

FIGURE 9.12   Chart Wizard and Resulting Modified Pivot Chart

REVIEW QUESTIONS

1. What are two functions of data tables?

2. What are the basic steps for creating a pivot table?

3. How do you add an additional variable to an existing pivot table?

4. What is "drilling down" and how is it accomplished in a pivot table?

5. How would you change data reported as frequencies in a column to percentages?

6. How do you create charts and graphs from a pivot table?

10 Single System Designs

Perhaps the most widely taught method of evaluating practice in social work and the social services is the single system design approach. Single subject designs as a method for evaluating practice have been reported in the literature since the late 1960s (Thyer, 1992). These designs have also been advocated for the evaluation of practice in leading social work textbooks (Bloom, Fischer, & Orme, 2003; Tripodi, 1994) and seminal research articles (Jayaratne, 1977; Kazi, 1997; Mattaini, 1996). They are sometimes referred to as single case designs or single subject designs. In this chapter we will use the term *single system design,* as we will describe how to use spreadsheets in this practice evaluation procedure with both individuals and groups. We will limit our discussion to spreadsheet procedures for collecting and graphically representing data generated through a variety of single system design procedures. Readers wishing to know more about the intricacies of practice evaluation, measurement conceptualization and application, and evaluation designs are referred to Bloom, Fischer, and Orme's (2003) *Evaluating Practice: Guidelines for the Accountable Professional,* perhaps the definitive text in the field.

Single system designs are a series of research designs for evaluating practice, not simply a single statistical procedure or a data analysis method (Bloom, Fischer, & Orme, 2003; Rubin & Babbie, 2001). In their most fundamental form, all single system designs require repeated measurement over time of an identified problem, experience of interest, behavioral change objective, or target behavior. Clearly, there are many possible terms for the range of phenomena that can be measured in a single system design. For the sake of simplicity, we will use the term *measurable change objective.* Measurable change objectives may be self-observations or self-ratings. Examples might include self-ratings of level of anxiety, depression, or some other emotional state. Measurable change objectives may also be some positive target behaviors or change goals such as minutes per day spent exercising, number of daily positive comments to one's spouse, or days per week without drinking. From the perspective of research design, a measurable change objective is the dependent variable. A measurable change objective is not always an observable behavior. As we will see, single system designs can involve the measurement of change over time for more than one measurable change objective.

A valid measurable change objective requires the measurement of change in one of three indicators: (1) frequency, (2) magnitude, or (3) duration. Frequency refers to how often the behavior, experience, or phenomenon occurs. In a single system design, we might measure the frequency of a wide range of experiences, thoughts, feelings, or behaviors such as self-defeating thoughts, use of stress management skills, or truancy. Magnitude refers to the size of the change. For instance, we might measure amount of weight loss per week, the level of anxiety experienced, or the miles walked per week. Duration refers to how long some behavior, experience, or phenomenon lasts. Examples of duration measured in valid change objectives might include daily length of time spent doing relaxation practices, hours worked per week, or number of days without a serious conflict between a parent and teenager. Measurable change objectives used in a single system design should specify change in one of these three indicators.

Time is the second variable of interest in single system designs. It is represented as the time interval at which the measurable change objective is recorded. Some target behaviors or change objectives are recorded on an hourly or daily basis, though target behaviors or change objectives more commonly are recorded on a weekly basis.

Spreadsheets offer four key advantages for conducting practice evaluation using single system designs. First, data are readily compiled in spreadsheets. A client's or group's daily, weekly, or monthly scores on the outcome measure can be entered and stored in a spreadsheet. Second, a critical feature of single system designs is the visual display of data points over time in order to discern change in the identified outcome measure. The graphing tools of spreadsheets make single system design graphs uncomplicated to produce and easy to update. Moreover, it is increasingly important in many social service practice environments to provide treatment progress updates for managed care purposes. Graphs, produced in spreadsheets, of single system designs evaluating client outcomes have a far more professional appearance than ones produced by hand on graph paper. Third, spreadsheet graphs are readily integrated into word processing documents for the purpose of professional or agency and managed care reporting (Carr & Burkholder, 1998; Patterson, 2000). Fourth, spreadsheets can aid the analysis of change through both visual and statistical procedures (J. G. Orme, personal communication, June 16, 2004).

Basic Elements of Single System Designs

The application of spreadsheets in practice evaluation using single system designs requires the understanding two basic procedures: (1) how to record in the spreadsheet data from the measurable change objective and (2) how to create an appropriate chart of the data.

Data Recording

The structure of the data recording of the measurable change objective in the spreadsheet is partially dependent on the specific type of single system design employed. The two fundamental principles for recording single system design data for individuals in a spreadsheet are (1) rows in the spreadsheet represent the time interval and (2) columns represent the phase of the design (Carr & Burkholder, 1998). These two single system design data recording principles are a departure from the data collection procedures presented in Chapter 2, where cases were recorded in the rows and variables in columns. For single system designs we record data from our specified time interval (hourly, daily, weekly, etc.) in a new row for each time period. So, if our measurable change objective is collected on a weekly basis, we record the data for each week in a new row. The particular column the time interval data is recorded in depends on the phase of the single system design.

As we will see in much greater detail, single system designs employ phases to indicate parts of the overall period of time in which data on the measurable change objective are recorded (Bloom, Fischer, & Orme, 2003). For instance, the A-B design is one of the most basic single system designs. It has two phases. The A phase is referred to as the baseline phase, which is the time period in which observations of the measurable change objective are made without any type of intervention occurring. It is often thought of as the assessment phase. Bloom, Fischer, and Orme (2003) suggest that the length of the baseline period should be determined by the usefulness of the assessment, the stability of the baseline data, and time. They advise collection of a minimum of three observations when possible.

The intervention or interventions begin in the B phase. Data for each phase are recorded in different columns of the single system design spreadsheet. Table 10.1 provides an example of data recorded in two columns for the two phases of an A-B design. Note that though the time interval is not specified in Table 10.1, each row represents a unique time period and that no row contains more than one entry. In Table 10.2, we have specified the time interval and actually recorded the week number. Generally, it is not necessary to do this, as Excel's Chart Wizard will display an appropriate numerical sequence. It is necessary to label the time interval on the x-axis of the single system design chart. This is described below.

TABLE 10.1   A-B Design Data Entry

Baseline	Intervention
9	
10	
9	
	7
	8
	5
	5
	4
	4
	5
	3
	2

TABLE 10.2   A-B Design Data Entry with Time Interval Included

Week	Baseline	Intervention
1	9	
2	10	
3	9	
4		7
5		8
6		5
7		5
8		4
9		4
10		5
11		3
13		2

Visual Display of Data

There are basic single system design rules established for the visual display of data in a chart. First, single system design data are almost always depicted in graphic form as a chart. Second, the time interval is displayed on the x-axis of the chart. Third, measurable change objective is displayed on the y-axis. Fourth, if there is more than one phase, a horizontal line is used to separate and distinguish the phases. Fifth, data points should stand out from the lines that connect them. Finally, lines should connect data points only within a phase; lines connecting data points do not cross phases. Each of these rules for the visual display of data can be accommodated with the Chart Wizard tool of Excel.

The creation of an A-B design single system chart from data in a spreadsheet is easily accomplished using the Chart Wizard. The basic steps are:

1. Label column A as Baseline and column B as Intervention.
2. Record baseline data in column A. When possible, a minimum of three observations is advisable.
3. Record intervention data in column B. Remember, data in columns A and B should not overlap. (If there are missed observations for one or more time periods, leave those cells empty.)
4. Select the range of data in columns A and B.
5. Select the Chart Wizard icon from the menu bar or from Insert, Chart in the menu bar dropdown menus.
6. The window entitled Chart Wizard–Step 1 of 4–Chart Type appears. Select Line Chart and then the line chart "with markers displayed at each data value." Then click Next. See Figure 10.1.
7. In Chart Wizard–Step 2 of 4–Chart Source Data there are two tabs at the top, Data Range and Series. The Data Range tab displays an image of how the data appears in the chart, the range of data the chart depicts, and the fact that the data for the chart is drawn from columns. The Series tab displays the chart and has fields indicating where the data in the chart are drawn from.
8. In Chart Wizard–Step 3 of 4–Chart Options add titles to the chart and to the axes. See Figure 10.2. Under the Legend tab, a legend labeling the lines in the chart can be added or removed.
9. In Chart Wizard–Step 4 of 4–Chart Location select either the option to place the chart in a new worksheet or in an existing worksheet. One option is to place it in the original worksheet adjacent to the data it represents.

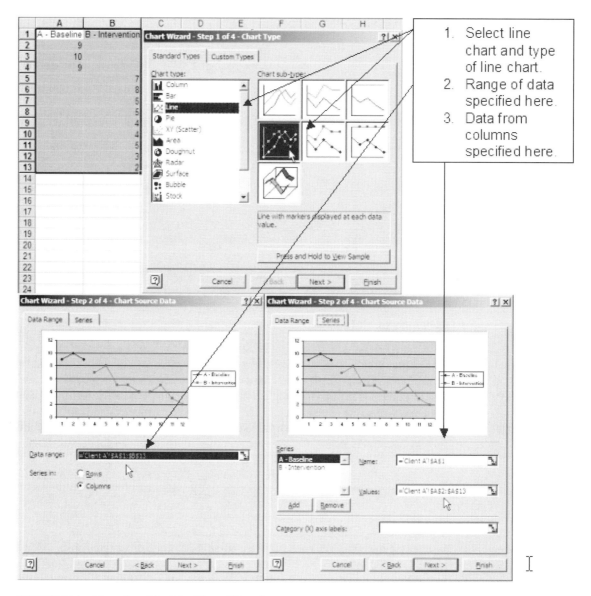

FIGURE 10.1   Steps 1 and 2 of the Chart Wizard

10. Once the chart is placed in a new or existing worksheet, select the Line tool from the Drawing Tools toolbar and create a vertical line separating the phases. Note the Drawing Tools toolbar and the Line tool in Figure 10.3.

11. The phases can be labeled as in Figure 10.3 with the Text Box tool, which is also available in the Drawing Tools toolbar. Also see the accompanying CD-ROM video animation: "SSD-AB Design Graphing."

Traditionally, single system design charts are formatted in black and white. We have elected to use a gray background in the plot area of all the single system design charts appearing in this chapter. This was done for three reasons. First, the default setting on Excel creates a gray plot area. Changing the plot area color from the default to white requires the extra step of clicking on the plot area and selecting Area, None. Second, retaining the gray plot area offers greater contrast of lines against background, especially when multiple baselines are plotted. Third, the convention of formatting single system design charts in black and white simply may be a residual tradition of the time before color computer monitors and inexpensive color and grayscale printing that is no longer useful or necessary.

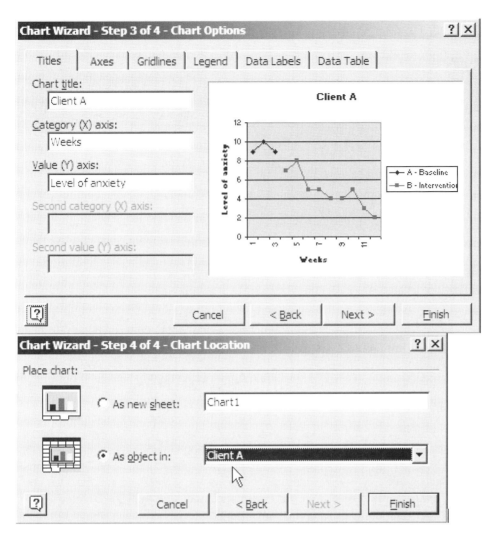

FIGURE 10.2   Chart Wizard Steps 3 and 4

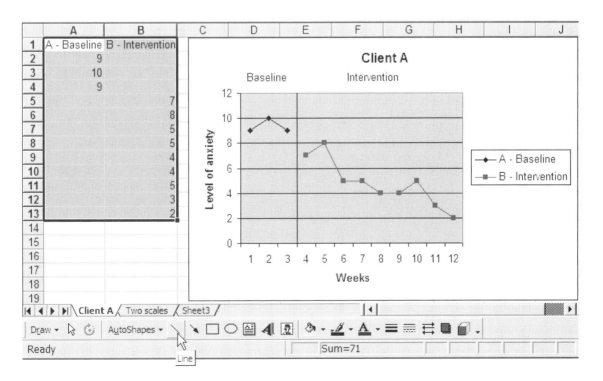

FIGURE 10.3   A-B Design with Phase Labeled and Separated by a Line

127

Advanced Designs

There are numerous single system designs beyond the A-B design. They include the A-B-A-B design, which is also called the experimental replication design, the A-B-A design or experimental removal of intervention design, and the B-A-B design or experimental repeat of invention design (Bloom, Fischer, & Orme, 2003). The data for each of these designs can be collected and represented in a chart following the basic procedures described previously. Here we will demonstrate applying these procedures to the A-B-A-B design.

The data for the A-B-A-B design is displayed in Table 10.3. Note that the data for each phase of the design are in their respective columns and that no row contains more than one value. Again, this is because observations for different phases are never taken in the same time period. Figure 10.4 contains the chart resulting from the data in Table 10.3. The line drawing tool was used to create lines between the phases. In this chart the phases are not labeled but instead are identified in the chart legend. See also the accompanying CD-ROM video animation: "SSD-A-B-A-B Design."

Dynamic Chart Production

Charts for single system designs do not have to be produced after all the data are collected. One of the values of single system designs is that they can be used to provide ongoing feedback to clients and for managed care and supervision reporting purposes. In this section we will demonstrate how to configure a spreadsheet for ongoing data entry and dynamic chart production. Let us suppose that we are undertaking a 16-week period of treatment with an individual who wishes to reduce his consumption of alcoholic beverages. During the baseline assessment phase we have asked this individual to record and report the number of drinks he consumes per week. Figure 10.5 displays the spreadsheet and resulting chart where these data are recorded. Note that we have selected columns A and B, rows 1–17. In creating the adjacent chart using the Chart Wizard we have included this range of data in the

TABLE 10.3   Spreadsheet Data for A-B-A-B Design

A1-Baseline	B1-Intervention	A2-Baseline	B2-Intervention
3			
2			
2			
3			
3			
	7		
	6		
	8		
	9		
	8		
		4	
		3	
		4	
		2	
		3	
			8
			7
			9
			8
			9

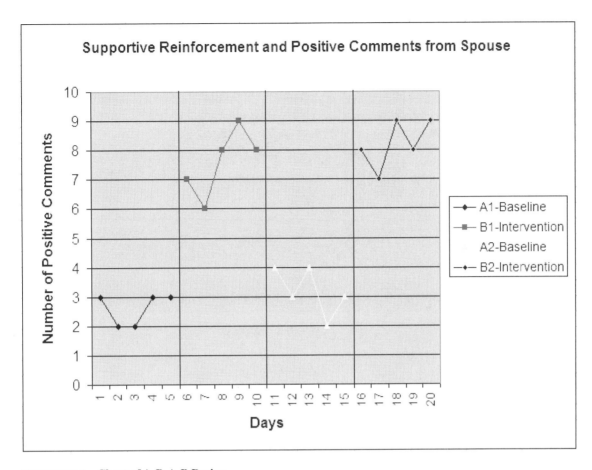

FIGURE 10.4   Chart of A-B-A-B Design

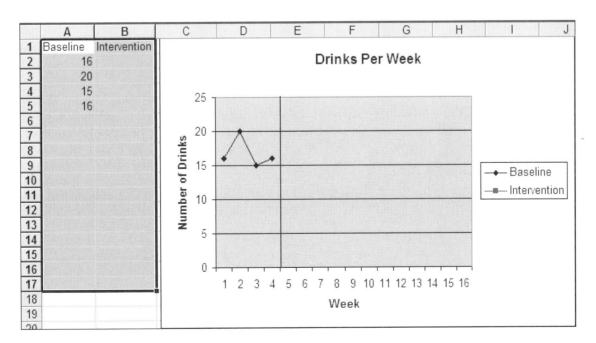

FIGURE 10.5   Dynamic A-B Design Chart Production

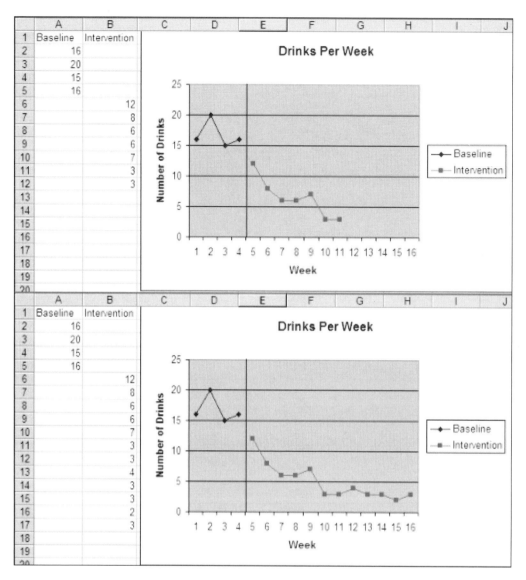

FIGURE 10.6   Dynamic A-B Design Charts at Weeks 12 and 16

chart specifications. Consequently, as we begin the intervention phase and enter new data into rows 6–17 of column B, the chart for that data is automatically updated as drinks per week are recorded. No further formatting of the chart is required. See Figure 10.6 for displays of this dynamic A-B design chart at weeks 12 and 16. The chief advantage of creating this type of dynamic chart is that weekly printouts of the chart can be provided to clients, graphically demonstrating progress, or sometimes the lack thereof, on the selected measurable change objective. Also see the accompanying CD-ROM video animation: "SSD-A-B Dynamic."

Analyzing Change

At times, one of the challenges to the use of single system designs in social work and social service practice evaluation is in interpreting the data. In charts such as those in Figure 10.6, the trend or directionality of the data is clear (Bloom, Fischer, & Orme, 2003). Unfortunately, distinct trends in single system design data are not always evident. Data instability can be an additional challenge to interpretation when using single system designs. Unstable data in the baseline makes it difficult, or impossible, to predict what would happen to the target behavior or problem without an intervention. Significant variability in the measurable change objective across observations in the baseline makes it much more difficult to evaluate the effect of an intervention on the target behavior or problem. Unstable data in the intervention phase complicates the determination of whether change is actually occurring. We now turn our attention to three methods of detecting trends and handling data instability: celeration lines, regression lines, and moving averages. We also will address a perennial conundrum of single system design data analysis, autocorrelation.

Celeration Line

A celeration line is a means to evaluate the directional trend in data either within the baseline or intervention phase or alternatively between phases (Bloom, Fischer, & Orme, 2003). Celeration lines are created within a phase by drawing a line between the midpoints of the two halves of the phase. This is accomplished by:

1. Dividing the phase in half,
2. Calculating the mean score for the two halves,
3. Plotting the mean score for the first half of the phase at the first quarter,
4. Plotting the mean score for the second half at the third quarter, and
5. Drawing a line that crosses the entire phase, intersecting the means for the first and second halves of the phase.

These steps are readily accomplished within a spreadsheet by adding a column beside each phase in which means for the two halves of the phase are calculated in the cells at the first and third quarter of the phase. In Table 10.4 we divided each phase in half and calculated

TABLE 10.4   Single System Design Spreadsheet for Generating Within Phase Celeration Lines

Baseline	Celeration 1	Intervention	Celeration 2
16			
20			
15	17.2		
16			
19			
21			
15			
17	18		
18			
19			
		15	
		12	
		8	
		6	8.5
		7	
		3	
		3	
		4	
		3	
		3	3
		2	
		3	

the means using the AVERAGE function, that is, =AVERAGE(A27:A31), for the two halves of both phases. We then created the chart in Figure 10.7 using the Chart Wizard steps described previously, including drawing a line between the two phases. The Chart Wizard did not plot a line between the two points in each phase. The celeration lines were drawn with the line drawing tool. We drew a line across the entire phase that intersected the data points at the first and third quarters of the phase. This procedure takes a little time and attention to adjusting the celeration line to ensure that it spans the phase and intersects both points. See also the accompanying CD-ROM video animation: "SSD-Celeration Lines."

The changes in direction of trends between the two phases are readily apparent in Figure 10.7. Unfortunately this is not always the case. Celeration lines are particularly useful in detecting trends when there is significant data instability. Figure 10.8 displays a spreadsheet with unstable data in each phase and a single system design chart created from the unstable data. The celeration lines in the two phases make it possible to see the change in trends between the two phases.

Regression Line

A readily employed alternative to the celeration line is the regression line (Bloom, Fischer, & Orme, 2003). The creation of a regression line in Excel requires neither alterations in the structure of the data display in the spreadsheet nor any additional calculations. Once a chart is produced with the Chart Wizard, click on the chart and then from the menu bar select Chart, Add Trendline. The Add Trendline dialog window appears in Figure 10.9. In the Add Trendline dialog window, select Linear, and then in the Based on Series window select the phase "Data for the regression line." Repeat this step for each data phase. In Figure 10.10

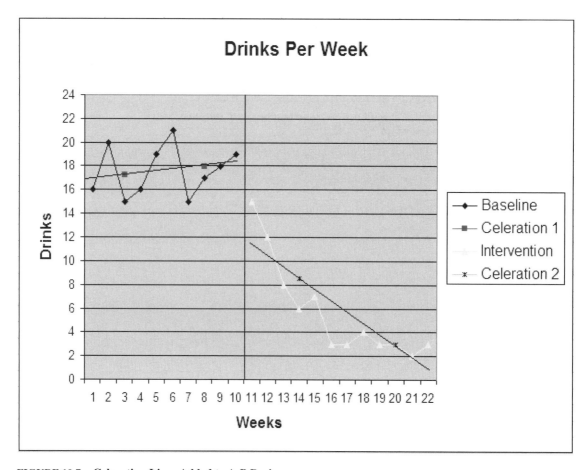

FIGURE 10.7   Celeration Lines Added to A-B Design

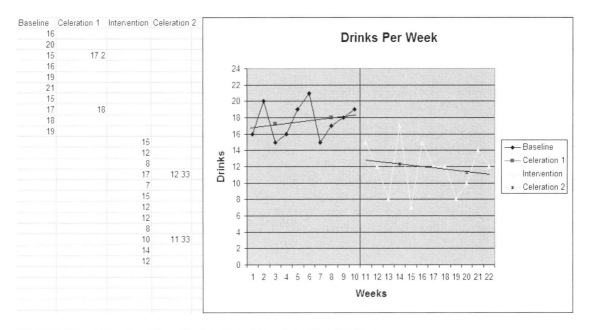

Baseline	Celeration 1	Intervention	Celeration 2
16			
20			
15	17.2		
16			
19			
21			
15			
17	18		
18			
19			
		15	
		12	
		8	
		17	12.33
		7	
		15	
		12	
		12	
		8	
		10	11.33
		14	
		12	

FIGURE 10.8   Celeration Lines Used to Detect Trends in Unstable Data

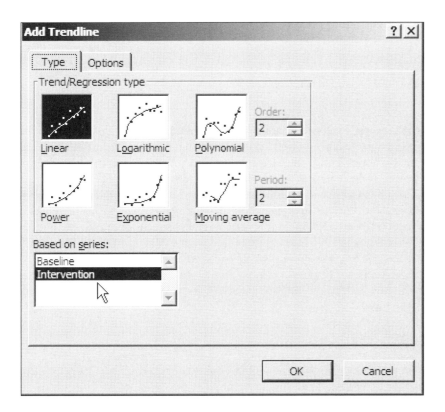

FIGURE 10.9   Add Trendline Dialog Window

the data from Figure 10.8 are displayed in a chart with regression lines added. The astute observer will note that the regression lines extend across phases. Despite the fact that the regression line is computed only from data within the phase, there appears to be no way in Excel to limit the generated regression line to width of the phase. On the positive side, the extension of the regression lines across phases clearly represents the contrast in trends, as

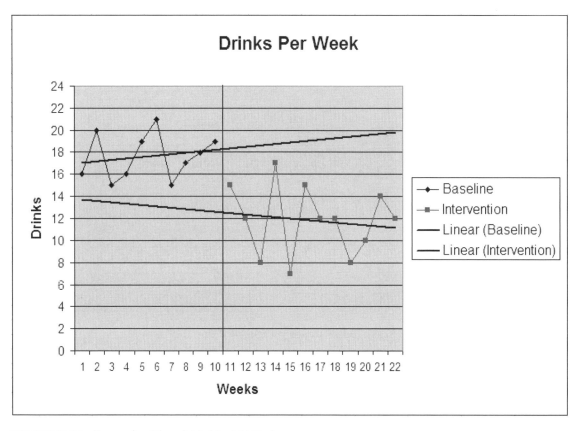

FIGURE 10.10   Regression Lines Added to A-B Design

evidenced by the respective slope of the lines across phases. If the regression line in the baseline phase is relatively horizontal and the regression line in the intervention phase has a notable positive or negative slope, then we may cautiously conclude that there was change between the phases. If the regression line in the baseline phase is relatively horizontal and the regression line in the intervention phase is also relatively horizontal, then interpretation is dependent on the level of the intervention phase regression line relative to the baseline. If the two lines overlap, then clearly there is no meaningful change between the two phases. Alternatively, if the intervention phase regression line is parallel to the baseline, but notably higher or lower than the baseline, the change has occurred between the two phases. Finally, the more the regression lines of the two phases slope in opposite directions, the greater the measured change between phases. Also see the accompanying CD-ROM video animation: "SSD-Regression Line."

Moving Average

A moving average is technically not a trend line, despite the fact that Excel includes moving average among other trend lines. Instead, a moving average is one way to smooth out data in order to better understand it. A moving average is particularly useful when there is considerable instability or fluctuation in the data within a phase (Bloom, Fischer, & Orme, 2003). Like the celeration line and the regression line, the moving average is a useful tool in detecting the slope or direction, or lack thereof, in the data. Unlike the celeration line and the regression line, the moving average does not depict the slope or direction with a straight line, but instead plots a nonlinear line based on a specified number of preceding periods. A minimum of two preceding periods are needed for the moving average formula.

The moving average is created in the Add Trendline dialog window previously described for the regression line. Instead of selecting regression line, select moving average

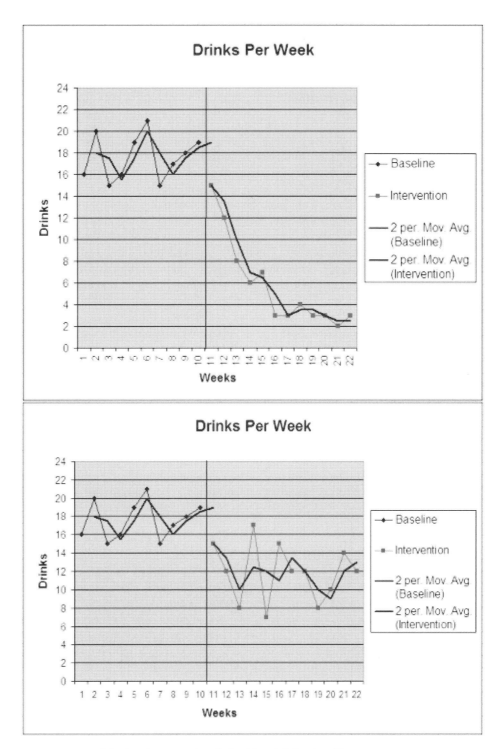

FIGURE 10.11   Moving Averages Applied to Two A-B Design Charts

and specify 2 periods. Figure 10.11 displays two charts. The upper chart is Figure 10.7 with moving averages added to both phases and the lower chart is Figure 10.8, also with moving averages in both phases. In comparing the charts in Figure 10.11 to their original representations in Figures 10.7 and 10.8 with celeration lines (pp. 132 and 133), it is clear that trends are much more evident with the celeration lines. Alternatively, the moving averages lines allow us to see the patterns beneath the fluctuation of the data across observations. All three methods—celeration lines, regression lines, and moving averages—have utility and may be employed to understand the same data from alternative perspectives. Also see the accompanying CD-ROM video animation: "SSD-Moving Average."

Autocorrelation

Serial dependency is the term used to describe the fact that the score on an outcome measure at one observation may influence the score on the same outcome measure at the next observation, or subsequent observations. Stated another way, the latter score is dependent on the previous score. The degree of this dependence or correlation between scores is quantified using a statistic known as autocorrelation.

The issue of autocorrelation is challenging for two reasons. The first challenge posed by autocorrelation is the fact that it may not be visually apparent. Visual examination of the graphed single system design data cannot reliably detect autocorrelation (Basham, 2002). The second challenge is that most statistical procedures used to evaluate the significance of change across phases in single system designs are based on the assumption that each observation is independent of all other observations. In other words, these statistical tests require that the data not be autocorrelated. Positive autocorrelation can result in statistical tests detecting a significant difference between phases that is not actually present. This is referred to as a Type 1 error. Alternatively, negative autocorrelation can cause a failure to detect significant differences between phases when in fact the differences are significant. This is referred to as a Type 2 error.

Given the challenges of autocorrelation, we recommend that readers wishing to conduct rigorous evaluations using single system designs should consult Bloom, Fischer, and Orme (2003) for detailed procedures and specialized software to detect and control for autocorrelation. For readers who wish to use spreadsheets to evaluate client change in social services practices settings, we recommend caution in the interpretation of change across phase. We are reminded of words of caution of a former professor who said that the gold standard for single system design data interpretation is "the 'inter-ocular trauma test;' if the change across phase hits you between the eyes, then maybe there is something there to pay attention to" (J. Yaffe, personal communication, September, 1990).

Single System Designs for Groups

Implicit in the notion of single system designs is the fact that individuals, groups, organizations, or any system may be evaluated or studied with these methods. Historically, group work has been an important mode of intervention in social work and social services practice (Marsh, 1931; Prath, 1945; Reid, 1997). Group methods have endured as an important practice modality. These methods are reported to be increasing in utilization in recent years as practitioners respond to health care needs for cost containment efforts (MacKenzie, 1995; Spitz, 1996).

Yalom (1995) describes group treatment as a "multidimensional laboratory of living" and suggests the necessity for recognizing the complexity of group phenomena in evaluation efforts (p. 530). Groups are composed of individuals who come together for either a single meeting at one point in time or multiple meetings over a period of time. There are a number of unique measurement considerations within group work practice. Each consideration will affect the measurement approach used for group evaluation (Toseland & Rivas, 2001). Group members may or may not have heterogeneity of problems, interests, and background. Members of groups may or may not enter the group process at the same time. Groups meet at specified time intervals and measurements of members, subgroups, and the entire group may be recorded on a number of dimensions. The number of total meeting times may vary from group to group, and from member to member. Groups may be difficult to compare to one another due to differences in group composition, leadership, intervention approach used, progression or course over time, frequency of group meetings, and duration of group service offering. Natural or cyclical events occurring in time may affect the responses of one or more group members, or one group as compared to another (Barlow & Hersen, 1984). The evaluator needs to determine the utility of evaluative efforts given these problems when rigorous research protocols are not possible in practice or service delivery settings (Hare, Blumberg, Davies, & Kent, 1994). Furthermore, there is a need to determine if information can be generated from group evaluative efforts that improve service accountability and reliability (Bloom, Fischer, & Orme, 2003).

When evaluating group level data there is a possibility of making an error in reasoning when attempting to generalize results and make inferences (Glisson, 1986). These errors, which are known as fallacies, are often due to mistaken assumptions made by the evaluator. Two common fallacies within group evaluation and group research are the ecological fallacy and the exception fallacy (Rubin & Babbie, 2001).

An ecological fallacy occurs when conclusions are drawn about individual group members based on the review of group-level data. For instance, a member of the group is presumed to be exceptional in some performance because the group data indicates that the average group performance is exceptional. In reality, the identified group member performs very poorly, but other group members are exceptional and so all members are mistakenly presumed to be performing well (Rubin & Babbie, 2001).

An exception fallacy occurs whenever conclusions about group performance are generalized from one or a few exceptional cases. This phenomenon is common and typical of stereotyping, profiling, or having prejudicial views for a group based on the performance of a few. Inferences are made about the group based on a few exceptional cases (Rubin & Babbie, 2001).

The multidimensional complexity that unfolds in treatment groups over time may cause some evaluators to condense evaluation to either a very constrained number of variables or to simply represent the mean of all dimensions as a single line plotted on a line chart, a standard single system design representation. This aggregation of multiple dimensions of the group process phenomenon impairs an evaluator's ability to detect fluctuations across dimensions for group sessions. Traditional approaches to single system design measurement have included the practice of using the individual as the unit of analysis but summarizing the total group outcome as a single measure such as the mean score for all individuals in the group (Bloom, Fischer, & Orme, 2003). The collapsing of individual group member responses into a single group mean impedes the ability to recognize either individual or subgroup variations across time or for a particular group session. A standard single system design line chart of group means for each session may be the simplest graphical representation for group evaluation, but its simplicity serves only parsimony, not understanding.

The use of aggregate line charts for the representation of individual group member responses also introduces the risk of an ecological fallacy. Evaluators and other viewers are at risk of assuming that the outcome for the group is also true for individual group members. Selection of unit of analysis can change the interpretation of the graphical representation of the data.

The challenge is to find methodologies for graphical representation of either multiple dimensions of group process data or individual responses across the life of a group that display both the richness and variation present in the data without overwhelming the viewer with excessive visual complexity. For instance, plotting the individual group participants' response scores on a weekly administered evaluation instrument as lines on a line chart may be visually intelligible if the group has four to five members. However, if the group has eight to ten members, the individuals' lines are likely to soon become an indecipherable tangle of lines from which the extraction of understanding of what is transpiring in the group is nearly impossible (Patterson, 2000). Figure 10.12 is an example of the visual complexity of a line graph plotting multiple group member responses. Representation group process measures as lines on a standard single system design line chart are feasible for a limited number of dimensions. The capacity of a line chart to convey discernable information degrades as a function of the addition of each new group dimension measured, the variability in the dimensions over time, and the duration of the group.

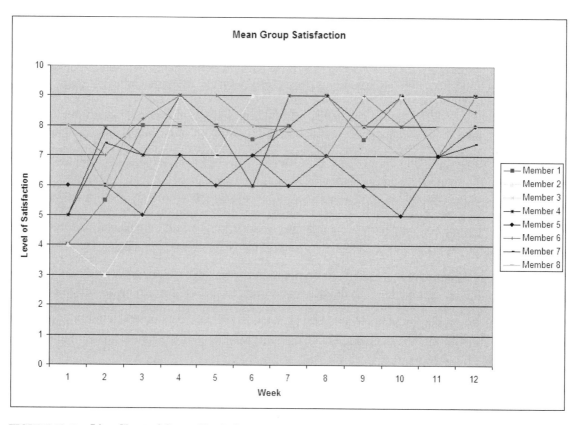

FIGURE 10.12   Line Chart of Group Single System Design Data

Standard Deviation Enhanced Line Graphs

One alternative is to display group evaluative data as both a measure of central tendency, the mean, and a measure of variability, the standard deviation, in a single chart (Basham, 2002; Patterson & Basham, 2002a). This standard deviation enhanced line graph (SDELG) presents both the commonality and the variability within the group at each point of observation (Patterson & Basham, 2002b).

The procedure for collection of single system design data for groups departs from the data collection procedures previously described for individuals. We return instead to the standard data collection format for multiple cases described in Chapter 2; variables are in columns and cases in rows. A portion of the data we will use to describe the steps to create a SDELG appears in the columns and rows of Table 10.5. The instrument used to collect these data contained eight items that group members rated their level of satisfaction with (from 1 to 9): (a) the amount of time I had to share my personal issues, (b) the leader's involvement in the group, (c) the comfort of the room, (d) the trust level in the group, (e) the other members' respect for each other, (f) the honesty during the group, (g) the degree of sharing that goes on in the group, and (h) the level of cohesion in the group. The data collection instrument was handed out to group members at the end of each session and collected before they departed (Patterson & Basham, 2002a). In addition to the eight variables on group satisfaction, we also included variables for group member identification, session number, and total satisfaction, representing the sum of scores on the eight group satisfaction variables. Therefore, the data summarized in the following procedures came from 13 group sessions with 10 group members where 11 different variables were collected. This constitutes 1,430 cells of data in the spreadsheet. This is a dramatic increase in the quantity of data we have dealt with in other single system design procedures in this chapter.

TABLE 10.5   Data Table of Single System Design Group Data

ID#	Group #	Time	Leader	Comfort	Trust	Respect	Honesty
0472	1	6	6	6	5	6	6
1981	1	9	9	8	6	9	9
1997	1	9	7	5	6	8	9
2079	1	9	8	6	8	9	8
2615	1	9	9	7	7	8	8
3873	1	9	8	8	7	7	9
4858	1	9	6	6	6	6	8
5114	1	8	6	7	6	9	9
8442	1	6	9	8	8	9	9
8638	1	6	6	3	6	9	9
8990	1	9	9	8	7	9	9
1981	2	6	6	6	6	9	9
1997	2	9	9	7	8	9	9
2079	2	8	6	4	4	9	9
2615	2	8	8	7	9	8	7
3873	2	8	9	8	6	8	7
3922	2	9	9	5	9	9	9
4858	2	6	8	8	8	8	8

To summarize this large amount of data, we will use a pivot table. In Figure 10.13 we have placed the Group # variable in Column area, the ID# in the Row area, and the Average of Satisfaction in the Data area. The Group # variable is the session number. Remember there are 13 sessions. The ID# variable is the group member identification number. We have placed the Satisfaction Total variable in the Data area and selected Average. Arranging the pivot table in this way will return the Satisfaction Total for each group member across the

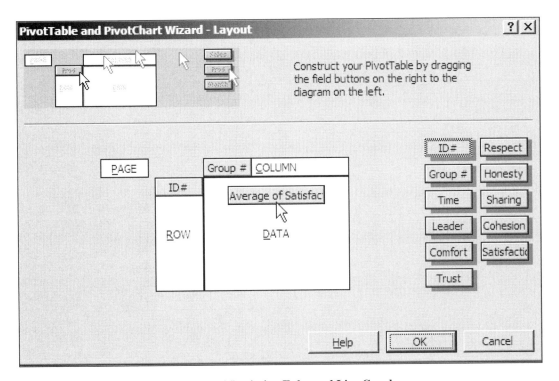

FIGURE 10.13   Pivot Table for Standard Deviation Enhanced Line Graph

13 sessions, the average level of satisfaction across group members for each session, and the average level of satisfaction for each group member across the 13 sessions.

Table 10.6 displays the copied results of the pivot table layout in Figure 10.13 plus some additional information we will use to create the SDELG. Once the pivot table is produced, we copy the entire pivot table. Then, in another open section of the worksheet, we select a cell, right click, and select Paste Special. In the Paste Special dialog window, we select Paste, Values, then click OK. This copying and special pasting of the pivot table is necessary in order to extract the values from the pivot table and create the chart.

The next step in creating a SDELG is to insert the standard deviation function in the third row below the mean in the column for session 1. In the standard deviation dialog window, we specify the range of values adjacent to each group member identification number. This function will return the standard deviation for the values in that column. For a reminder of how to use functions, see Chapters 1 and 2. We then copy and paste the standard deviation function we just created into each cell in the same row beneath the columns containing section data. This row will now display the standard deviations for the 13 sessions. Next we want to add the standard deviation for each session to the mean value for that session. We have done that in the row labeled Mean + S.D. To do this we click on the cell adjacent to the row label and write a simple formula such as =SUM(B15+B18), which tells the spreadsheet to add the value in cell B15 (the mean) to the value in cell B18 (the standard deviation). We then copy this formula and paste it into each cell in the same row beneath the columns containing section data. We repeat this procedure with the row labeled Mean − S.D., only the formula would be =SUM(B15 − B18). Table 10.6, therefore, also shows the standard deviation for each session as well as the mean plus the standard deviation and the mean minus the standard deviation.

We use the Chart Wizard to create a SDELG by plotting the mean, the mean plus the standard deviation, and the mean minus the standard deviation. The resultant SDELG chart appears in Figure 10.14. This chart allows us to see beyond the mean level of group satisfaction over the 13 sessions of the group and view the variability in the level of group satisfaction over time. See also the accompanying CD-ROM video animation: "SSD-SDELG."

TABLE 10.6   Data Table for Standard Deviation Enhanced Line Graph

ID#	1	2	3	4	5	6	7	8	9	10	11	12	13	Mean
1997	59	69	72	72	72	72	72	72	66	72	63	72	72	69.62
8442	65	71	72	69	71	72	67	71	55	61	67	72	70	67.92
5114	60	70	71	71	72	65	72	71	62	57	63	72	70	67.38
3922		64	68	68	68	71		72	60		59	69	68	66.7
0472	46		71	69		68	68	70	67	71	61		72	66.3
8638	51		68	67	72	68	69		56	71	61	71	71	65.91
2615	62	60	68	58	63	71	71	71	59		63	72	68	65.5
8990	69	60	70	68	65	65	69	64	58	68	58	65	65	64.92
4858	57	58		65	69	66	67	66		66	56	66	65	63.73
2079	64	50	66	61	65	60	63	63		65	65	64	69	62.92
3873	61	62		57	59	65	64	64	61	63	55	65	72	62.33
1981	67	54	60	54	57	60	62	64		64	51	66	68	60.85
Mean	60.09	61.8	68.6	64.92	66.64	66.9	67.64	68	60.4	65.64	60.17	68.5	69.17	
Mean + S.D.	66.89	68.71	72.2	70.86	71.95	71.1	71.11	71.74	64.5	70.46	64.74	71.9	71.65	
Mean − S.D.	53.29	54.89	65	58.97	61.32	62.7	64.16	64.26	56.3	60.81	55.6	65.2	66.69	
S.D.	6.804	6.909	3.63	5.946	5.316	4.21	3.472	3.742	4.1	4.826	4.569	3.36	2.48	

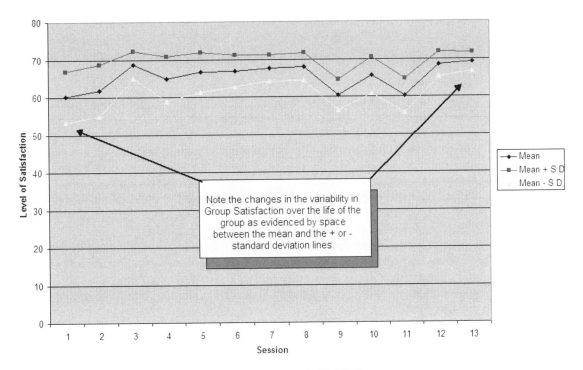

FIGURE 10.14   Standard Deviation Enhanced Line Graph (SDELG)

Surface Plots

The chief advantage of the SDELG is that it allows us to see the variability and a measure of central tendency, the mean, in group data over time. The disadvantage is that we are unable to see change in the outcome measures of the individual group members over time. The next single system design graphical procedure, surface plots, makes it possible to see data from every group member across all group sessions.

Surface plots are one option for representation of group session evaluation information over time. A surface plot is a multivariate, three-dimensional graphical representation displaying variables on the x and z horizontal axes and data values of the variables that are plotted on the y-axis, thereby creating a topography on the resultant surface. For example, with group evaluation information the topography of the group's satisfaction over time is formed by plotting each group member's group satisfaction score on the z-axis, the repeated measurement of those scores are displayed on the x-axis, and the level of group satisfaction is plotted on the y-axis. More specifically, each point on the surface plot represents the intersection of three variables, the individual group members' group satisfaction score, the group session in which the dimension was measured, and the level of the dimension measured. The resultant grid of plotted points forms a three-dimensional topography displaying the peaks and valleys of the group's life.

As will be demonstrated below, surface plots are readily generated with graphing tools of most widely available spreadsheet software such as Microsoft Excel. Once created, these three-dimensional images can be rotated, allowing for examination of the surface plot from multiple perspectives. The grid of the surface plots makes it possible to locate the points of intersection between variables. Moreover, the grids aid in the perception of variation across the range of dimensions measured and duration of the group. Gradients of color or shadings of gray representing the level of measurement on the y-axis further aid the perception of variation. This additional visual information aids in interpreting the information represented in the surface plot.

We can use the pivot table generated data in Table 10.6 to create a surface plot of group satisfaction. We right click on the original pivot table and select Pivot Chart. A column chart is produced by default. We select the chart and from the menu bar select Chart, Chart Type, Surface. Then in Chart Sub-type we select 3-D Surface. It may be initially challenging to comprehend what is being displayed in the resultant surface plot. If we move the cursor slowly around the perimeter of the cube in which the surface plot appears, at each corner of the cube a pop-up window will appear with the word "Corner." If we click on the "Corner," and hold down the left mouse button, we can the rotate the surface plot cube. This allows us to examine the surface plot from multiple perspectives. In Figure 10.15 we have rotated the cube of the surface plot so the intersection of the x- and z-axes is pointing to the bottom of the page (or screen on a computer). The cube is also titled downward so the topography of the surface plot is visible. In order to see the values for each session and for each group member, click on each axis. The Format Axis dialog window appears. Click on the Scale tab and then select Number of series between tick-mark labels = 1 and Number of series between tick marks = 1. Also see the accompanying CD-ROM video animation: "SSD-PivotChart-Surface Plot."

Examining Figure 10.15 we see several points of the graph extending downward. If we review Table 10.6 we see there are data missing from the table. These missing data are due to group members missing particular group sessions. We can correct this element of the graph and improve the overall appearance of surface plot with three procedural steps we will now detail.

We will first copy the data in the pivot table and special paste it into another location in the worksheet, in the manner that we did when creating the SDELG. Then using mean substitution, described in Chapter 4, we copy and paste the mean value for each session into the blank cells of the data table. Note that in Table 10.7, values in the data table with two decimal places are the means substituted for missing data.

On the far right side of the copied pivot table is the mean for each row. In Table 10.7, it is of course labeled Mean. When we copied and used Special Paste, Values

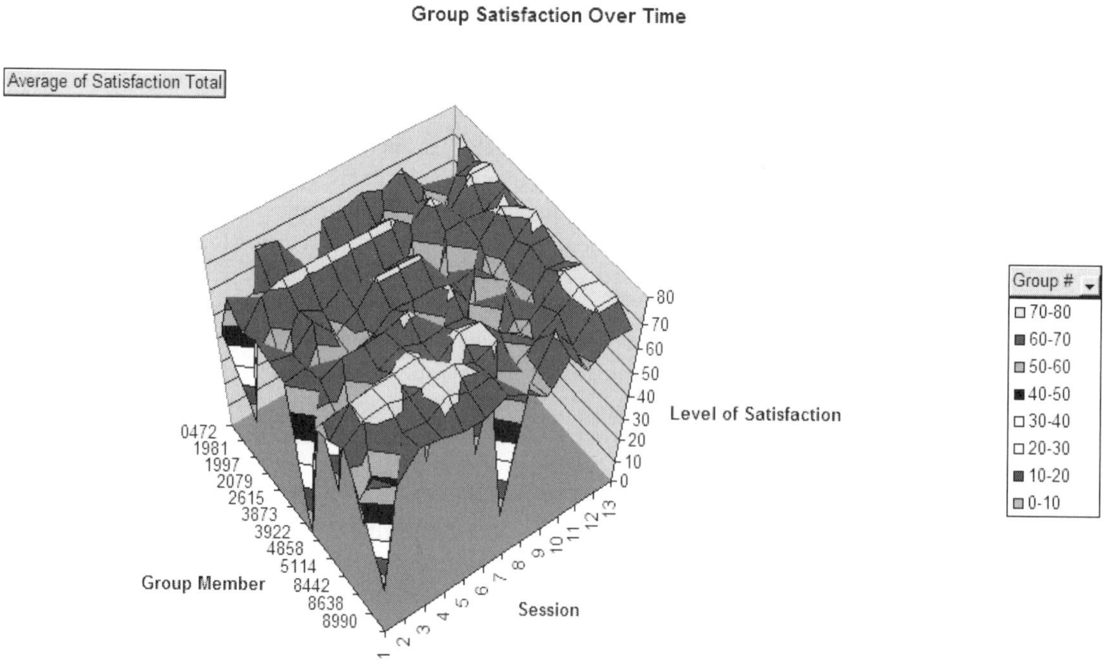

FIGURE 10.15   Surface Plot of Group Data Created Directly from Pivot Table

TABLE 10.7 Data Table for Creating Surface Plot

ID#	1	2	3	4	5	6	7	8	9	10	11	12	13	Mean
						Session								
1997	59	69	72	72	72	72	72	72	66	72	63	72	72	69.62
8442	65	71	72	69	71	72	67	71	55	61	67	72	70	67.92
5114	60	70	71	71	72	65	72	71	62	57	63	72	70	67.38
3922	60.09	64	68	68	68	71	67.64	72	60	65.64	59	69	68	66.18
0472	46	61.80	71	69	66.64	68	68	70	67	71	61	68.55	72	66.15
8638	51	61.80	68	67	72	68	69	68.00	56	71	61	71	71	65.75
2615	62	60	68	58	63	71	71	71	59	65.64	63	72	68	65.51
8990	69	60	70	68	65	65	69	64	58	68	58	65	65	64.92
4858	57	58	68.60	65	69	66	67	66	60.44	66	56	66	65	63.85
3873	61	62	68.60	57	59	65	64	64	61	63	55	65	72	62.82
2079	64	50	66	61	65	60	63	63	60.44	65	65	64	69	62.73
1981	67	54	60	54	57	60	62	64	60.44	64	51	66	68	60.57
Mean	60.09	61.80	68.60	64.92	66.64	66.92	67.64	68.00	60.44	65.64	60.17	68.55	69.17	

to paste the pivot table data, formulas for computing the row mean were lost. Because the mean substitution has now added values to the data table, we must delete or clear the contents of this column and recompute the row means. We select the range of value and right click, selecting Clear Contents. In the cell to the right of the last session of the group for the first group member, we would insert a formula to calculate the mean for that row, for instance =AVERAGE(B3:N3). We then copy and paste this formula into each cell in the column adjacent to data from the group sessions. Finally, we select the range of cells all of these data, with exception of the row containing the means for each session. From the menu bar we select Data, Sort, Descending, and sort on the last column in the selected data. Note that in Table 10.7 the values in the column labeled mean appear in descending order.

Once these data are sorted we are ready to produce a new surface plot. Again, select the range of data, this time excluding the row containing the column means and the column containing the row means. We only want to include actual group satisfaction data in the surface plot, therefore we do not select the cells containing the calculated means. Once the data are selected, we click on the Chart Wizard and again select Chart, Chart Type, Surface. Then in Chart Sub-type we select 3-D Surface. In Step 2, under the Series tab, we remove the group member identifier variable from the list of variables that are graphed in the surface plot. We then proceed through the Chart Wizard and give names to the chart and each of the axes.

Figure 10.16 displays the data from Table 10.7. In this figure it is much easier to see the topography of change that occurred in this group over the 13 sessions of its life. Note the variability evident both across group members in each session and for each individual group member across the 13 sessions. Compare Figure 10.16 to Figure 10.14. Both are based on the same data, but the data are graphically displayed in two very different forms. The challenges of using surface plots in single system designs for groups is in learning the procedures to produce them and then learning to interpret them to gain the maximum understanding of the available rich and complex information about group changes over time. Once these two challenges are mastered, using surface plot to evaluate groups opens a new window to understanding the complexity of group interactions over the life of a group. Also see the accompanying CD-ROM video animation: "SSD-Surface Plot."

Group Satisfaction Over Time

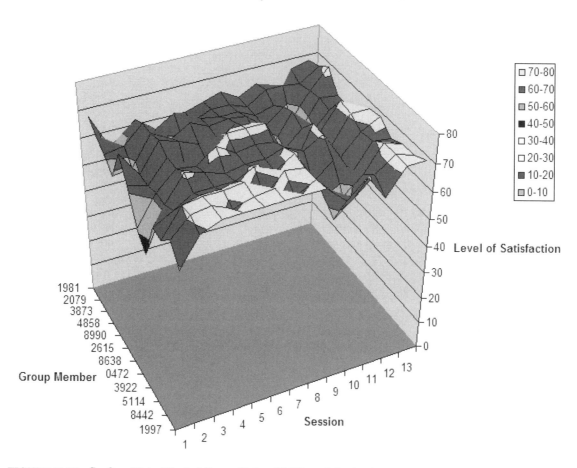

FIGURE 10.16   Surface Plot of Sorted Group Data with Mean Substitution for Missing Data

Summary

Single system designs are widely recognized as an evaluation method essential for social workers, social service practitioners, and researchers who wish to evaluate practice outcomes. Spreadsheets are extremely well suited as tools for conducting single system design evaluations. Spreadsheets are widely available, enable easy data entry and analysis, and can readily produce a variety of single system design charts. Single system designs require the collection over time of one or more measurable change objectives. Valid measurable change objectives require the observation of change in one of three indicators: (1) frequency, (2) magnitude, or (3) duration. Time is the second variable of interest in single system designs. Observations are recorded over time intervals varying from minutes to months. The two fundamental principles for recording single system design data for individuals in a spreadsheet are (1) rows in the spreadsheet represent the time interval and (2) columns represent the phase of the design. The two primary types of phases are the baseline phase, in which observations are made over time without intervention, and the intervention phase, in which observations are recorded during the period of time that some intervention is used to attempt to alter the measurable change objective. In this chapter we describe the rules for visual displays of data in single system designs and how they are applied with spreadsheets. We detail the production of A-B designs, A-B-A-B designs, and how to create dynamic spreadsheets in which the charts are automatically updated as data is entered into the spreadsheet. We describe how to detect trends and handle data instability with celeration lines, regression lines, and moving averages. The complex issue of autocorrelation in single system designs is discussed. We offer two spreadsheet methods for evaluating groups with single system designs: standard deviation enhanced line graphs and pivot table generated surface plots. We discuss the utility of both approaches in understanding changes in outcomes for group members and groups over the life of a group.

REVIEW QUESTIONS

1. What does the term "measurable change objective" refer to?

2. What are the three dimensions or indicators of measurable change in single system designs?

3. What are the three key advantages of conducting practice evaluations using single system designs?

4. What are the two basic spreadsheet procedures one must know to use spreadsheets for single system designs?

5. How do you create an A-B design in a spreadsheet?

6. What are the basic rules for the visual display of data in a chart in single system designs?

7. How do you enter the data and configure the chart to create an A-B-A-B design in a spreadsheet?

8. How do you create a dynamic, automatically updateable single system design chart in a spreadsheet?

9. How do you create a celeration line, a regression line, and a moving average for single system design charts in a spreadsheet?

10. What is autocorrelation and why should we care about it?

11. How do you create a standard deviation enhanced line graph (SDELG) to evaluate group data?

12. How do you create a surface plot to evaluate group and individual changes over time?

11 Correlation and Regression

Up until now we have seen the descriptive and inferential data analysis methods that are the most familiar to practitioners in various agency or organizational settings. However, spreadsheet applications also have the capacity to examine relationships between variables and to perform predictive analysis on dependent variables with multiple causal variables affecting the dependent variable (Dretzke & Heilman, 1998).

Spreadsheet technology can be a useful and reliable aide in the calculation of complex relationships between variables of interest. Decision makers and practitioners in various human service settings are often interested in the amount of change that occurs in one variable as compared to, or associated with, another variable (Jantzen & Lewis, 1990). They are also frequently interested in the direction of the associated change. In more advanced human service delivery problems, decision makers will want to know if a change to one or more variables within a set of related variables will create a reliable and predictable change in another variable and the direction of change, either positive or negative (Black, 1999). However, until recently, smaller organizations could not readily analyze these changes without employing external resources such as research consultants and expensive data analytic software designed for research settings (Mather, 1999). Now, computing applications that are spreadsheet based have made this level of analysis a possibility for those employing widely available personal computer technology (Patterson, 2000a). Although much of the following discussion on measures of association and regression can be located in any number of statistical methods texts, some of the key aspects are presented here as a review and orientation to the use of spreadsheets to accomplish these data analytic procedures often identified with costly and not widely distributed statistical software (Hendry & Green, 1994).

Pearson's r and R^2

Correlation as a measure of association is well known to those who seek to understand the process or interventions associated with the determinants of change. Both Pearson's r and R^2 are measures of association that are popular data analytic procedures in the social sciences when determining causality, cause and effect, and prediction of preferred outcomes are needed information to facilitate decision making with respect to resource allocation (Lacher, 1997) and to determining intervention or service delivery effectiveness (Patterson, 2000b).

The degree to which two variables are related to each other constitutes a correlation often expressed as a Pearson's r correlation. This correlation consists of a linear relationship between the two variables, expressed as a numerical value that is identified as a correlation coefficient, or a number that indicates the magnitude and direction of the association (Cohen & Cohen, 1983). Though a measure of correlation between two variables does not mean that there is a causal relationship between the variables, the likelihood that one variable may influence another, or simply change as another variable changes, is an important consideration for agency decision makers and practitioners.

A correlation's degree and direction of change is expressed either as a positive correlation coefficient that approaches the value of 1.00 (represented as an inclined association in a traditional line graph), or as a negative correlation with an inverse direction in association that is expressed as a correlation coefficient that approaches the value of -1.00 (represented as declined association in a traditional line graph). Pearson's product moment correlation coefficient is a well-known statistic that reports the degree of linear relationship between two variables when their scale of measurement is either interval or ratio. The term "product moment" refers to the process of determining the z scores, or standardized scores, of each variable and then multiplying them by each other. Then the average value of the multiplied z score product is calculated to determine the moment for the variables. Pearson's correlation coefficient is commonly symbolized as r.

Pearson's r correlations are of interest to service providers as an applied issue, to determine if services, policies, and interventions are increasing or decreasing the value of an associated variable. On the one hand, a practitioner may want to know if a proposed intervention will serve to increase or decrease a client's functioning as measured by one or more indices. On the other hand, an agency decision maker may be interested in whether increasing manpower in a service delivery unit of an organization is likely to improve some measure of outcomes for either a service recipient group or the organization as a whole (Montcalm & Royse, 2002).

For example, in a spreadsheet application such as Microsoft Excel, Pearson's r may be calculated by selecting the Pearson's function from the menu of statistical categories of functions and inserting the function as a formula into an empty cell. Then the range of data for the two variables of interest is selected. Once selected, the user will click the OK button to confirm the selection. Both Pearson's r and R^2 will be calculated and displayed. The R^2 value represents the percentage of variance in the dependent variable explained by the effect of the selected independent variable.

To compute Pearson's r in the Excel spreadsheet application, simply select two sets of values or scores that you wish to determine the relationship between for a particular subject of interest and follow the following sequence of steps.

Step 1. After the values are entered into the spreadsheet cells, another cell is selected with the cursor to display the value of the calculated correlation by clicking the computer mouse once.

Step 2. Next the function box is selected; a scroll-down menu presents a series of calculations including correlation under the statistical functions. After selecting the correlation function (abbreviated as "CORREL") click on the button marked "Finish."

Step 3. A second menu will ask for an array of cells or data to be included for each of the two variables to be correlated.

Step 4. Select the range of data cells to be included for each variable and click on the finish button for this menu. The correlation value will be calculated and appear in the cell that you selected earlier as seen in Figure 11.1 (see also the accompanying CD-ROM video animation: "Correlation").

Step 5. By using the graphing wizard tool and selecting the values of the two variables being evaluated for a measure of correlation, we can also plot the variables on a scatterplot. Simply select scatterplot (xy) on the wizard menu and then select the second graphic choice. Press the finish button to see the completed graphic.

There are any number of situations where more than one aspect or variable of an intervention, such as changes in service policy or organizational changes in a service delivery system, may have a positive or negative influence on some variable of interest. Such is the case where there are several independent variables that may be correlated with a change in a measured dependent variable. In this instance a multiple coefficient of determination is needed to derive a measure of association between a dependent variable and several independent

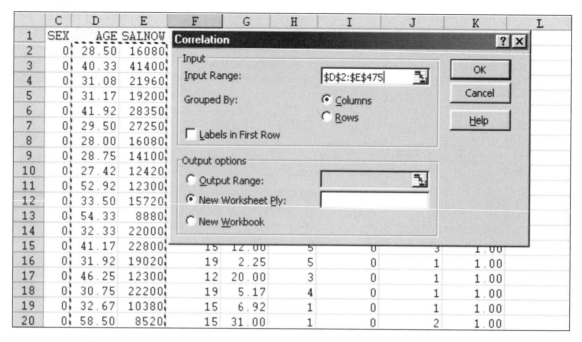

	C	D	E	F	G	H	I	J	K	L
1	SEX	AGE	SALNOW							
2	0	28.50	16080							
3	0	40.33	41400							
4	0	31.08	21960							
5	0	31.17	19200							
6	0	41.92	28350							
7	0	29.50	27250							
8	0	28.00	16080							
9	0	28.75	14100							
10	0	27.42	12420							
11	0	52.92	12300							
12	0	33.50	15720							
13	0	54.33	8880							
14	0	32.33	22000							
15	0	41.17	22800	15	12.00	5	0	3	1.00	
16	0	31.92	19020	19	2.25	5	0	1	1.00	
17	0	46.25	12300	12	20.00	3	0	1	1.00	
18	0	30.75	22200	19	5.17	4	0	1	1.00	
19	0	32.67	10380	15	6.92	1	0	1	1.00	
20	0	58.50	8520	15	31.00	1	0	2	1.00	

FIGURE 11.1   Preparing the Correlation Function in Excel

variables, the statistic used as a measure of the goodness of fit for a linear relationship is expressed as R^2, or "R-squared." The set of independent variables may then be reported by a coefficient that explains or predicts the linear change expected in the dependent variable. Practitioners and agency decision makers may then seek to determine whether changes in several variables might be expected to have either a beneficial or negative effect as indicated in the direction of association for a measured dependent variable of interest.

R^2, the coefficient of multiple determination, is a numerical value that is less than one, such as .20. However, the fraction of 1.0 is reported as a percentage (e.g., 20%) such that the set of independent variables together provide a measure of positive association, or prediction, that explains the percentage of the variance in the dependent variable of interest. This coefficient is often useful for practitioners attempting to determine the likely change that could result from multiple interventions. It can also be useful for service delivery systems in estimating the effects of changes in multiple demographic and economic factors in the efficacy of a service delivery model or the distribution plan for scarce resources.

Bivariate Regressions

A two-variable regression or "bivariate" regression is essentially the same as a correlation in that a bivariate regression is concerned with measuring the association between two variables, a dependent variable and an independent variable. A multivariate regression is concerned with measuring the relationship between a single dependent variable and several independent variables. There are a number of data analytic procedures that measure the relationship between two variables depending on the numerical scale of the data or other considerations. Bivariate regression, then, estimates the measurable difference in a dependent variable for each one-unit change in an independent variable. If the bivariate regression coefficient is reported in a standardized form, then it has the same value as a Pearson's r correlation coefficient. Spreadsheet applications that can perform data analytic functions are capable of performing either the correlation or the regression analysis. Although these procedures are detailed here, the accompanying CD-ROM will present more information on how to perform these procedures.

Regression

Regression includes a variety of methods that use several statistical procedures to explain the variation in a dependent variable from data derived from one or more independent variables. Regression is more concerned with the prediction or determination of the expected change in the dependent variable of interest resultant from changes in the independent variables. Regression analysis makes use of a number of spreadsheet and graphing functions to evaluate the data and form predictive inferences about the data. Predictive regression analysis relies on a number of assumptions about the quality and nature of the data being evaluated (Pedhazer, 1999).

Assumptions about the data necessary for reliable and valid predictions using regression include:

1. *Normality:* scores or observations obtained would be normally distributed in the population of interest assumed if sampling is random or includes random assignment (explore with a normal probability scatterplot). Normality means that the distribution of probability values tend to cluster around the mean for all possible values to form a symmetrical and unimodal normal (or bell-shaped) curve. In such a distribution, the mean, the median, and the mode are represented by the same value.

2. *Heterogeneity:* a quality of being diverse and not comparable in kind. This essentially means that there is enough variation in data to determine the presence or absence of a relationship between variables. The opposite condition of little variation is known as homoscedasticity and can be explored through plotting the data on a scatterplot. Homoscedasticity would indicate that there may be too little variation between the dependent and independent variables to make inferences due to variations for the samples of the population being evaluated.

3. *Linearity:* a linear relationship exists between variables (explore with a scatterplot). Linearity means that the relationship between the variables forms a relatively straight line when plotted on a graph.

4. *Independence:* scores or observations are independent from each other (controlled through the research design). Independence means that the observations or values are independently derived and that one event or value will not depend on another event or value. Any association between the two or more sets of values are incidental and not "significant."

Two-Variable Regression

Bivariate or two-variable regression includes statistical procedures that are concerned with demonstrating the relationship between two variables. One variable, the predictor variable, is the independent variable. When changed by one unit of measurement, it results in an estimated associated change in the criterion, or dependent variable. The estimation of associated change in the dependent variable is referred to as the bivariate regression coefficient. However, a standardized bivariate regression coefficient is the same as a Pearson's R^2 correlation.

The formula for calculating a bivariate linear relationship between a single criterion and a single predictor variable is:

$$y = a + Bx$$

Where:

y = Predicted value of Dependent Variable (D.V.)
a = Intercept value of D.V. when the Independent Variable (I.V.) = 0
B = Slope = Average change of D.V. associated with a 1 point increase in the I.V.
x = Value of I.V.

A residual value in regression analysis refers to the value derived from the difference for a particular person or case of their actual value minus their predicted value.

Multiple Regression

Multiple regression is used to examine the relationship between one criterion variable (Y, a dependent variable) and more than one predictor variable (X1, X2, . . . etc., independent variables). Ordinary least squares (OLS) regression requires that these variables contain continuous data (interval or ratio, but not categorical variables such as Likert Scales and True/False items). A model for predicting change in the dependent or criterion variable can be tested to determine the amount of change accounted for by the set of predictor variables. The formula for calculating a multivariate linear relationship between a single criterion and a multiple predictor variable is the same as the bivariate formula, with the following modifications: $Y = a + (X1)(B1) + (X2)(B2) + \ldots$ (Pedhazer, 1999).

Creating Scatterplots

A scatterplot can be defined as a graph or illustration that is made up of a series of dots or points that are the end product of plotting values for two variables. Each dot or point indicates a value of a single unit. The point is where that unit, or subject, is represented for the two variables. This pattern of dots can be represented as a nearly straight line or at some level of dispersion and variability. The degree of clustering along a line suggests a stronger degree of correlation or association. The linear association may represent a positive or negative direction or slope of relatedness. Points on the scatterplot that are randomly dispersed suggest no association or a limited association between the two variables of interest.

A scatterplot can be used to visually examine variables to determine if data is normally distributed and to determine if a linear relationship exists between a criterion variable (Y) and a predictor variable (X). There are a number of steps in creating a scatterplot in a spreadsheet application such as Microsoft Excel. These are listed as follows:

Step 1. Select variables (interval or ratio data) from spreadsheet data for generating a scatterplot of variables of interest.

Step 2. Select Insert on the menu bar, and then select Chart to display the Chart Wizard.

Step 3. Confirm the input range of data for X (independent) and Y (dependent) variables. On the Source Data tab, determine the source data configuration preferred (rows or columns) and whether variables are to be added or removed.

Step 4. Click on the Next button.

Step 5. Use the Chart Options tabs to add titles, variable labels, legends, and data labels as well as to adjust or format gridlines and axis choices as seen in Figure 11.2 (see also the accompanying CD-ROM video animation: "Scatterplot and Trendline").

Step 6. Click on the Next button.

Trendlines in Scatterplots

A trendline may be drawn into the scatterplot to best fit or represent the linear association between clustered values on the graph and to determine the direction of values in the association over time. Often a trendline enhances the presentation of the data and clearly communicates the nature of the association between the two variables. Here are the steps to add

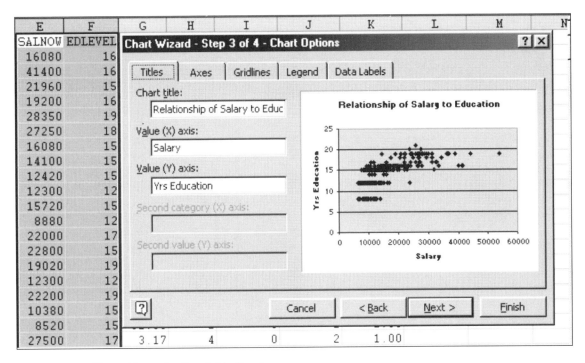

E	F	G	H	I	J	K	L	M	N
SALNOW	EDLEVEL								
16080	16								
41400	16								
21960	15								
19200	16								
28350	19								
27250	18								
16080	15								
14100	15								
12420	15								
12300	12								
15720	15								
8880	12								
22000	17								
22800	15								
19020	19								
12300	12								
22200	19								
10380	15								
8520	15								
27500	17	3.17	4	0	2	1.00			

FIGURE 11.2   Formatting a Scatterplot in Excel

a trendline to a scatterplot to represent the associated values from a spreadsheet analysis in Microsoft Excel.

Step 1. Add a trendline to the scatterplot by selecting Chart from the menu bar and then selecting Add Trendline.

Step 2. From the Add Trendline tabs, select the Trend/Regression type for the line and from the Options tab, check any desired customizations and click on the "OK" button. Note: Select "Linear" to plot a trendline of a linear relationship between variables and select "Polynomial" to plot a line to check for a curvilinear relationship between variables.

Step 3. To format a trendline so that it is colorized for enhanced visualization, click on the trendline, select format trendline, and single click on the computer mouse.

Step 4. From the Format Trendline dialog box, select preferred changes from the Patterns, Type, or Options tabs and click on OK. The trendline will appear as drawn on the graph. See Figure 11.3 (see also the accompanying CD-ROM video animation: "Scatterplot and Trendline").

Interpreting Scatterplots

Interpreting scatterplots is somewhat difficult if there is not a clear linear association between the two variables plotted. Fitting a line of best fit to the data points is helpful, but at times the scatter of the data points suggests an alternate association. By examining a number of scatterplots or by viewing the examples on the accompanying CD-ROM, some skill can be acquired in differentiating four possibilities of data scattering or clustering. These are:

1. A curvilinear relationship between variables is suspected, though not confirmed, by the fitting of a polynomial trendline.
2. A curvilinear relationship between variables is illustrated and confirmed by the adding of a polynomial trendline.

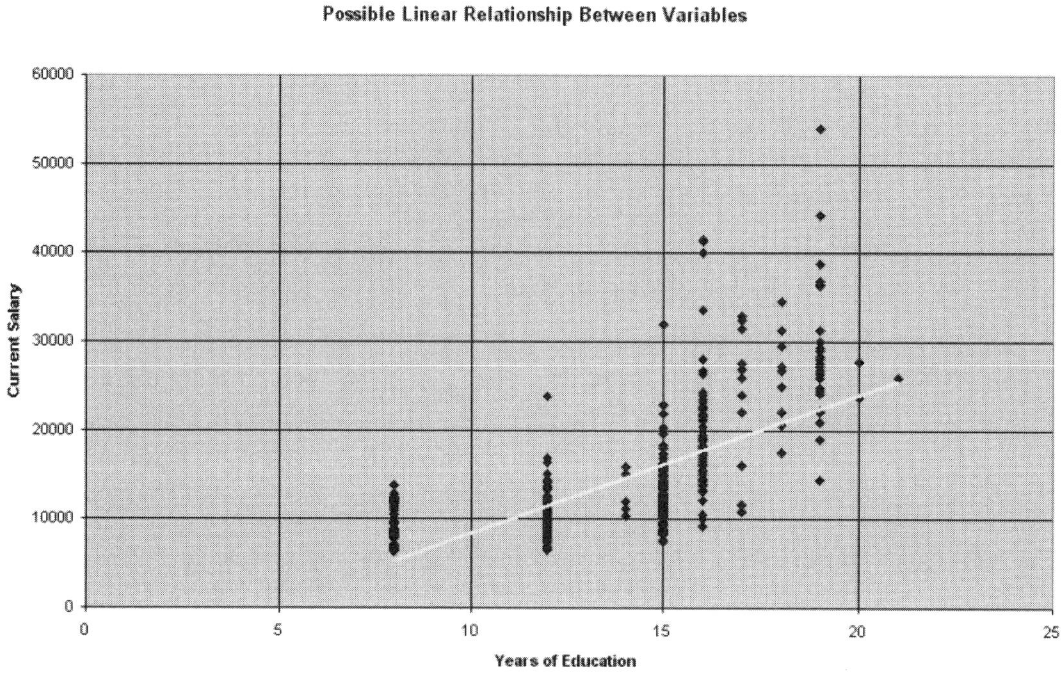

Possible Linear Relationship Between Variables

FIGURE 11.3   A Trendline Formatted to Show a Possible Linear Relationship

3. A linear relationship between variables is suspected, though not confirmed, by the fitting of a linear trendline.
4. A linear relationship between variables illustrated and confirmed by the adding of a linear trendline.

Depending on your interpretation, you may wish to select other data for analysis methods or use another analysis procedure for the variables selected. If the scatterplot suggests a linear relationship between variables and meets the other assumptions required, then you will want to compute a regression analysis, though not under the following conditions:

1. *Nonhomoscedasticity:* If the variance in one variable is unequal in the dependent variable for the same values in the independent variable, heteroscedasticity (different scattering) is evident and a nonparametric test is called for.
2. *Nonlinearity:* If the trendline does not illustrate some linear relationship between the criterion variable (Y) and the predictor variables (X), then there may be a nonlinear relationship such as a curvilinear relationship, or another relationship.
3. *Nonnormality:* A scatterplot of normal probability distribution can be selected when running the regression analysis procedure. The results and plot will appear on the output worksheet. If the scatterplot approaches a straight line, the sample is assumed to be drawn form a normally distributed population.

Ordinary Least Squares Regression

Ordinary least squares (OLS) regression is the data analysis procedure that derives an equation to represent the relationship between or among variables. The mean of the least sum of squared deviation scores or errors is calculated to generate the values to plot the best fit regression line for a distribution of values.

For example, we are interested in learning whether higher wages are associated with seniority and age in a particular organization or whether higher salaries are due to training and education. We have data available on age, education, and wages. Wages are the dependent variable that may be due to either age or education. A regression model can be hypothesized, given the available set of data, to determine whether age or education predicts wages, and to what degree. Using a spreadsheet database we can begin to compute an OLS regression, using the information on interpreting outputs to bring meaning to the results.

Computing OLS Regression

To compute OLS regression from spreadsheet data using the data analysis tools in Excel, use the following procedure:

Step 1. Select variables (interval or ratio data) from spreadsheet data for a multivariate research problem. In OLS multivariate regression, the independent variable (predictor variable) and dependent variables must include a continuous scale of data (not categorical). Arrange these variables in the order that you wish to examine their relationship to each other.

Step 2. Select Tools from the menu bar and then Data analysis.

Step 3. Select Regression and click on the OK button.

Step 4. In the regression dialog box, perform the following:

A. Select the data column for the criterion (Y) variable and observe the included value range in the Input *Y* Range of the dialog box. Do not include the column label cell.

B. Select the data columns for the predictor (X) variables and observe the included value range in the Input *X* Range of the dialog box. Do not include the column label cell.

C. Confirm the input range of data for X (independent) and Y (dependent) variables.

Step 5. Set preferences in the regression dialog box:

Uncheck "Labels": Variables will show up as variable X1, X2, and so on in the output in the order of being entered into the input range.

If "labels" is checked, variable names will be included in the data ranges, but this function does not perform consistently well in multivariate data ranges.

Constant is zero remains unchecked unless you wish to force the regression line through the zero value. In most instances this will not be preferred.

Confidence level is set to 95% by default. Check the box and enter 90% or some other value for a secondary confidence level report as needed.

Output range: Check the option for "New Worksheet Ply"; a blank spreadsheet in the same workbook will be created and output will begin in cell A1. If instead the button for the "Output Range" is checked, the output will be placed on the same spreadsheet as the original variable data. Indicate the upper left cell value where you wish to insert the output into the spreadsheet. Output will vary but requires a minimum of seven columns and twenty rows. Alternatively, checking the "New Workbook" option will create a separate workbook for the output.

Residuals: Check residuals to create a table that lists the actual value of data points, the predicted value, and the difference (the residual) for each predicted data point of the regression equation. Select other options such as Standardized Residuals, Residual Plots, and Line Fit Plots to compute additional values and chart plots for regression-predicted data points.

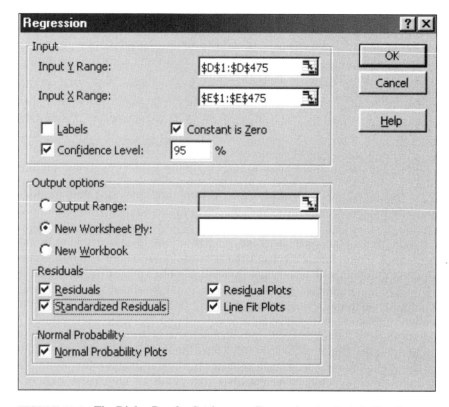

FIGURE 11.4   **The Dialog Box for Setting up a Regression Analysis in Excel**

Normal probability: Select to compute a plot of normal probabilities in the regression output.

Your final dialog box choices will look like Figure 11.4 (see also the accompanying CD-ROM video animation: "Bivariate Regression Example").

Step 6. Click on the OK button in the regression dialog box.

Step 7. The visible portion of the table output from a regression analysis (without annotation) is displayed.

Step 8. Click on worksheet tab output with no control variables.

Interpreting Multivariate Regression (OLS) Output in Excel

Spreadsheet results for the regression analysis procedures do not include the narrative information necessary to readily translate numerical values into meaningful findings. Therefore, the content needed necessary to understanding the results are included along with the steps required to interpret and begin to write up findings. The tables and steps are presented as follows:

Step 1: Examine the summary output worksheet and interpret the regression statistics. Regression statistics test the null hypothesis (H_0: $R^2 = 0$) and the alternate hypothesis (H_A: $R^2 \neq 0$). Row values under the heading of regression statistics correspond to the following outputs:

Multiple R: The correlation between R and the independent, predictor, or X variables selected.

R^2: The amount of variance in the dependent, criterion, or Y variable expressed as a fraction of one (when multiplied by 100, it will be expressed as percent accounted for).

Adjusted R^2: The amount of variance accounted for by the set of independent, predictor, or X variables expressed as a fraction of one (when multiplied by 100, it will be expressed as percent accounted for).

Standard Error: The average error when making this regression prediction.

Observations: The number of subjects or observations included.

Step 2: Examine the summary output worksheet and interpret the ANOVA outputs. To review, analysis of variance is a statistical test of the null hypotheses of no relationship between predictor variables and the criterion variable. Row values under the heading of ANOVA correspond to the following outputs:

Regression: The variation in Y that is explained by the predictor variables.

Residual: The variation in Y that is not explained by the predictor variables.

Total: Total variation that may be ascribed to regression and residual variation.

Column values under the heading of ANOVA correspond to the following outputs:

df: Degrees of freedom.

SS: Sum of squares value.

MS: Mean square values; MS regression and MS residual values are derived by dividing the SS by the df (degrees of freedom).

F: The F value, obtained by dividing the regression MS value by the residual MS value.

Significance F: The probability value (P-value) associated with the obtained F.

Step 3: Examine the summary output worksheet and interpret the coefficient summary outputs. Row values under the heading of coefficient summary correspond to the following outputs:

Intercept: The intercept point of the X variables and Y variable of the regression equation.

X Variable 1: The beta score weight for the first predictor variable entered into the regression equation or model.

X Variable 2: The beta score weight for the second predictor variable entered into the regression equation or model.

Further X Variables: Up to 16 predictor, independent, or X variables may be analyzed.

Column values under the heading of coefficient summary correspond to the following outputs:

Coefficients: The unstandardized values of the dependent variable associated with the independent variables.

Standard Error: A measure of sampling error due to random fluctuations in the sample.

t Stat: A statistical test of the hypothesis that the intercept value is equal to zero. For each predictor, variable beta weight tests the hypothesis that the beta weight is equal to zero.

P Value: The probability that the result could have been produced by chance or random error is less than 5 percent if the value is below .05.

Lower 95 percent: The lower bound value of a confidence interval that the sample statistic contains the population parameter 95 percent of the time.

Upper 95 percent: The upper bound value of a confidence interval that the sample statistic contains the population parameter 95 percent of the time.

Step 4: Examine the summary output worksheet and interpret the residual outputs. Column values under the heading of residual outputs correspond to the following outputs:

Observation: The number of the person, case, or observation is given.

Predicted Y: Generates a prediction value for each person, case, or observation.

Residuals: Derived by subtracting the predicted value of the person, case, or observation from the actual value.

Standard residuals: Derived by transforming residuals to a unit of normal distribution with a mean of 0 and standard deviation of 1.

Step 5. Examine and interpret the line plot graphs included with the regression output. Three line plots are generated to assist in the interpretation of output.

Residual plots: Compare the actual (Y) values with the predicted (Y) values for each prediction (X) variable selected.

Line fit plots: A plot is created for each predictor variable. Each plot depicts a view of the mathematical plane created by regression analysis.

Normal probability output and plot: Examines the assumption of normal distribution. The data points approximate a straight line if the sample is drawn from a normally distributed population.

Step 6. Annotate, colorize, and summarize the regression output to communicate findings in an understandable way.

A sample regression summary based on the example as given in the accompanying CD-ROM could be briefly written as follows:

Higher number of years of age do not have a strong linear association with salary ($24.91) NS (not significant). The higher the number of years of education (1 year), the higher the salary ($1,592.55). No control variables were included in the analysis. An earlier review of a scatterplot depicting the relationship between age and current salary suggests a possible curvilinear relationship between age and current salary.

See Figure 11.5 and the accompanying CD-ROM video animation: "Annotating Regression Output."

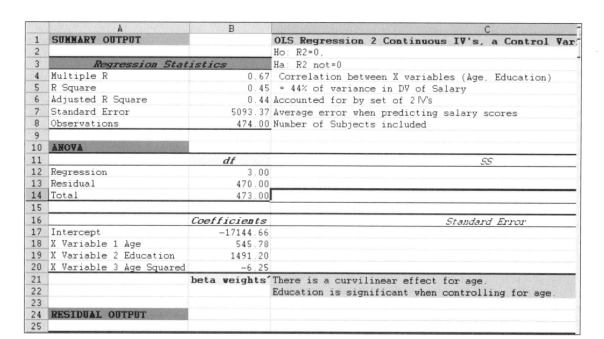

	A	B	C
1	**SUMMARY OUTPUT**		OLS Regression 2 Continuous IV's, a Control Var
2			Ho: R2=0,
3	*Regression Statistics*		Ha: R2 not=0
4	Multiple R	0.67	Correlation between X variables (Age, Education)
5	R Square	0.45	= 44% of variance in DV of Salary
6	Adjusted R Square	0.44	Accounted for by set of 2 IV's
7	Standard Error	5093.37	Average error when predicting salary scores
8	Observations	474.00	Number of Subjects included
9			
10	**ANOVA**		
11		*df*	*SS*
12	Regression	3.00	
13	Residual	470.00	
14	Total	473.00	
15			
16		*Coefficients*	*Standard Error*
17	Intercept	-17144.66	
18	X Variable 1 Age	545.78	
19	X Variable 2 Education	1491.20	
20	X Variable 3 Age Squared	-6.25	
21		beta weights	There is a curvilinear effect for age.
22			Education is significant when controlling for age.
23			
24	**RESIDUAL OUTPUT**		
25			

FIGURE 11.5   An Annotated and Colorized Regression Analysis Output Summary

Creating a Control Variable for Regression Analysis in Excel

A control variable statistically subtracts the effects of a predictor variable to see what a relationship between another predictor variable, or a set of predictor variables, would be on a criterion variable without it. An example of this is available on the Web at http://web.utk.edu/~dap/Random/Order/Start.htm. This link is included in the bonus section of the accompanying CD-ROM.

Step 1. Select the variable that you wish to control for while regressing a predictor variable (X) of interest on a criterion variable (Y) on the raw data spreadsheet.

Step 2. Copy and arrange the variables of interest on a separate spreadsheet in the workbook so that the dependent variable (Y) precedes the independent variables (X). You may place the variable to be controlled last in the sequence; however, the output summary will reflect the order of entry into the model.

Step 3. In a new column, multiply the control variable by itself to create squared values.

Step 4. Enter the variables into the regression equation with the variable to be controlled, with the created independent control variable entered last into the model.

Step 5. Run the regression analysis (see the previous procedure: include the control variable with the independent variables in the data input range).

Interpreting Results of Multivariate Regression Using a Control Variable

Interpret the results as before, with the exception of the addition of the control variable. Otherwise, the hypothesis being tested and the reported outcomes in the spreadsheet analysis are the same. However, the summary following interpretation of results may be different due to the need to use a control variable. A sample regression summary based on the example as given in the accompanying CD-ROM could be briefly written as follows:

The control variable is introduced into a statistical analysis to see if a statistical relationship holds among subjects in a sample who are alike on a particular characteristic. In multivariate analysis, the control variable removes the effect of a third variable on extraneous variables so that the remaining effect is limited to that of the prediction variable, X, acting on or related to the criterion variable, Y.

To examine the curvilinear effect of age on current salary, age was entered into the regression equation first, then educational level was added, and then the control variable of age squared was added to the equation. There is a curvilinear effect for age.

Education is significant when controlling for age. The higher the number of years of education (1 year), the higher the salary ($1,491.20) when controlling for age. Approximately 44% of the variance in salary is due to education.

Summary

Spreadsheets have the capacity to perform complex analysis of measures of association and to hypothesize models of the relationships between variables to control for multiple variables affecting a dependent variable or to offer a measure of predictive reliability for interventions and change processes. Models of analysis for correlation and regression can be developed and rapidly reproduced by service providers and practitioners who do not have access to advanced data analytic research-oriented software applications to measure associations and change over multiple measures or over time.

Spreadsheets can also be used as an educational tool (Lentini, Nardi, & Simonetta, 1999) or to orient direct service providers rapidly to the utility of advanced evaluation concepts (Kerr & Payne, 1994).

REVIEW QUESTIONS

1. What is Pearson's *r* used for in hypothesis testing?

2. What does the R^2 value designate in a test of the association between two variables?

3. What is an array of values used for in spreadsheet data analysis?

4. Regression statistical procedures are used for what?

5. Describe the heterogeneity of variance assumption in performing a regression analysis.

6. In the linear regression formula, what does the symbol "B" designate?

7. How are scatterplots used to evaluate the statistical assumptions of data needed to perform regression analysis?

12 Graphical Representation of Practice Information

One of the most remarkable advances in personal computers in their brief history is their expanding capacity to manage images and the visual representation of information. For the purposes of this discussion the term *image* is used to denote drawings, illustrations, and digitized photographs. Following the convention of Henry (1998), the terms *graph* and *chart* are used interchangeably. The term *diagram* refers to a drawing that shows a relationship or arrangement. The term *graphics* is used in a more general sense to refer to images, charts, diagrams, graphics, and other visual representations.

The introduction of the Apple Macintosh computer in 1984 opened vast possibilities of computer generated graphics to the imaginations of a broad spectrum of first-time computer buyers. It ushered in the age of graphical computing in which the potential to express ideas and represent information is continually spurred by the growing facility of both hardware and software to produce images and graphics. As a result, present-day computing is characterized by a graphical user interface (GUI) in all widely used operating systems, manuscripts and reports are seeded with diagrams and charts, e-mail arrives with accompanying animation, and web pages are filled with digital images, animations, and graphics.

The application of graphics in the social service practice to date has been limited. Three noteworthy exceptions are the use of graphs in single system designs for practice evaluation (Bloom, Fischer, & Orme, 2003), ecomaps for the representation of clients in social contexts (Hartman, 1978), and genograms for the representation of the intergenerational structure families (Hartman, 1978; Mattaini, 1993). This constrained use of graphical information as a tool of social service practice exists as a result of a reciprocally determined interaction. Until recently there has been an absence of tools for ready production of graphics, little social service educational emphasis on the use of graphics in practice, and limited theory and practice experience to guide and drive experimentation with graphics applications. These interacting impediments are showing signs of erosion. Though there has been virtually no discussion in the social service education literature specifically related to the expanded use of graphics in social service practice, texts on practice evaluation increasingly emphasize the importance of visual representation of client/system change data (Alter & Evens, 1990; Bloom, Fischer, & Orme, 1999; Nurius & Hudson, 1993; Orme & Cox, 2001; Royse, 1992). Mattaini (1993) describes and illustrates multiple applications for the use of graphics in social service practice. A number of researchers have created assessment instruments and packages that employ graphics to illustrate client social or behavioral status and change (Benbenishty, 1991; Hudson & McMurtry, 1997; Lachiusa, 1996; Ogilvie, 1996). Spreadsheets now commonly provide an array of tools for the production and manipulation of graphics and images.

Despite the heretofore constrained use of graphics in social service practice, the potential applications are numerous. The use of single system design graphs for individuals, groups, and systems is described in Chapter 10. Many practice situations call for the development of educational materials for clients and families. The infusion of such materials with carefully selected graphics both captures the reader's attention and conveys the core message of the pamphlet or brochure. The use of spreadsheet-generated charts and graphs in reports to supervisors or for supervisees can concisely summarize service delivery data. Agencies' newsletters and public relations releases employing diagrams, flowcharts, and graphs convey far more information than simple text-based materials. Computer-based slideshow presentations containing graphical materials from spreadsheets can engage and hold an audience's attention. Web pages with graphics and charts are far more likely to be reviewed than those relying solely on text for communication. In each of these examples, spreadsheet-created graphics are employed with the intention of capturing attention and conveying information.

This chapter describes and provides illustrations of the use of spreadsheet graphics tools in the visual representation of social service practice information. More specifically, this chapter addresses how to use spreadsheets for the production of graphs and the application of spreadsheet drawing tools to create diagrams and illustrations. Many of the drawing and graphics tools available in spreadsheets also are found in the companion word processors of their respective software suites.

Thinking Visually

At the core of most social services education and professional development is listening. We are trained to listen accurately, to listen empathetically, and to listen for the subtext or underlying meaning in verbal communication. Along with the development of listening skills, but perhaps to a lesser degree, social service practitioners are taught to visually observe behavior, body language, and social setting. Historically, much of our reporting of what we have heard and observed is conveyed in text and written reports. Managers and administrators also are trained to varying degrees to listen, observe, and communicate findings in written format. The use of graphical information and images for communication has not played a major role in the training of most social service professionals. Therefore, before embarking on a description and demonstration of how to use spreadsheets in the generation and display of graphics and images, we will first consider the role of graphics in communication.

Meyer (1993) points out that throughout history, images have played a major role in communicating our understanding of the world, others, and ourselves. The use of images, of course, predates the written word. Images have been used over time by humankind to communicate about both real events and to symbolically represent experiences from the corporal to the transcendental. Images evoke emotions, tell stories, and provoke thought. Images make it possible to communicate complex information in a simple and direct way. One of the enduring images of the 1989 Tiananmen Square uprising in Bejing, China, was the photograph of a single student standing in front of a line of tanks. For many in western democratic countries, this photograph is deeply symbolic of the struggle of the pro-democracy movement in China at that moment in history. The same image likely elicits an entirely different response from Chinese leaders.

The precarious balance in the use of images is always between the message or experience the creator wishes to communicate or evoke and the interpretation of the viewer. Images are open to greater interpretation than text alone (Meyer, 1993), so the use of words in communication allows for the careful crafting of a precise message. Images can reflect the cultural tradition and biases of the creator; conversely, images are commonly interpreted through the lens of the viewer's cultural worldview. For instance, a child raised in the religious traditions of India might draw a picture of Lakshmi, the goddess of beauty and abundance. In the picture, Lakshmi appears with four arms, as she is traditionally represented in Indian art. A clinical social worker who looked at the picture without any information about the child or her cultural tradition could conclude the image was suggestive of possible sexual abuse, the four arms symbolizing unwanted touching. In this example, a single image evokes two dramatically different responses as a result of differences in cultural backgrounds and the social worker's professional training. The continuing struggle in graphical representation is the selection of images that carefully match the intended message with consideration of the anticipated audience.

Graphical Representation

Although the expression of human experience through drawings, paintings, and other media predates recorded history, the use of charts and graphs to symbolically represent quantitative information developed only in the last 400 years (Holmes, 1984). Perhaps most noteworthy is the work of René Descartes (1596–1650), whose development of the Cartesian grid laid the foundation for plotting numerical information on a grid in the form of graphs and charts. The use of graphs and charts for the expression of financial and other information was left to William Playfair (1759–1823), who is credited with the invention the line graph, the bar chart, and the pie chart. In doing so, he devised a means of making the abstract visible, as in the relationship between time and rising national debt. According to Holmes (1984), wide interest in the use of graphs in the United States did not develop until the late 1920s, concurrent with the crash of the stock market.

Prior to the advent of personal computer software for the production of charts and graphs, they were created by hand with drawing tools, a time-consuming and exacting endeavor. The ease with which charts and graphs are now produced with spreadsheet software can lead to the quick creation of graphics that are visually compelling without adequate consideration for the accuracy or the parsimony of the message they convey. Poorly designed graphs can confuse and frustrate viewers' attempts to decipher the data expressed in the graph (Henry, 1998). Conversely, when graphs are carefully planned and well designed, they reveal information to viewers. Henry (1998) argues that the visual representation of quantitative information in a well-executed graph draws on viewers' spatial intelligence and conveys information more directly than text-based material.

The question that then arises is what are the characteristics of a well-designed and useful graph. White (1984) proposes six characteristics evident in the design of a useful graph.

1. *Elegance:* The graph should express the information present in the data in a simple and direct manner. The graph displays the essence of the idea or finding present in the data.
2. *Clarity:* The meaning of the graph should be clear to the viewer. The graph should be designed to facilitate the transmission of information. The graph's title, axis labels, and legend should use unambiguous language that requires no further explanation.
3. *Ease:* A well-designed graph is easy to understand. It engages and stimulates viewers' interest. Text and graphics should be easy to read, their respective sizes balanced with each other.
4. *Pattern:* Use the same type of graph when presenting the same type of information to an audience. Once an audience understands the information contained in a particular type of graph, changes in the style or format will likely produce only confusion. Mixing bar charts and column charts without any reason directly related to the data does not enhance comprehension.
5. *Simplicity:* Design the graph to focus viewers' attention on the information evident in the data. Many software applications have tools to add visual bells and whistles to graphs, but their parsimonious application is recommended. Any element added to a graph should be used in the service of enhancing the conveyance of the intended message. Too much information on a single graph may confuse the audience. Sometimes the use of multiple simple graphs to convey elaborate information is far better than a single, visually complex graph.
6. *Validity:* The graph should accurately portray the relationships present in the original data without distortion. Distortion can occur, for instance, through the use of scales in a graph that create overly steep upward or downward slopes.

Henry (1998) emphasizes the necessity of giving primacy to the data. Comparisons are the primary means by which graphical information is understood. Therefore, viewers should be able to clearly see differences and similarities between groups as displayed in a chart. They should be able to detect trend changes in a measured behavior or attitude over time. Graphs should display the relationships that exist or do not exist between subjects or variables. Patterns and trends in the data should be emphasized in the design. Consideration must also be given to the intended audience of the graph. Viewers vary in their experience and sophistication in understanding charts and graphs. Some viewers are better prepared to appreciate complex relationships displayed in graphs, while for others, parsing complex data into two or more graphs maximizes communication.

The best graphs both answer questions for viewers and stimulate the desire to know more (Henry, 1998). The questions raised by a graph should not be related to its meaning, but instead in response to the ideas conveyed in its representation of data. Having a clear intention about the information one wishes to express with a graph facilitates the likelihood of heightened viewer response and interest. By using preliminary graphs as tools for considering what the data show, one can assist the development of a clear intention for a final version of a graph (Drew, 1985). This preliminary graphing is a thinking tool used to contemplate the relationships, or lack there of, in the data. Visual examination of the data in preliminary graphs can stimulate further ideas about the information present in the data. This visual inspection of the information can also further clarify one's intentions on how to display it for maximum information transmission to the prospective audience. This iterative process results in refining a graph's communicative effect through the creation of multiple versions. This process is facilitated by spreadsheet software, which makes possible the ready generation of multiple versions of a graph along with an enhanced capacity to edit many of the elements composing a graph.

Tools for Graphical Representation of Information

Spreadsheets

As described throughout this text, spreadsheets are robust tools for the collection and analysis of quantitative information. Commonly available spreadsheet applications such as Corel Quattro Pro, Microsoft Excel, and Lotus 1-2-3 all have graphing tools for the generation of a broad spectrum of charts and graphs. The approaches of these spreadsheets to graph production are remarkably similar. Figure 12.1 displays the basic steps in the graphing process in Microsoft Excel utilizing the Chart Wizard. The essential process is (1) select the data to be graphed, (2) choose a type of graph, (3) specify title and labels for the graph and if desired, (4) modify formatting and appearance, and select the location of the chart. Notice that in the first screen, the Chart Wizard displays icons that pictorially represent the available choices in chart type. Each of these steps are described and illustrated in the following sections. Readers unfamiliar with graphing are encouraged to review the terms in Table 12.1 to prepare themselves for the ensuing discussion. Also see the accompanying CD-ROM video animation, "Chart Wizard—Basic Steps."

Data Selection Prior to Graphing

The first step in creating a graph with a spreadsheet is to have the data arranged in a table of columns and rows. At times the data are already in a format from which they can be graphed. For instance, data on the number of people attending a weekly support group, week number, and attendance might be entered in two columns of a spreadsheet as in Table 12.2. In Figure 12.2 this data table is converted into a bar graph displaying a frequency count (attendance) over time (weeks).

Another example of creating a graph directly from unsummarized data is a scattergram. A scattergram represents the relationship between two interval or ratio level variables as single points on a two-dimensional graph. Scattergrams are useful in displaying the strength of association or correlation between two variables. The strength of the relation-

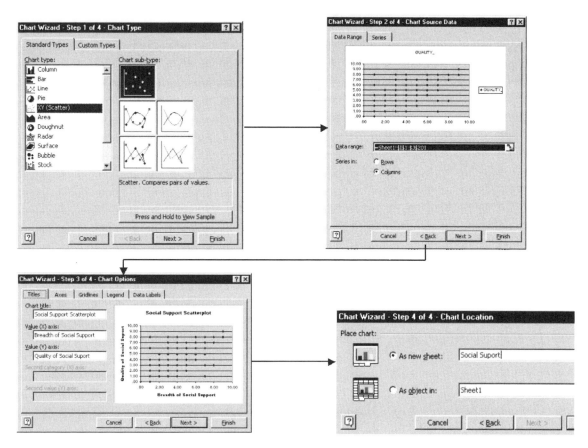

FIGURE 12.1   The Four Steps of the Microsoft Excel Chart Wizard

ship between the two variables is evidenced in how tightly the points are grouped together. Widely dispersed points on a scattergram indicate a lack of relationship between the plotted variables. In Figure 12.3, there appears to be a strong, positive relationship between Age and GAFS-M (social and occupational functioning) scores. The relationship is said to be positive as the data points move in an upward slope from left to right. A negative relationship between two variables forms a downward slope from left to right. In a negative relationship, the values of one variable increase as the values of the second variable decrease. A regression line is displayed in Figure 12.3 to emphasize the apparent linear relationship between the two variables in this hypothetical example.

Line graphs used in single system designs, as described in Chapter 10, are yet another example of graphs that require no prior summarization of data. Line graphs plot the change over time of one or more outcome measures. The use of two or more outcome measures in the same graph requires that the outcome measures have the same scale. This is necessary in order to detect differences and have a common means of comparison of the two or more measures. For instance, an agency that aids former welfare recipients in securing and holding jobs wishes to measure on a weekly basis each client's overall satisfaction with their job and the client's perception of their supervisor's supportiveness. The first measure uses a 0–100 scale to measure job satisfaction and the second measure uses a 1–10 scale to measure perceived supportiveness of a supervisor. When these two measures were plotted on the same line graph, changes in the smaller scale are dwarfed by the larger scale, despite the fact that both of them may be of equal importance in job retention. Therefore, if multiple measures are to be used in construction of a line graph for a single system design, careful consideration must be given to the selection of measures in order to make appropriate and meaningful comparisons. Figure 12.4 displays data from two self-rating measures that use the same scale (1–10) measuring anxiety and relaxation. Notice that because the measures

TABLE 12.1   Graphing Terms

Area graph	Displays one or more series of data points over a time period. By stacking data series on each other it shows the sum of the combined series over time.
Bar graph	Used to horizontally or vertically represent quantitative information on two or more categories. Usually has space between the bars.
Column graph	Used to vertically represent quantitative information on two or more categories. Usually has space between the bars. AKA bar graph.
Data series	Variables plotted in the graph.
Fever chart	Plots quantities over time as a rising and falling line.
Grid line	A line extending vertically and/or horizontally from points of measurement on the x-and/or y-axis.
Histogram	Chart used to represent a frequency distribution of interval or ratio data. The bars must be joined.
Legend	A key that indicates name and/or pattern of each data series.
Line chart	Plots trends or changes over time or frequency distributions on which the x-axis represents some quantity (e.g., age or income).
Pie chart	Displays proportions of a whole (e.g., ethnic composition of a city's population). Used with nominal level data.
Plot	The body of the graph in which the data are graphically displayed.
Scattergram	Displays the paired observations of two variables as single points on a two-dimensional graph. Used to represent the relationship between two variables.
Series	A set of data plotted on a graph.
Table	The columns and rows containing the data for the graph.
Tick mark	Short line identifying a value on a graph.
Time-series	A line graph representing the repeated measurement of some phenomenon over time.
Title	The name or heading given to a graph.
Trend	A line graph on which time is measured on the x-axis and a dependent variable is measured on the y-axis.
X-axis	The horizontal axis (abscissa) used for the independent variable.
Y-axis	The vertical axis (ordinate) used for the dependent variable.
Z-axis	The vertical axis present in three-dimensional graphs. Often indicates a frequency count.

Sources: Boyce et al., 1997; Drew & Hardman, 1985; Eddy, 1997; Holmes, 1984; Lefferts, 1981; Weinbach & Grinnell, 2001.

TABLE 12.2   Support Group Attendance Data Table

Week Number	Attendance	Week Number	Attendance
1	15	5	15
2	13	6	16
3	16	7	17
4	12	8	16

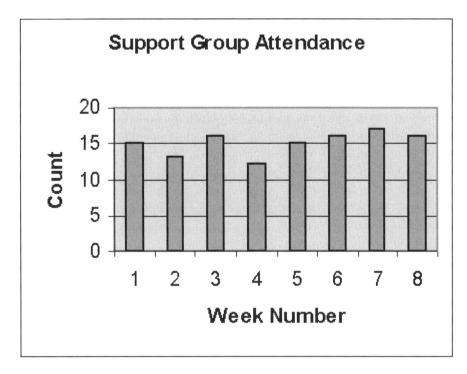

FIGURE 12.2   Bar Graph of Support Group Attendance over Time

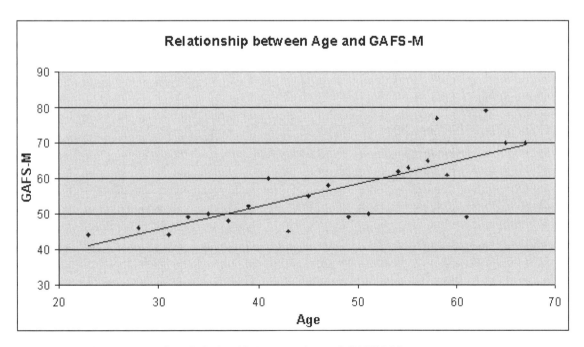

FIGURE 12.3   Scattergram of the Relationship between Age and GAFS-M Scores

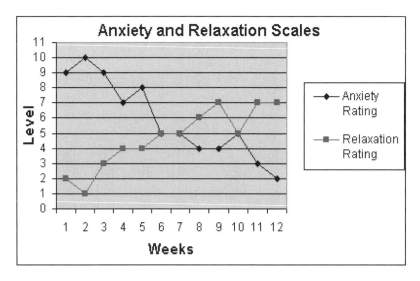

FIGURE 12.4   Single System Line Graph Plotting Anxiety and Relaxation Ratings

use the same scale, a visual comparison of the relationship between the two scales over time is possible.

In some situations it is necessary to summarize a dataset before attempting to graph the information. For example, in order to graphically depict the relative proportion of clients in an agency's different treatment programs, it is first necessary to have a frequency distribution of the number of clients in each program. Once a frequency distribution is produced (see Chapter 5 for the procedure), the data are arrayed in two columns, one column containing either a label or number representing each attribute (e.g., the different treatment programs) and a second column with a frequency count of each attribute. The summarized information in these two columns may then be graphed in a pie chart or bar graph.

A second means of summarizing two or more variables is a cross-tabulation table. The use of a cross-tabulation table makes possible the reduction of complex information from two or more variables into a table displaying summary information on the variables. Depending on the purpose of the table, this summary information in the cells could include frequency count, average, standard deviation, or percentage frequency. Table 12.3 reports,

TABLE 12.3   Degree of Medication Compliance across Treatment Groups

Medication Compliance	Treatment Group		Grand Total
	.00	*1.00*	
.00	3.41%	4.63%	4.08%
1.00	5.68%	0.93%	3.06%
2.00	6.82%	2.78%	4.59%
3.00	13.64%	0.93%	6.63%
4.00	7.95%	5.56%	6.63%
5.00	5.68%	12.04%	9.18%
6.00	11.36%	11.11%	11.22%
7.00	13.64%	11.11%	12.24%
8.00	13.64%	25.00%	19.90%
9.00	18.18%	25.93%	22.45%
Grand Total	100.00%	100.00%	100.00%

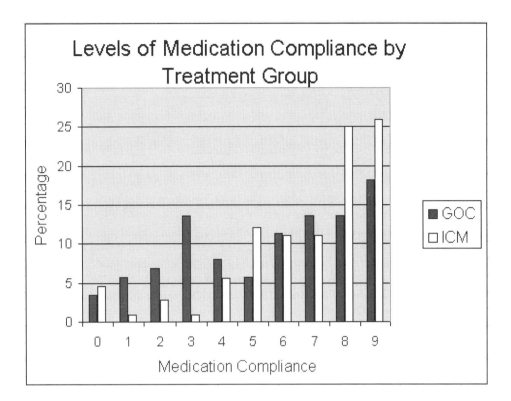

FIGURE 12.5   Bar Graph Produced from Cross-Tabulation Table 12.3

by percentage, the level of medication compliance for clients in two treatment groups: general outpatient care (GOC) and intensive case management (ICM). The data contained in Table 12.3 was compiled with a cross-tabulation procedure. Figure 12.5 displays the first three columns of Table 12.3 in a bar graph. The resultant bar graph enables the viewer to readily discern the fact that medication compliance was higher for the ICM group, while noncompliance was higher for the GOC group. Another way to think about Figure 12.5 is that it represents the summary of information contained in 196 cases across two variables: treatment group and level of medication compliance. Moreover, for most viewers the relationship apparent in the bar graph is likely much more quickly understood than through examination of Table 12.3.

In summary, the first step in creating a graph with a spreadsheet is compiling the data intended for graphing into columns representing the variables and rows representing the cases. Data are either entered directly or summarized with a frequency distribution or cross-tabulation table. To graph these data, select the columns and rows containing the information. Microsoft Excel and other spreadsheets have a toolbar icon for graphs, which when clicked initiate graph creation procedures. Selecting data and clicking the graph icon in Microsoft Excel activates a Chart Wizard. The Chart Wizard walks the users through the four steps in creating a graph: (1) specification of chart type, (2) designation of the location of the data source for the graph, (3) selection of options for the appearance of the graph, and (4) location of the final chart. The location options are in the spreadsheet or on a new worksheet (see Figure 12.1, p. 163). This Chart Wizard readily transforms data in the spreadsheet into its corresponding graphical representation.

Matching Data to Type of Graph

The next consideration is what type of graph to use with what type of data and for what purpose. The proper match between the purpose of the graph, the type of graph, and the type of data enhances the capacity of a visual representation to transmit information. Graphs are used to describe data and as analytic tools for understanding the complex relationships intrinsic to some data. We will return to the use of graphs as analytic tools later and retain our present focus on graphs as tools to visually describe data. Graphs work best as descriptive tools when they are selected with consideration to the type of data they are to describe. For instance, a pie chart is a good choice for nominal data to illustrate the relative proportions of parts of a whole. Conversely, a pie chart is an inappropriate choice to display the relationship between two continuous (interval or ratio) variables such as are represented with a scattergram in Figure 12.3 (p. 165). The question that now arises for our consideration is what types of graphs work best with what types of data?

Pie Charts and Bar Graphs. Henry (1998) suggests that pie charts and bar graphs are frequently used in descriptive displays that represent parts of a whole. These two graphics are commonly employed to illustrate the proportions of a budget allocated to different spending categories, the relative frequency of individuals of different ethnic groups being served by an agency, or the percentage of clients served by distinct treatment programs in an agency. However, research has shown that viewers are able to derive information from bar graphs faster and with greater accuracy than from pie charts (Cleveland & McGill, 1984; Simkin & Hastie, 1987). Henry recommends that a pie chart is appropriate only for presenting the relationship of parts to a whole when there are a limited number of categories or attributes (parts) in a variable and their relative proportions are distinct. In other words, it is difficult in a pie chart to visually distinguish between three categories of 36 percent, 34 percent, and 30 percent. One of the graphical drawbacks of the use of graphing tools in spreadsheets is they offer multiple possible configurations and enhancements to pie charts that can ultimately result in distorted comprehension. Henry contends that effects such as pseudo 3-D, contrasting shading, the use of legends, and arbitrary pullout (slice of the pie set apart) all represent possible impediments to comprehension and should therefore be avoided in pie chart production.

The pie chart in Figure 12.6 conforms to Henry's guidelines. It displays budgetary information drawn from Table 12.4. This pie chart illustrates the relative proportions of non-personnel expenses allocated to expenditure categories. Because the percentage of non-personnel expenses are shown, but not the actual dollar amounts for the categories, it would be necessary to provide an accompanying table with those figures. In this case, the pie chart proportionally communicates the expenditure categories where dollars will be spent and raises the question of how much will be spent. This pie chart is intended to capture the viewers' attention, raise the question of how much will be spent, and draw their attention to the table containing the actual amounts.

The second and more highly recommended means to visually describe data about parts of a whole is the bar graph. The bars of bar graphs are oriented either horizontally or vertically, in which case they are sometimes referred to as column graphs. Henry (1998) points out that an important advantage of using horizontally arranged bars is that if labels (values or names) are attached to the bars, they are easier to read than labels set at the base of columns. Moreover, attaching values to bars improves the accuracy with which viewers comprehend the graph (Jarvenpaa & Dickson, 1988). Figure 12.7 illustrates the use of a horizontally oriented bar graph with attached values. This graph is an alternative representation of the same data displayed in the pie chart in Figure 12.6. The vertical grid lines offer a visual cue to assist in judging the relative lengths of the bars. The use of grid lines is especially important if values are not attached to the ends of the bars. The bars in Figure 12.7 are arranged in descending order in order to display the relative magnitude of the nonpersonnel expenditures. The arrangement of the bars in ascending or descending order is achieved by sorting the data in the spreadsheet. The choice of ascending or descending order is a matter of the message the graph is intended to convey. Remember that viewers read from top to bottom, so it is important to consider which category the viewer will see first when deciding whether to use ascending or descending order. In the example in Figure 12.7, the bar graph clearly displays the emphasis placed on equipment expenditures in the budget.

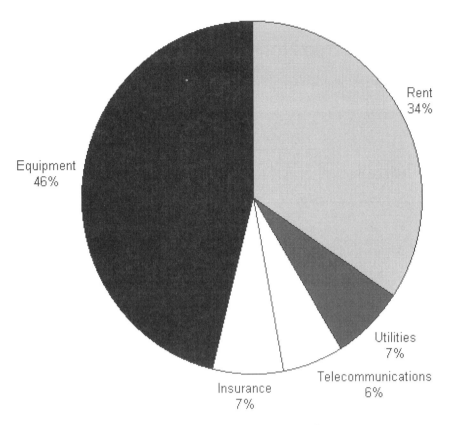

Projected Non-personnel Expenses for 2005

Rent
34%

Utilities
7%

Telecommunications
6%

Insurance
7%

Equipment
46%

FIGURE 12.6   A Pie Chart of Budgetary Expenditures by Category

TABLE 12.4   A Spreadsheet Budget

	A	B	C	D	E	F
1	**Maximum Mental Health—Budget for 2005**					
2						
3	**Income**	**Actual for 2004**	**Projected for 2005**	**Allocated for 2005**	**Difference**	**Percent**
4	State Contracts	500,000	525,000	510,000	15,000	2.94%
5	Federal Grants	150,000	175,000	155,000	20,000	12.90%
6	Fees	300,000	325,000	305,000	20,000	6.56%
7	Fund Raising	100,000	120,000	115,000	5,000	4.35%
8	**Total**	1,050,000	1,145,000	1,085,000	60,000	5.53%
9						
10	**Expenses**					
11	Personnel	850,000	884,000	875,000	9,000	1.03%
12	Rent	60,000	62,400	62,400	0	0.00%
13	Utilities	12,000	12,480	12,000	480	4.00%
14	Telecommunications	10,000	10,400	12,000	−1,600	−13.33%
15	Insurance	12,000	12,480	12,480	0	0.00%
16	Equipment	80,000	83,200	90,000	−6,800	−7.56%
17	**Total**	1,024,000	1,064,960	1,063,880	1,080	0
18						
19	**Grand Total**	**26,000**	**80,040**	**21,120**	**58,920**	

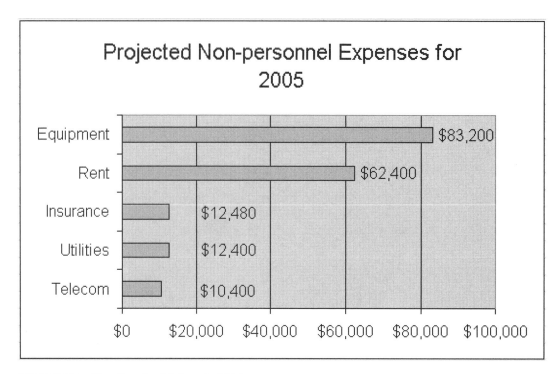

FIGURE 12.7   Bar Graph with Attached Values

Line graphs. In its most basic form, a line graph depicts the relationship between two continuous (interval or ratio level) variables with a line crossing a plane created by the x- and y-axes. Variants of line graphs include fever charts, trend lines, and time-series graphs. Line graphs are most frequently used as either a frequency distribution or display change in a dependent variable over time (Lefferts, 1981).

A line graph used as a frequency distribution displays the shape of the distribution of that which is being counted across a range of values. Frequency distribution graphs also are called frequency polygons (Weinbach & Grinnell, 2001). Figure 12.8 is a frequency distribution of GAFS-M scores for 196 severely and persistently mentally ill outpatients (Patterson & Lee, 1995). Frequency distribution graphs are important for both describing the relative frequency of values in a variable and as an analytic tool in understanding and raising questions about the variable. For instance, the values in Figure 12.8 are not distributed in a normal distribution. Instead, the three major peaks in the frequency distribution occur at 10-point intervals (40, 50, 60), while the remaining minor peaks are generally at five-point intervals. Examination of this frequency distribution suggests that the therapists who provided these ratings of social and occupational function either did not or could not differentiate on this 0–100-point scale at increments less than five points. Instead, they tended to use five-point increments in rating social and occupational functioning. Applications of frequency distribution graphs in social service settings include examination of lengths of treatment of service recipients, family income of clients, age of program participants, lengths of stay in residential care, and so on. Frequency distribution graphs are particularly useful in visually describing some client characteristics (age, income) and service use indicators (number of services, length of stay, cost of treatment).

A second type of line graph displays changes in a dependent variable over time. For the purposes of this discussion, a dependent variable is an event, behavior, or indicator that is repeatedly measured over time, such as income, customer satisfaction, or rate of unemployment. This type of line graph often depicts trends in the dependent variable over time, such as declines in rates of juvenile violence or increases in childhood poverty rates. The line chart in Figure 12.4 (p. 166) displays the relationship between two variables (anxiety

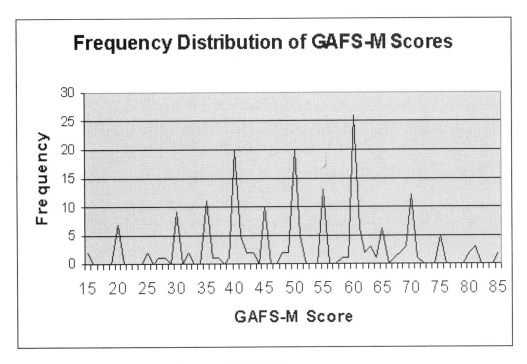

FIGURE 12.8   Frequency Distribution of GAFS-M Scores

and relaxation levels) over a 12-week period. Illustrating the relationship between two or more dependent variables for the purpose of comparison is a second function of line charts. Almost all types of spreadsheets allow for the display of multiple dependent variables in a line chart. However, as with many software features, just because it is possible to apply it to data does not necessarily mean the intended message of the graph is served by plotting multiple dependent variables on the same line graph. For example, Figure 12.9 contains a line graph labeled "Group Cohesion—All Students" that depicts the ratings from eight students of group cohesion for each group session over the life of the group. The multiple dependent variables (students' cohesion ratings) were graphed with the intent of displaying the complexity of group process. The graph in Figure 12.9 requires the viewer to expend time and energy to appreciate its meaning. Readers are cautioned to carefully consider the intended message and purpose of a line graph before creating a graph with more than three dependent variables. Despite this cautionary note, line graphs, particularly as applied in single system evaluation, remain an important graphing tool for data description and analysis.

Area Graphs.   Area graphs display data from one or more variables over time. The filled portion of the graph depicts the relative contribution to the whole of each variable. Area graphs are particularly useful in showing a comparison of variation over time in the proportion of the sum of a phenomenon accounted for by its parts. For instance, Figure 12.10 displays six months of nonpersonnel expenditures for Maximum Mental Health. Each section of the graph represents a budgetary cost category. Notice how declines in equipment expenditures impact the overall budget, while costs in the other categories remain relatively stable. This stability of nonequipment costs over time is evidenced by the lack of changes in the size of the areas of each cost category. This graph shows both the relationship of each cost category to the whole and to the other categories over time. Area graphs are essentially a multivariate form of the line graph. They are applicable for displaying data collected over time for categories of fiscal information, for population or demographic groups, or for comparing groups on outcome measures.

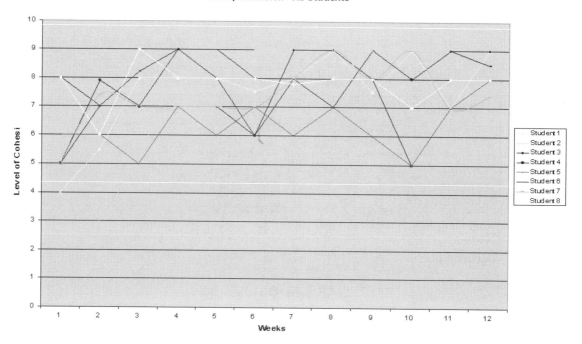

FIGURE 12.9   An Example of Too Many Dependent Variables (Students) Used in a Line Graph

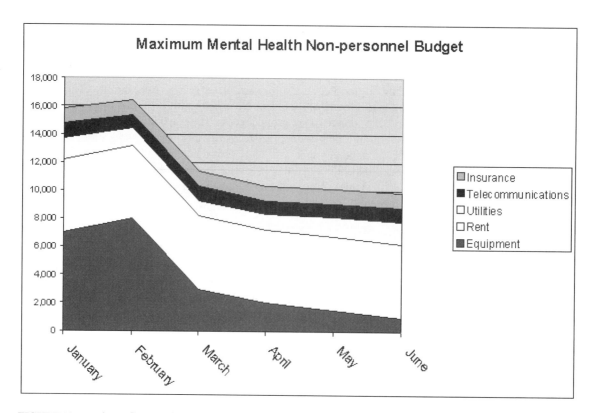

FIGURE 12.10   Area Graph of Nonpersonnel Budget Expenditures

3-D Area Graphs.   Three-dimensional graphs add depth and dimension to the display of variables or subjects, allowing for ready visual comparison and contrast. The Chart Wizard in Microsoft Excel has the option of creating a 3-D area graph. Sanders and Patterson (2003) utilized this graphing option in their Par-Fit Excel template to illustrate the goodness of fit between family members for the purpose of custody evaluation. A psychologist or clinical social worker rates each family member across eight dimensions of psychological and interpersonal functioning. These ratings are transformed into a 3-D area graph that allows for the examination of the areas of alignment or fit between parents and children in a family. These graphs have been employed in custody hearings as a means to illustrate to the court the areas of function and dysfunction between parents and children involved in custody battles. Figure 12.11 uses a 3-D area graph to illustrate the goodness-of-fit in a hypothetical family.

Surface Plots.   In Chapter 10 we demonstrated the use of surface plots in the evaluation of groups using single system design procedures. Surface plots make possible representation of multivariate information in a three-dimensional graph. Surface plots are particularly well suited to illustrate the change in some indicator, such as outcome measure or frequency counts over time across subjects (individuals, groups, communities), treatment conditions, or settings. Stated another way, surface plots are useful in displaying the change dynamics of a system of interest. For instance, Figures 12.12 and 12.13 use data drawn from the 1988 National Survey of Families and Households to provide alternative views of the change

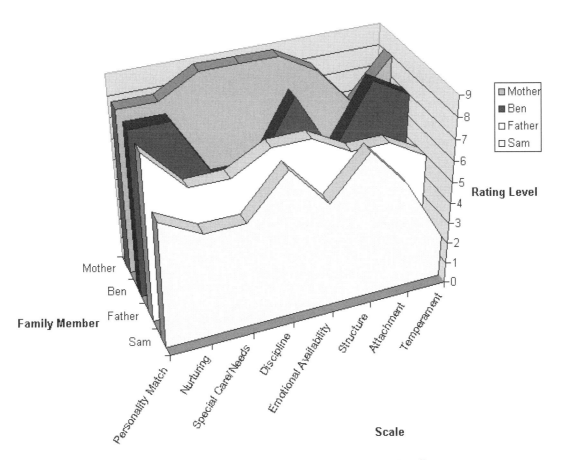

FIGURE 12.11   3-D Area Graph Used to Evaluate the Goodness of Fit in a Family

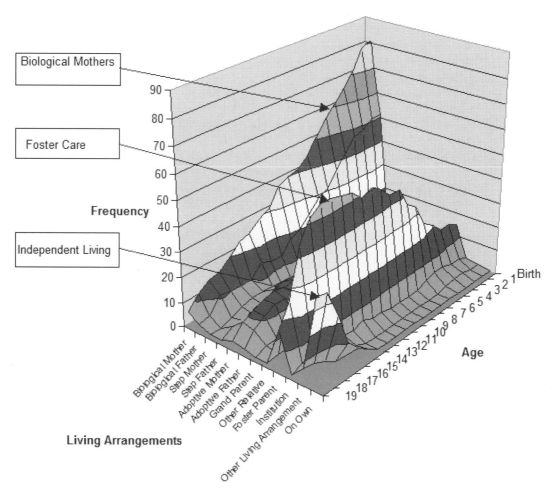

FIGURE 12.12   Childhood Living Arrangements Over Time of Children Who Experienced
Foster Care—Diagonal View

over time in the living arrangements of 101 individuals who were in foster care before age 19 (Patterson, Post, & Buehler, 1999). The topography or shape of this surface plot is produced by the spreadsheet graphing software displaying time, expressed as "Age" on the horizontal x-axis, the categorical variable "Living Arrangement" on the horizontal z-axis, and the "Frequency" count, a continuous variable, is plotted on the y-axis, producing the resultant surface (Yu & Behrens, 1995).

The alternative views or perspectives of the foster care surface plot displayed in Figures 12.12 and 12.13 were produced by the rotation of a surface plot. This rotation allows for consideration of the contours of the information represented in it from multiple perspectives. Spreadsheets commonly have graphing functions that enable the user to rotate the orientation of the surface plot. Clicking on a corner of the surface plot and dragging it in a desired direction produces a different orientation of the image. Alternatively, in Microsoft Excel, surface plots may also be rotated by specifying degrees of horizontal and vertical rotation in a 3-D view dialog box that is available when the three-dimensional graph is selected. This capacity to manipulate graphic objects enables the exploration of the data representation from multiple perspectives.

Surface plots commonly have a grid, enabling viewers to identify points of intersection between variables. Grids also assist in the perception of the variability of the variable across the duration or range of its measurement. Each point on the grid represents three val-

Foster Care Group - Living Arrangements Over Time

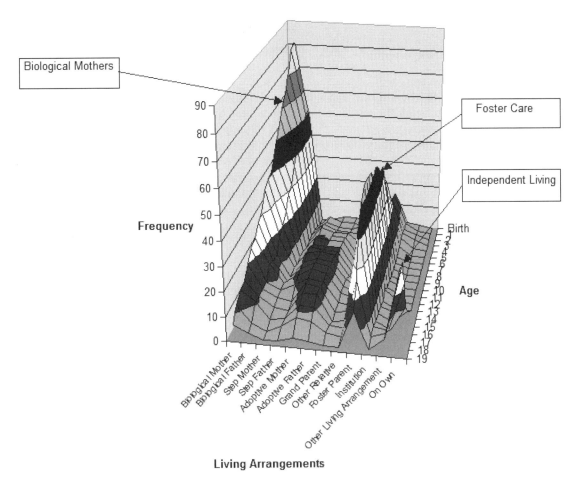

FIGURE 12.13   Childhood Living Arrangements over Time of Children Who Experienced Foster Care—Longitudinal View

ues, for example, age, living arrangement, and a frequency count. Surface plots also employ variation in coloring or shading of gray to represent relative height on the y-axis. The use of coloring or gray shading offers a visual cue by which the viewer can interpret the information contained in the surface plot.

In summary, the graphs reviewed here represent the major types of charts commonly found in the social service literature. Moreover, social service agency audiences such as clients, contributors, and board members are likely to be familiar with many of these types of graphs through newspapers, magazines, the Web, and television. These basic types of graphs have become part of a common visual vocabulary for most literate people in the developed world. This visual familiarity aids comprehension of the intended message of these basic graph types. These graphs do not, however, represent the full range of graph types available in spreadsheets. A partial list of additional choices available in most spreadsheets includes doughnut, radar, surface, bubble, and stock charts. The drawback to using any of these options is that they may be unfamiliar to the intended audience and therefore produce confusion as opposed to communicating a clear message. Henry (1998) urges careful consideration of the ability of an audience to retrieve the meaning of a graph type. This caution extends to selection of a graph type. The choice of an unfamiliar graph is at times justified by its capacity to display a particular type of data or the clarity with which it depicts a set of relationships in the data. The use of a commonly unfamiliar type of graph with a suitable audience should be supplemented by explanatory text. If used in a presentation, accompanying oral explanation will aid the audience in grasping the graph's meaning.

Enhancing Graphs

Clear communication of an intended message with a graph requires not only preparation of the data in a spreadsheet and selection of an appropriate type of graph, but also careful choices regarding its augmentation. Each of the graphs presented in this chapter contain the basic graphic representation of the data: a title, labels for the axes when necessary, numerical scales or category names on the axes, and in some cases legends to identify components of the graph. Beyond the graph itself, each of these components conveys information that, when appropriately used, informs viewers and clarifies the intended message of the graph.

The specific procedures for creating and editing the components of a graph vary among spreadsheet publishers, though the steps are largely analogous (Patterson, 2000). Microsoft Excel offers a Chart Wizard for graph production. The Chart Wizard has four steps; to review, they are (1) selection of chart type, (2) specification of source data, (3) choosing chart options, and (4) designation of the completed chart's location in the spreadsheet. The choices in the third step, choosing chart options, include titles, axes, gridlines, legends, data labels, and data tables to be specified. Review Figure 12.1 (p. 163). Chart modification options are selected by clicking the tabs at the top of the window.

Once a chart is created, modifications to the chart are made by clicking on the component of the chart intended for alteration. For instance, Excel charts are created with a gray background by default. Some agencies and institutions require the use of only black and white for charts and graphs. To modify the chart area from gray to white, one would simply double click on the chart area. This produces a dialog window entitled Format Plot Area, which offers multiple color choices for the chart area. Selecting white for the chart (plot) area removes the gray background and substitutes a white background.

To reiterate, once a graph is produced with the Chart Wizard, modifications to the chart can be made by clicking any component of the graph. A dialog window will appear from which modification to the "clicked on" component of the chart can be made.

Alternatively, simply clicking once on the chart alters the menu bar to include a Chart option. Under this menu option, each of the steps in the Chart Wizard are available so decisions made in the original graph production with the Chart Wizard can be revisited. Also see the accompanying CD-ROM video animation: "Chart Modification."

The judicious application of the graph component application tools described above facilitates the conveyance of the graph's intended message. Listed here are several guiding principles for the labeling and enhancement of graphs.

1. Titles should clearly describe what the graph displays so the viewer knows what it represents (Drew & Hardman, 1985; Lefferts, 1981).
2. The label of each axis should be specific and clear. The unit of measurement of each axis should be identified (APA, 1994). "Place the axis label parallel to the proper axes. Do not stack letters so that the label reads vertically" (APA, 1994, p. 158).
3. Numbers for the grid points on both axes should be horizontal.
4. Make sure that the scales used on the x- and y-axes on line graphs do not distort the data by creating inappropriately steep slopes.
5. Use a legend to identify symbols used in graphs. The letters in a legend should be of the same font and size of letters used in the graph. Legends can distract the viewer by forcing them to look back and forth between the graph and the legend. Consider using labels with the graph to identify data.

In summary, the enhancement of graphs with careful choices regarding components improves the likelihood that viewers will comprehend their intended meaning. Spreadsheets have an array of options for modification and enhancement of graphs. These tools enable the user to carefully format graphs so the information contained in the data is clearly expressed. The temptation for a user learning the graph enhancement tools is to add extraneous information and formatting to the graph that can distract viewers' attention away from the core message of the graph. Henry (1998) emphasizes the importance, while developing a graph, of continually asking, "What is the purpose of this graph?" (p. 554). Consideration of this question can both guide the application of enhancements to a graph and further improve its clarity.

Spreadsheet Drawing Tools

Spreadsheets commonly have drawing tools, which are a set of graphic functions that can either be used for the augmentation of charts or for the creation of original graphics such as flowcharts, organizational charts, and, as we will demonstrate, graphics for the description and representation of families and social systems. These drawing tools are applicable in spreadsheet data analysis both for the informational enhancement of graphs presenting quantitative information and for the visual representation of qualitative information, such as the creation of a genogram depicting a family across generations. These drawing tools are activated in Excel by selecting View, Toolbars, Drawing from the menu bar. Doing this places a Drawing Tools menu bar at the bottom of the worksheet. Figure 12.14 shows the Drawing Tools menu bar. Described here are the uses of spreadsheet drawing tools for the creation of ecomaps and genograms. In each of the figures in this section, the gridlines of the spreadsheets have been turned off in order to enhance the visual representation of the information. Gridlines are turned off in Excel by selecting from the menu bar Tools, Options, View, Windows Options, and then deselecting Gridlines. Also see the accompanying CD-ROM video animation: "Drawing Tools—Eco Maps."

Ecomaps

A commonly used graphic tool in social service practice is the ecomap (Mattaini, 1993). Hartman (1978) described the ecomap as a tool to facilitate a worker's thinking about issues of assessment and intervention with cases. An ecomap graphically represents a client's relationships with individuals, family, friends, organizations, and institutions. The relative strength and nature of these relationships or interactions are depicted with choices of types of lines and their relative thickness. Colored lines may be used to add graphic information to the ecomap. Mattani (1993) suggests red lines to represent negative relationships and black lines for positive relationships.

Ecomaps can be developed with the drawing tools in most spreadsheets. Figure 12.15 displays ecomap symbols (Mattaini, 1993) produced with the drawing tools in Excel. Mattaini reports that the ecomap is useful for intakes and crisis situations to produce a quick graphical representation of a client's psychosocial environment. The basic graphical objects of the ecomap are circles, text boxes, and bi-directional arrows. Notice at the bottom of Figure 12.15, the drawing tools of Excel appear in the toolbar at the bottom of the screen. To use any of these drawing tools, click the tool, then click the location on the spreadsheet it will appear. Drag the resulting object to a desired size and shape (Gilgen, 1997). Once in place, modifications are made to the object by right clicking it. This produces a dialog window with a number of options including Cut, Copy, Paste, Order, and Format Auto-Shape. The "Order" option is useful when objects are arranged on top of one another, as in the Family or Household circle in Figure 12.15. The order of the larger circle was changed from

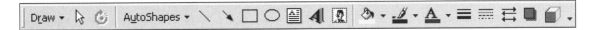

FIGURE 12.14   Microsoft Excel Drawing Tools Menu Bar

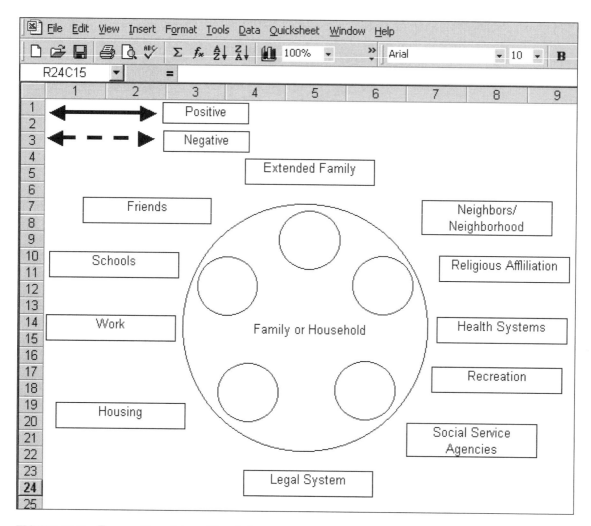

FIGURE 12.15   Ecomap Template and Symbols

front to back, to make the smaller circles visible. In other words, the smaller circles now sit on top of the larger circle. The Format Auto-Shape option in the dialog window produces another dialog window in which changes to color, size, and line characteristics are made.

The ecomap template in Figure 12.15 contains multiple copies of the same text box. This uniformity of size and shape is achieved by creating one box with the desired dimensions, which is then copied. Once copied, repeat the paste command until the requisite number of boxes is produced. Use clicking and dragging to position the new objects. See also the accompanying CD-ROM video animation: "EcoMap Creation."

After producing an ecomap template, save a backup copy that will not be used. The ecomap can either be printed and used with clients or completed within the spreadsheet. With each new client, open the template file and immediately use the Save As command to save the new version with some identifier of the client. Use of the spreadsheet version allows for rearranging objects and the addition or subtraction of family members, organizations, social constellations, or institutions. Moreover, if new ecomaps are completed over time, discussion of changes between ecomaps can provide evidence of change (Mattaini, 1993).

Figure 12.16 shows an ecomap produced from the ecomap template. Extraneous social connections were removed from the template in order to produce an ecomap that clearly depicts sources of support and conflict present in the client's life at this time. Note the lines indicating the client reports negativity toward the husband, but also is aware of his

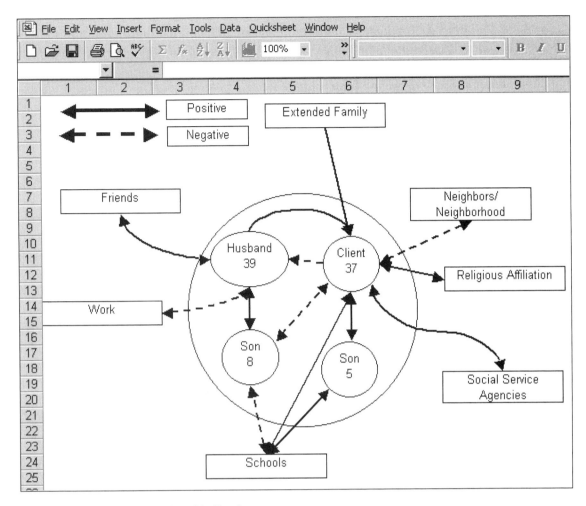

FIGURE 12.16   Ecomap Developed in Excel

positive support. The line from friends to the client runs through the husband, reflecting his mediation of contact with friends. What else is evident in this ecomap about the client's other relationships? Note that the size of the line indicates the strength of the relationship.

Genograms

Genograms are a graphic tool used in social work, medicine, and other applied health sciences to create an intergenerational picture of family relationships (Mattaini, 1993; McGoldrick & Gerson, 1985). They are commonly used to represent family functioning and to detect intergenerational patterns in biopsychosocial processes. Figure 12.17 is an Excel screen image in which the commonly agreed-on symbols of genograms have been created with the application's drawing tools. The triangle was created with a drawing tool called Basic Shapes, which is found under Auto-Shapes in the Drawing Tools menu bar.

Once a set of genogram symbols are created and saved in a file as a template, the creation of a genogram in a spreadsheet becomes a matter of copying and pasting the symbols into a new worksheet in the genogram spreadsheet. To copy a genogram symbol in a spreadsheet, select the range of cells beneath the symbol, then click Copy under Edit in the menu bar. Figure 12.18 displays a genogram of an extended family that was created as part of a forensic social work investigation. As genograms are created in a genogram spreadsheet, each family's genogram can be labeled within the spreadsheet on a worksheet tab at the bottom of the spreadsheet. Double clicking on a worksheet tab highlights it and allows one to

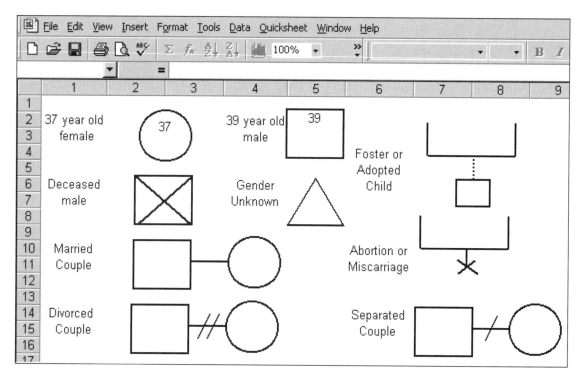

FIGURE 12.17   Genogram Symbols Created in Excel

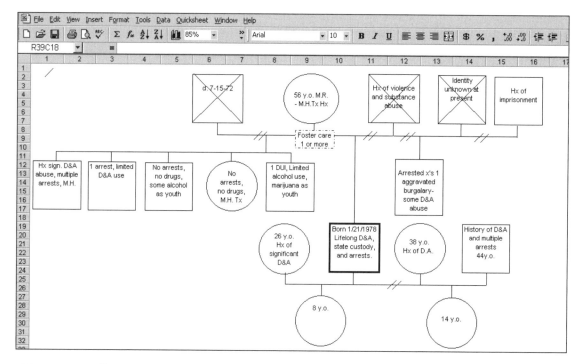

FIGURE 12.18   Genogram of Forensic Social Work Case Created in Excel

type in a unique label for each tab. As a result, one can create a spreadsheet workbook containing the genogram symbols on one worksheet and then separate worksheets and genograms for each family in one's caseload. Also see the accompanying CD-ROM video animation: "Genogram Construction."

Summary

This chapter describes the role of visual representation in the presentation of practice information. The core message of the chapter is that social service workers can now employ the multiple graphics tools available in spreadsheets to describe, analyze, and communicate practice information. In this chapter, consideration is given to the balance between the intended message of a graphical representation and the anticipated audience of viewers. The characteristics of well-designed and useful graphs are presented. The use of spreadsheets for graphical representation of information is described. Also discussed are the topics of selection of data prior to graphing, matching data to type of graph, the enhancement of graphs, and their subsequent export to other documents. The application of spreadsheet graphics tools for the creation of ecomaps and genograms are reviewed here.

REVIEW QUESTIONS

1. Briefly describe the reasons for the historical constraints on the use of graphics in social service practice and the noteworthy exceptions. What are some of the potential applications of graphics in social service practice?

2. Briefly describe the "precarious balance" inherent in the use of images.

3. Briefly list and describe the characteristics evident in the design of a useful graph.

4. What is the role and result of a graph designer's intention in the creation of a graph?

5. What are the four basic steps in producing a graph with a spreadsheet?

6. Why is it important to use measures that use the same scale, for example 1–10, when constructing a line graph displaying multiple measures?

7. What is the importance of data summarization in the creation of graphs?

8. Briefly discuss the relative advantages of using bar charts instead of pie charts to visually describe data about parts of a whole.

9. Describe the basic steps in creating a graph in a spreadsheet.

10. List five guiding principles for labeling and enhancing graphs.

11. What are spreadsheet drawing tools and how are they used?

12. What are ecomaps and how are they used?

13. What are genograms and how are they used?

GLOSSARY

absolute percentage   The actual percentage of times that an observation within a particular value occurs in the distribution.

alpha level   An estimate of making a Type I error and rejecting a null hypothesis of no difference that is actually true. The alpha level is selected as the "significance level" for the test statistic.

alternative (research) hypothesis   The alternative hypothesis states that there is a difference or relationship between the variables x and y.

analysis of variance (ANOVA)   Used to test hypotheses about differences between two or more means.

attribute   A quality, property, or characteristic of something or somebody. The attributes of a variable are said to be exhaustive if they include all the possible responses, conditions, or categories.

Auto filter   A tool used in detecting data problems, it displays in the dropdown boxes of each variable all the attributes or values found in the data of each variable. It displays only those cases that have that particular invalid code in a particular variable and can also be used to identify values outside of the expected range. The tool allows one to select a value or word in a specified column and filter the dataset for only cases containing that value or label, the filtering criteria. The filtered dataset displays only the rows that meet the specified criteria.

Bartlett's Test   Used to test if k samples have equal variances. The Bartlett test can be used to verify that assumption.

bell curve   A normal curve of distribution, a unimodal curve, or a symmetrical curve. A normal distribution is visually represented as a bell-shaped curve that is symmetrical on both sides of the mean or average score.

bimodal   Wherever two scores occur most often within a group of scores.

bit   The presence or absence of an electronic pulse, a magnetized spot on a disk or hard drive, or a microscopic pit on the plastic-coated aluminum disk of a CD-ROM.

bivariate regression   A two-variable regression that is concerned with measuring the association between two variables: a dependent variable and an independent variable.

bivariate statistics   Used to describe the relationship between two variables and attempt to ascertain the strength of association between two variables.

central tendency of a distribution of values   The point in a distribution of scores that corresponds to the typical score in the distribution.

chi-square (test of independence)   A nonparametric analysis test of statistical significance for bivariate data that is in a tabular form such as cross-tabs or cross-break tabulation. Chi-square is used as a test of independence of two variables and is also used as a goodness of fit test. Sample data is not required to be normally distributed, but it is assumed the variable is normally distributed in the population from which the sample is drawn. The chi-square test has the following requirements: the sample must be randomly drawn from the population, data must be reported in raw frequencies, measured variables must be independent, and values or categories on independent and dependent variables must be mutually exclusive and exhaustive. The test may be converted to one of a number of similar measures of association.

codebook   A document of one or more pages containing information about each variable, including a short form of each variables' name; a longer, more descriptive variable name; each question or instrument item; and each category or label in the variable with its respective numerical value.

comment window   A window into which information pertaining to a cell in a spreadsheet is entered. Comment windows can be created for each variable containing all the codebook information germane to the variable.

confidence interval   The value that, when added to the sample mean and subtracted from the sample mean, yields a confidence level for the population mean.

confidence level   Represents the level or degree to which the evaluator or researcher is confident in or certain of a prediction. If an alpha level of .05 is selected, and the statistical result is found to be significant, then the alpha of .05 may be subtracted from 1.00 and multiplied by 100 to derive the confidence level of 95% confident.

contingency cleaning   A data cleaning procedure that looks for logical inconsistencies or impossibilities between two variables.

correlation   A measure of association. Both Pearson's r and R^2 are measures of association.

count of scores   The frequency or number of scores in the distribution of scores.

cumulative frequency Based on summing the frequencies observed for each value, or for each class interval in a frequency distribution, or the total of frequencies up to and including a specified value or interval.

cumulative percentage Based on summing the percentage observed for each value, or for each class interval, in a frequency distribution.

data Factual information encoded into a form allowing for transmission and processing.

data coding The process of organizing data through the creation and assignment of numerical values for nominal data and ordinal data.

data cleaning A precursor of data analysis intended to detect and eliminate errors made during data entry.

database A means to store information, like an electronic filing system (Margolis, 1996). Beyond information storage, most databases provide options for summarizing data in reports, basic data analysis, sorting data on specified parameters, and finding specific information. Databases store information in one or more tables. Each table is composed of fields and records.

downloading The term given to the process of copying data to a personal computer from a network file server or from a computer on the Web (a web server).

degrees of freedom (*df*) The number of values free to vary when computing a statistic. Degrees generally tell us how much data was used to calculate a statistic, and this value is usually one less than the number of variables.

descriptive statistics Procedures that summarize data through summary measures, organization of data, and graphical representation. Descriptive statistics are used only to describe quantitative information and are not concerned with making inferences about a population derived from information for a representative sample of the population.

drilling down A means of determining the frequency count for any cell in a pivot table. It allows one to look beneath the values on the surface of the pivot table to see and conduct subgroup analysis of the underlying data. Outlier values can readily be found. The size of subgroups can be determined. Drilling down is also used in server-based technologies to differentiate layers of data.

Duncan's Test (or Duncan's Multiple Range Test) Performed after an ANOVA (Analysis of Variance) has been conducted, to determine which group means are significantly different from one another (Black, 1999).

effect size ("d") An estimation of the difference between an average subject in a sample who received an intervention and an average subject in a sample who did not receive the intervention, or the mean difference between groups in standard score form. An effect size may be thought of as the ratio of the difference between the means to the standard deviation.

empirical probability distribution of obtaining a result This is a construct of the range of all possible probabilities and outcomes.

expected frequencies The frequencies that would be predicted in a chi-square tabulation, if the marginal total of frequencies is known and the variables being tested are assumed to be independent.

filter A criterion or set of criteria that is applied to a dataset in order to select a subset of the dataset.

flat file The resulting file when a data query is run that could be imported into a spreadsheet for an analysis.

formulas Calculations performed as a means through which data in a spreadsheet is analyzed.

frequency The number of times that an observation or score occurred with a category of values.

frequency distribution A distribution that counts the number of scores or observations in each category of values.

frequency polygram A histogram, or a graphical representation of a distribution.

function "A special prewritten formula that provides a shortcut for commonly used calculations" (Parsons, Oja, & Auer, 1995, p. 32).

Gaussian distribution The range of normal distributions possible for an infinite number of samples drawn from a population.

goodness-of-fit test Checks on whether all such data are reasonable or highly unlikely, given an assumed distribution model.

homogeneity of variance Equal variances across samples.

hypothesis A statement that is testable regarding the relationship between or among variables that a researcher intends to study.

IF function A logical test that evaluates whether a condition is true, in which case it returns one value; if the condition is false, it returns another value.

interval level data Variables are rank ordered and the distance between attributes of interval variables are equally spaced and constant. There is a known distance between attributes.

intranet　A network internal to an organization or company that uses Internet software to share information on internal web servers.

kurtosis　A measure of the peakedness or flatness of a distribution of scores. Positive kurtosis represents a relatively peaked distribution. Negative kurtosis represents a relatively flat distribution. Normal bell-shaped distributions of scores produce a kurtosis statistic of about zero.

labels　Explanatory text, such as the name of a variable, that appears at the top of a column and identifies the information contained in the column.

leptokurtic distribution　A more positive value indicates the possibility of a distribution that is too tall.

Levine's Test　Used to test if k samples have equal variances. The Levine test can be used to verify the assumption that variances are equal across groups or samples.

listwise deletion　A procedure that removes all cases with missing data from variables used in a particular analysis.

maximum score　The largest score in the distribution of scores.

mean　The average value obtained by adding the values of all cases or observations within the group and dividing this total by the number of cases or observations. The mean, considered the most powerful measure of central tendency, is used most commonly for interval scale data.

mean substitution　A procedure that uses the mean or average value of the variable in place of the missing data in the variable.

measure of central tendency　Attempts to capture the value within a group of numbers that represent the middle or typical value through a statistical summary of the numbers. Measures that summarize the central tendency are the mean, median, and mode.

median　The middle score or measurement in a set of scores that are ranked. The median, obtained through averaging the value of the two middle scores, is used most commonly as the measure for central tendency for ordinal scale data.

minimum score　The smallest score in the distribution of scores.

mode　The most frequently occuring score within a set or group of scores. The mode is used most commonly as the measure for central tendency for nominal scale data.

multivariate regression　Concerned with measuring the relationship between a single dependent variable and several independent variables.

mutually exclusive　An attribute that means a respondent or client should not have or qualify for two or more attributes in a variable at the same time.

negatively skewed distribution　The distribution has an asymmetrical tail that extends downward around the mean toward more negative values.

nominal level data　Data that specify the differences in the attributes of the variable that are not quantifiable. It is sometimes referred to as qualitative or categorical data. Nominal level variables are frequently used as socio-demographic descriptors.

nonprobability sampling　Relies on nonrandomly selected or available subjects, selected by methods that offer no assurance that each subject in the population has an equal chance of being selected for the sample. Subjects are often selected because the researcher has access to them, or because other subjects in a sample know them. The subject selection methods of nonprobability sampling call into question whether the subjects in the sample actually constitute a representative sample of subjects within the population. The findings from studies that employ nonprobability sampling cannot be generalized to the population from which the sample was drawn.

normal distribution　A theoretical construct based on the concept that all possible values of a continuous probability distribution can be plotted on the horizontal or x-axis of a graph, while the probability of each value occurring can be plotted on a vertical or y-axis of a graph.

null hypothesis　A statement that there will be no difference or change between a sample exposed to an intervention condition and a sample that is not. A null hypothesis that holds true suggests no effect or no change for a condition or intervention. There may be change or effect, but to an insufficient degree to reject chance as the reason for the change. The null hypothesis states that there is no relationship between two variables in the population, or that there is no difference between a sample statistic and a population statistic.

observed frequencies　The actual data in the chi-square tabulation. These are compared to expected frequencies.

operators　Used in formulas for arithmetic calculations to reference cells, to link portions of equations, and to segment portions of equations.

ordinal level data　Expresses information about the rank of the categories contained within the range of measurement in the variable. Ordinal data expresses a rank ordering, providing information on the relative position of each attribute in relationship to the others, but not conveying information on the relative distance between the attributes.

Pearson's product moment correlation coefficient A common and well-known statistic that reports the degree of linear relationship between two variables when their scale of measurement is either interval or ratio. The term "product moment" refers to the process of determining the z-scores, or standardized scores, of each variable and then multiplying them by each other. Then the average value of the multiplied z-score product is calculated to determine the moment for the variables. Pearson's correlation coefficient is commonly symbolized as r.

pivot tables Data tables, also referred to as contingency tables or cross-tabulation tables, that are a means to collapse and summarize data in order to understand the relationship between two or more variables displayed in the table format.

pivot table and duplicate detection An alternative approach to finding duplicate cases in a dataset by examining the client identifier codes to find duplicate cases.

platykurtic distribution A negative value indicates the possibility of a distribution that is too flat.

population Understood to be the total theoretically specified collection of subjects or cases of interest to the researcher (Healey, 1993).

positively skewed distribution The distribution has an asymmetrical tail that extends upward around the mean toward more positive values.

probability sampling methods Use some form of random sampling in order to select subjects for the sample from the population of interest. Random sampling enables the selection of a sample of subjects whose characteristics will approximate those of the population from which the sample is drawn. Probability sampling makes it possible to generalize findings from the sample to the population.

probability value, or "p-value" An estimate of probability that the obtained value for an outcome of a statistical test would have been due to chance or random error. The smaller the values for "p," the greater the likelihood that the obtained result could have been due to chance.

query The extraction of data from database tables based on specifically defined criteria.

R^2, coefficient of multiple determination A numerical value that is a fraction of the number "1.0," such as ".20." However, the fraction is reported as a percentage such that the set of independent variables when taken together provides a measure of positive association or prediction that explains, for example, 20% of the variance (or change) in the dependent variable of interest. This coefficient is often useful for practitioners attempting to determine the likely change that could result from multiple interventions or to service delivery systems in estimating the effects of changes in multiple demographic and economic factors in the efficacy of a service delivery model or the distribution plan for scarce resources.

random assignment A process of assigning clients or cases to equivalent groups for the purpose of making comparisons between the two groups.

random sampling A sampling method that enables the selection of a sample of subjects whose characteristics will approximate those of the population from which the sample is drawn. Random sampling controls for the possibility of selection bias.

range of scores Derived by determining the lowest and highest value of the scores. The lowest value is subtracted from the highest value.

ratio level data Has all the attributes of interval level data along with the presence of a true or absolute zero. Ratio level measures do not have negative values. Because a ratio level variable has a true zero, it is possible to specify the magnitude of difference between values (attributes) in the variable.

relative frequency The proportion of times that a particular value occurs in the distribution.

representativeness The degree to which a sample is similar to the population.

sample A subset of a population from which inferences about and descriptions of the population under study are made.

skewed distribution An asymmetrical distribution around the mean.

spreadsheet A table composed of rows, columns, and cells.

standard deviation A statistic that measures the average amount of deviation of scores in a distribution, or how much the scores deviate from the mean or average score. A standard deviation measure can be derived by calculating the square root of the variance of scores.

standard error (of a statistic) The standard deviation of the sampling distribution of a statistic. Standard errors are considered important because they reflect how much of a sampling fluctuation a statistic will show. How good an estimate of the population the sample statistic is depends on the sampling or measurement error. The standard error of any statistic depends on the sample size. Larger sample sizes tend to have a smaller standard error or standard error of the mean (S_M).

statistical power   Refers to the capacity of the selected statistical test to identify or detect a relationship between variables and to correctly reject the null hypothesis when it is false. The power estimate of a statistical test is determined by subtracting beta from 1.00, or the probability of making a Type II error from 1.00. The convention for most studies using statistical tests is a power estimate of at least .80.

stratified sampling   Another probability sampling method that is widely used and readily produced with a spreadsheet is stratified sampling. Stratified sampling reduces the sampling error through random selection from subsets of the population (Rubin & Babbie, 2001). Stratified sampling is commonly used to ensure the representation of subgroups or strata of the population.

study population   The collection or aggregation of subjects or cases from which the sample will actually be selected.

sum of scores   The total value of all scores in the distribution.

systematic sampling   An alternative procedure for selecting a random sample. Rubin and Babbie (2001) and Williams, Unrau, and Grinnell (1998) describe the process of creating a systematic sample in which every *k*th case is selected.

text box   A rectangular space in an application into which text may be inserted or typed.

theoretical probability distribution   Refers to the possibility that scores may not distribute in a normal curve distribution, but may distribute unevenly such that there is a bunching up effect on one side of the measure of central tendency. There is also a corresponding thinning out of scores on the other side of the measure of central tendency. The direction of the thinning scores determines the direction of skew in the distribution (left and negatively skewed, or right and positively skewed).

There is also a greater variability of scores relative to the degree of skewness in the distribution.

Tukey's b test   When completing an ANOVA (Analysis of Variance) to determine the difference between group means, the ANOVA will indicate that some group means may be significantly different from other group means. A post hoc comparison test such as Tukey's HSD or Tukey's b is performed to determine which group means are significantly different.

Type I error   Associated with drawing a false conclusion that a relationship exists between two variables where none exists. Type I errors are known as "alpha" errors and are due to wrongly accepting that a value of a sample statistic is greater than it would be due to chance.

Type II error   Concerned with denying a legitimate effect that does exist by failing to reject a null hypothesis. Type II errors are known as "beta" errors.

unimodal   Only one score occurs most often within a group of scores.

variable   Something that can change or vary. The two fundamental characteristics of a variable are that its attributes are exhaustive and that the attributes in the variable are mutually exclusive.

variance   The spread or dispersion of scores within a distribution of scores. As variance of scores increases the farther the individual cases are from the mean value, and as the variance of scores decreases the closer the individual cases are to the mean value in the distribution.

z-score   A standardized score that is represented as a normal distribution by converting scores to a standard score. The z-score is used to compare different groups of scores that are sometimes produced or assessed on differing scales or metrics. The z-score has a mean of 0.00 and a standard deviation of 1.00.

BIBLIOGRAPHY

Albright, S. C., Winston, W. L., & Zappe, C. (2003). *Data analysis and decision making with Microsoft Excel*. Pacific Grove, CA: Brooks/Cole-Thomson Learning.

Alter, C., & Evens, W. (1990). *Evaluating your practice: A guide to self-assessment*. New York: Springer.

American Psychological Association. (1994). *Publication manual of the American Psychological Association* (4th ed.). Washington, DC: American Psychological Association.

Aron, A., & Aron, E. (2001). *Statistics for the behavioral and social sciences* (2nd ed.). Upper Saddle River, NJ: Prentice Hall.

Barlow, D., & Herson, N. (1984). *Single case experimental designs* (2nd ed.). New York: Pergamon.

Basham, R. E. (2002). *Data visualization: Graphical representation in the evaluation of experiential group therapy education outcomes. Proquest Digital Dissertations (UMI Dissertation Abstracts Database)*, Vol. 64, 02A.

Benbenishty, R. (1991). Monitoring practice on the agency level: An application in a residential care facility. *Research on Social Work Practice, 1*(4), 371–86.

Black, T. R. (1999). *Doing quantitative research in the social sciences: An integrated approach to research design, measurement, and statistics*. Thousand Oaks, CA: Sage.

Bloom, M., Fischer, J., & Orme, J. G. (2003) *Evaluating practice: Guidelines of the accountable professional* (4th ed.). Boston: Allyn & Bacon.

Boyce, J. (1997). Using outlines, templates, and styles. In T. F. Hayes (Ed.), *Special edition using Microsoft Office 97 Professional, best sellers edition* (pp. 85–107). Indianapolis: Que.

Bricklin, D. (2003). "Was VisiCalc the "first" spreadsheet? Available at www.bricklin.com/firstspreadsheetquestion.htm.

Carr, J. E., & Burkholder, E. O. (1998). Creating single-subject design graphs with Microsoft Excel. *Journal of Applied Behavior Analysis, 31,* 245–251.

Chapple, M. (2003). Choosing a database product. Retrieved December 1, 2003, from http://databases.about.com/library.weekly/aa050601a.htm

Cleveland, W. S., & McGill, R. (1984). Graphical perception: Theory, experimentation, and application to the development of graphical methods. *Journal of the American Statistical Association, 79,* 531–554.

Cohen, J. (1988). *Statistical power analysis for the behavioral sciences* (2nd ed.). Hillsdale, NJ: Erlbaum.

Cohen J., & Cohen P. (1983). *Applied multiple regression/correlation analysis for the behavioral sciences* (2nd ed.). Hillsdale, NJ: Erlbaum.

Dretzke, B. J., & Heilman, K. A. (1998). *Statistics with Microsoft Excel.* Upper Saddle River, NJ: Prentice Hall.

Drew, C. J., & Hardman, M. L. (1985). *Designing and conducting behavioral research.* New York: Pergamon.

Eddy, S. (1997). *Mastering Lotus SmartSuite 97 for Windows 95.* San Francisco: Sybex.

Fuller, S., & Pagan, K. (1997). Access quick start guide. In T. F. Hayes (Ed.), *Special edition using Microsoft Office 97 Professional, best sellers edition* (pp. 583–590). Indianapolis: Que.

Gaffikin, M. J. R.(1996, June). Seeking the foundations for accounting research. *Asia-Pacific Journal of Accounting,* 102–103.

Gilgen, R. (1997). PowerPoint quick start guide. In T. F. Hayes (Ed.), *Special edition using Microsoft Office 97 Professional, best sellers edition* (pp. 475–488). Indianapolis: Que.

Glass, G. V. (1976). Primary, secondary, and meta-analysis of research. *Educational Researcher, 5,* 3–8.

Glass, G. V., McGraw, B., & Smith, M. L. (1981). *Meta-analysis in social research.* Beverly Hills, CA: Sage.

Glisson, C. (1986). The group versus the individual as the unit of analysis in small group research. *Social Work with Groups, 9*(3), 15–30.

Gravetter, F. J., & Wallnau, L. B. (1999). *Statistics for the Behavioral Sciences* (6th ed.). Minneapolis: West.

Hare, P. A., Blumberg H. H., Davies M. F., & Kent M. V. (1994). *Small group research: A handbook.* Norwood, NJ: Ablex.

Hartman, A. (1978). Diagrammatic assessment of family relationships. *Social Casework, 59,* 465–476.

Healey, J. F. (1993). *Statistics: A tool for social research* (3rd ed.). Belmont, CA: Wadsworth.

Hendry, D. G., & Green, T. R. G. (1994). Creating, comprehending and explaining spreadsheets: A cognitive interpretation of what discretionary users think of the spreadsheet model. *International Journal of Human–Computer Studies, 40,* 1033–1065.

Henry, G. T. (1998). Graphing data. In L. Bickman & D. J. Rog (Eds.), *Handbook of applied social research methods.* Thousand Oaks, CA: Sage.

Holmes, N. (1984). *Designer's guide to creating charts and diagrams.* New York: Watson-Guptill.

Hudson, W. W., & McMurtry, S. L. (1997). Comprehensive assessment in social work practice. *Research on Social Work Practice, 7*(1), 79–98.

Jantzen, F. V., & Lewis, R. E. (1990). Spreadsheet analysis in human services. *Computers in Human Services, 6*(1–3), 51–67.

Jarvenpaa, S. L., & Dickson, G. W. (1988). Graphics and managerial decision making: Research based guidelines. *Communications of the ACM, 31,* 764–774.

Jayaratne, S. (1977). Single-subject and group designs in treatment evaluation. *Social Work Research and Abstracts, 13*(3), 35–42.

Johnson, N. (2001, September). Selecting software tools for outcomes projects: Which tools are best suited for what activities? *Formulary, 36,* 656–663.

Kazi, M. A. F., Mantysaari, M., & Rostila, I. (1997). Promoting the use of single-case designs: Social work experiences from England and Finland. *Research on Social Work Practice, 7*(3), 311–328.

Kerr, M. P., & Payne, S. J. (1994). Learning to use a spreadsheet by doing and watching. *Interacting with Computers, 6*(1), 3–32.

Krazit, T. (2002). *StarOffice set to challenge Microsoft's Office.* Retrieved July 24, 2003, from World Wide Web, http://www.pcworld.com/news/article/0,aid,99643,00.asp

Lacher, J. (1997). The power of spreadsheets. *Journal of Accountancy, 183*(5), 66–72.

Lachiusa, T. A. (1996). Development of the graphic social network measure. *Journal of Social Service Research, 21*(4), 1–35.

LaMorte, W. (1999). *LaMorte's Calculator.* Available at www.bumc.bu.edu/Departments/PageMain.asp?DepartmentID=287&Page=2120.

Lefferts, R. (1981). *Elements of graphics: How to prepare charts and graphs for effective reports.* New York: Harper & Row.

Legg, H. (1988, Summer). Ricco Mattessich: Acclaimed researcher. *Viewpoints, 15.*

Lentini, M., Nardi, D., & Simonetta, A. (1999). Self-instructive spreadsheets: An environment for automatic knowledge acquisition and tutor generation. *International Journal of Human–Computer Studies, 52,* 775–803.

Levene, H. (1960). I. Olkin et al. (Eds.), In *Contributions to probability and statistics: Essays in honor of Harold Hotelling* (pp. 278–292). Palo Alto, CA: Stanford University Press.

MacKenzie, R. (Ed.) (1995). *Effective use of group therapy in managed care.* Washington, DC: American Psychiatric Press.

maranGraphics (1996). *Teach yourself computers and the Internet visually.* Foster City, CA: IDG.

Margolis, P. E. (1996). *Random House personal computer dictionary* (2nd ed.). New York: Random House.

Marsh, C. (1931). Group treatment of the psychosis by the psychological equivalent of the revival. *Mental Hygiene, 15,* 328–349.

Mather, D. (1999). A framework for building spreadsheet based decision models. *Journal of the Operational Research Society, 50,* 70–74.

Mattaini, M. A. (1993). *More than a thousand words: Graphics for clinical practice.* Washington, DC: NASW Press.

Mattaini, M. A. (1996). The abuse and neglect of single-case designs. *Research on Social Work Practice, 6*(1), 83–90.

Mattessich, R. (1961). Budgeting Models and System Simulation, *The Accounting Review,* July: 384–397.

Mattessich, R. (1964a). *Accounting and analytical methods.* Homewood, IL: R. D. Irwin.

Mattessich, R. (1964b). *Simulation of the firm through a budget computer program,* Homewood, IL: R. D. Irwin.

McGoldrick, M., & Gerson, R. (1985). *Genograms in family assessment.* New York: W. W. Norton.

Meyer, C. H. (1993). The impact of visualization on practice. In M. A. Mattaini (Ed.), *More than a thousand words: Graphics for clinical practice* (pp. 261–270). Washington, DC: NASW Press.

Montcalm, D., & Royse, D. (2002). *Data analysis for social workers.* Allyn & Bacon: Boston.

Murphy, G. J. (1997). Mattessich, Richard V. in M. Chatfield and R. Vangermeersch (Eds.), *The history of accounting—An international encyclopedia* (p. 405). New York: Garland.

Nash, J. C., & Quon, T. K. (1996). Issues in teaching statistical thinking with spreadsheets. *Journal of Statistics Education, 4*(1). Retrieved July 30, 2003, from www.amstat.org/publications/jse/v4nl/nash.html.

National Association of Social Workers (2003). *Code of ethics.* Retrieved July 28, 2003, from www.socialworkers.org/pubs/code/code.asp.

Negroponte, N. (1995). *Being digital.* New York: Knopf.

Neuman, W. L., & Kreuger, L. W. (2003). *Social work research methods: Qualitative and quantitative approaches.* Boston: Allyn & Bacon.

Nurius, P. S., & Hudson, W. W. (1993). *Human services practice, evaluation, and computers: A practical guide for today and beyond.* Grove Park, CA: Brooks/Cole.

Ogilvie, D. M. (1996). Use of graphic representation of self-dynamisms in clinical treatment. *Crisis-Intervention, 1*(2), 125–40.

Orme, J. G., & Cox, M. E. (2001). Analyzing single-subject design data using statistical process control charts. *Social Work Research, 25*(2), 115–28.

Parsons, J. J., Oja, D., & Auer, D. (1995), *Comprehensive Microsoft Excel 5.0 for Windows.* Cambridge, MA: Course Technology.

Patterson, D. A. (2000a). *Personal computer applications in the social services.* Boston: Allyn & Bacon.

Patterson, D. A. (2000b). *Using spreadsheets for data collection, statistical analysis, and graphical representation* [Online]. Available at http://web.utk.edu/~dap/Random/Order/Start.htm.

Patterson, D. A., & Basham, R. E. (2002a). Data visualization procedures in the analysis of group treatment outcomes across units of analysis. *Small Group Research, 33*(2), 209–33.

Patterson, D. A., & Basham, R. E. (2002b). Visualizing change: Spreadsheets and graphical representation across domains in human service practice. *The Journal of Technology for Human Services, 21*(4), 1–16.

Patterson, D. A., & Lee, M. S. (1995). A field trial of Global Assessment of Functioning Scale–Modified. *The American Journal of Psychiatry, 152*(9), 1386–1388.

Patterson, D. A., & Lee, M. S. (1998). Intensive care management and rehospitalization: A survival analysis. *Research on Social Work Practice, 8*(2), 152–171.

Patterson, D. A., Post, J. A., & Buchler, C. (January, 1999). *The application of data visualization in understanding lives in foster care.* Third Annual Conference of the Society for Social Work and Research, Austin, TX. Retrieved August 15, 2003, from http://web.utk.edu/~dap/Austin%20Presentation/index.htm.

Patterson, D. A., Basham, R. E., & DeCoster, V. (in preparation). *The absence of spreadsheets in social work research education.* http://www.amstat.org/publications/jse/v4n1/nash.html

Pedhazer, E. J. (1999). *Multiple regression in behavioral research* (3rd ed.). Fort Worth, TX: Harcourt Brace College Publishers.

Pinto, J. (2001). *BA201 and BA321 Hypothesis testing.* Available at www.cba.nau.edu/pinto-j/Commands/HypothesisExEq.html#WebMail.

Power, D. J. (1999). A brief history of spreadsheets. Retrieved September 24, 2002, from http://dssresources.com/history/sshistory.html.

Pratt, J. (1945). The group method in the treatment of psychosomatic disorders. *Sociometry, 8,* 323–331.

Proctor, E. (2002). Decision making in social work practice. *Social Work Research, 26*(1), 3–7.

Reid, K. E. (1997). *Social work practice with groups: A clinical perspective* (2nd ed.). Pacific Grove, CA: Brooks/Cole.

Royse, D. (1992). *Program Evaluation.* Nelson-Hall: Chicago.

Rubin, A., & Babbie, E. (2001). *Research Methods for Social Work* (3rd ed.). Pacific Grove, CA: Brooks/Cole.

Rutledge, P. A. (1997). Using lists and databases. In J. Boyce (Ed.), *Using Microsoft Office 97 Professional.* Indianapolis: Que.

Sanders, J. D., & Patterson, D. A. (2003, June). *The science and craft of writing reports and testifying in custody cases.* Paper presented at the Florida Psychological Association annual conference, Hutchinson Island, FL.

Simkin, D., & Hastie, R. (1987). An information-processing analysis of graph perception. *Journal of the American Statistical Association, 82,* 454–465.

Snedecor, G. W., & Cochran, W. G. (1989). *Statistical methods* (8th ed.). Ames: Iowa State University Press.

Spitz, H. I. (1996). *Group psychotherapy and managed mental health care: A clinical guide for providers.* New York: Bruner Mazel.

Thyer, B., & Thyer, K. (1992). Single-system research designs in social work practice: A bibliography from 1965 to 1990. *Research of Social Work Practice, 2*(1), 99–116.

Toseland, R. W., & Rivas, R. F. (2001). *An introduction to group work practice* (4th ed.). Boston: Allyn & Bacon.

Tripodi, T. (1994). *A primer on single subject design for clinical social workers.* Washington DC: NASW Press.

Tufte, E. R. (1983). *The visual display of quantitative information.* Cheshire, CT: Graphics Press.

U.S. Census Bureau. (2003). *Current population survey (CPS)—Definitions and explanations.* Retrieved September 15, 2003, from www.census.gov/population/www/cps/cpsdef.html

Vogt, W. P. (1999). *Dictionary of statistics and methodology: A nontechnical guide for the social sciences.* Thousand Oaks, CA: Sage.

Walkenbach, J. (2003). *Microsoft Excel: The spreadsheet page.* Retrieved July 24, 2003, from www.j-walk.com/ss/excel/index.htm.

Weinbach, R. W., & Grinnell, R. M., Jr. (2001). *Statistics for social workers* (5th ed.). Boston: Allyn & Bacon.

Welkowitz, J., Ewen, R. B., & Cohen, J. (1982). *Introductory statistics for the behavioral sciences.* San Diego, CA: Harcourt Brace Jovanovich.

White, J. V. (1984). *Using charts and graphs: 1000 ideas for visual persuasion.* New York: R. R. Bowker.

Williams, M., Unrau, Y. A., & Grinnell, R. M. (1998). *Introduction to social work research.* Itasca, IL: F. E. Peacock.

Yalom, I. D. (1995). *The theory and practice of group psychotherapy* (4th ed.). New York: Basic Books.

Yu, C. H., & Behrens, J. T. (1995), *Applications of multivariate visualization to behavioral sciences.* Retrieved June 21, 2000, from http://research.ed.asu.edu/reports/multi-vis/multi-vis.html#what-is.

WEB LINKS

Web links to spreadsheet data analysis resources

www.wa.gov/esd/lmea/download/download.htm

Web links to public access data sets

www.lttechno.com/links/spreadsheets.html

www.cdc.gov/nedss/DataModels/index.html

Web links to statistical analysis information

Exploratory Data Analysis

www.itl.nist.gov/div898/handbook/eda/eda.htm

HyperStat Online Textbook

http://davidmlane.com/hyperstat/index.html

Rice Virtual Lab in Statistics

www.ruf.rice.edu/%7Elane/rvls.html

MedCalc Statistics Menu

www.medcalc.be/manual/mpage06.php

Statistics Demonstrations with Excel

http://sunsite.univie.ac.at/Spreadsite/statexamp/

Visual Statistics with Multimedia

www.visualstatistics.net/Visual%20Statistics%20Multimedia/Outline%20of%20Visual%20Statistics.htm

StatPrimer, Version 6

http://www2.sjsu.edu/faculty/gerstman/StatPrimer/

Spreadsheets, Mathematics, Science, and Statistics Education

http://sunsite.univie.ac.at/Spreadsite/

Chapter 1: An Introduction to Spreadsheets

A Brief History of Spreadsheets

www.j-walk.com/ss/

Why Use Spreadsheets for Data Analysis in the Social Services?

www.usd.edu/trio/tut/excel/1.html

www.qualitydigest.com/oct97/html/excel.html

A Comparison of Spreadsheets to Statistical Analysis Software

http://sunsite.univie.ac.at/Spreadsite/

http://edn.schoolnet.org.za/cd-19dec01/spread/Content/Education.htm

Spreadsheet Basics
www.csubak.edu/~jross/classes/GS390/Spreadsheets/ss_basics/ss_basics.html

Using Formulas and Functions
www.meadinkent.co.uk/excel.htm

Simple Formulas
www.barasch.com/excel/xlformulas.htm

Excel Functions
www.du.edu/uts/training/handouts/excel2000/stats2000.htm
www.bridgewater.edu/cescc/acadcomp/ExcelDataAnalysis

Setting Up Data Analysis Tools
www-micro.msb.le.ac.uk/1010/toolpak.html

Getting Help
www.lacher.com/toc.htm
www.mrexcel.com/articles.shtml

Chapter 2: Data Collection Ways and Means

Creating Data Entry Forms
http://business.unisa.edu.au/innovres/research/excelforsurveys/dataentry.htm

Downloading Data
www.mcpressonline.com/mc/.5bfb6b55

Importing Data
http://info.wlu.edu/working_with_data/excel.html

Relating to Database Software
http://databases.about.com/library/weekly/aa123100a.htm

Chapter 3: Selecting Samples

Why Use Random Samples?
www.mis.coventry.ac.uk/~nhunt/sampling.htm

Chapter 4: Data Cleaning

The Burdens of Dirty Data
www.audiencedialogue.org/excel1.html

Chapter 5: Frequency Distributions and Histograms

Cumulative Percentage
www.emory.edu/EMORY_CLASS/PSYCH230/p230sm.html
Using the Pivot Table Option
www.audiencedialogue.org/excel4.html

Using the Data Analysis Histogram Option
www.wtamu.edu/~crobinson/5516/excel1.htm
www.audiencedialogue.org/excel3.html

Chapter 6: Descriptive Statistics

Data Analysis Tools: Descriptive Statistics
http://commfaculty.fullerton.edu/jreinard/bookweb/computer1.htm

Producing Frequency Polygrams
www.mnstate.edu/wasson/ed602createfreqpoly.htm

Chapter 7: Statistical Inference and Hypothesis Testing

Probability Distributions
http://home.clara.net/sisa/spreadsh/distribs.htm

Statistical Significance, p-Values
www.ubalt.edu/arc/math_resources/stat_means2.html

Effect Size
http://cem.dur.ac.uk/ebeuk/research/effectsize/EffectSizeCalculator.xls

Chapter 8: Bivariate Statistics

Chi-Square Test of Independence
www.elon.edu/econ/sac/chisquare.htm

Expected Frequencies
www.gifted.uconn.edu/siegle/research/ChiSquare/chiexcel.htm

One-Sample t-Test
www.kean.edu/~breid/CAB/student.html

t-Test for Two Independent Samples
www.mnstate.edu/wasson/ed602excelss11.htm

Paired Samples t-Test (Dependent)
www.mnstate.edu/wasson/ed602excelss12.htm

ANOVA, One-Way Between-Groups
www.mnstate.edu/wasson/ed602excelss13.htm

Chapter 9: Pivot Tables

Using the Pivot Tables Wizard
www.botany.hawaii.edu/faculty/bridges/eschool/lectures/20a_PivotTables/20a_
PivotTables1.htm
www.marymount.edu/telcom/mutts/Using%20Pivot%20Tables.pdf

Graphing Cross-Tabulation Tables
http://edtech.tennessee.edu/itc/grants/twt2000/modules/dpatter2/Patterson%20-%
20ITC%20Grant%20Project/Cross-tabs.htm

Chapter 10: Single System Designs

http://edtech.tennessee.edu/itc/grants/twt2000/modules/dpatter2/Patterson%20-%
20ITC%20Grant%20Project/Single-system.htm

Chapter 11: Correlation and Regression

Pearson's r *and* R^2

www.econ.ucdavis.edu/faculty/cameron/excel/excorr.html

www.mnstate.edu/wasson/ed602calccorr.htm

www.mnstate.edu/wasson/ed602lesson8.htm

Creating Scatterplots

www.ksu.edu/stats/tch/malone/computers/excel/graphs/scatter.html

Trendlines in Scatterplots

www.ncsu.edu/chemistry/resource/excel/excel.html

Interpreting Scatterplots

www.ed.uiuc.edu/courses/edpsy390a/notes/l2324.htm

*Computing Ordinary Least Squares
(OLS) Two-Variable Regression*

www.econ.ucdavis.edu/faculty/cameron/excel/exregfn.html

Computing OLS Multiple Regression

www.sbaer.uca.edu/Research/1999/WDSI/99wds594.htm

www.econ.ucdavis.edu/faculty/cameron/excel/exmreg.html

Chapter 12: Graphical Representations

Basic Graphing Procedures

www.kcl.ac.uk/humanities/cch/pg/course/graphical_rep/graphmain.html

www.nova.edu/~gmoserc/SS101-Lesson5.htm

Guidelines for Graphical Presentation

www.du.edu/uts/training/student/handouts/excel/excel2000charts.htm